THE ARMY

Other National Historical Society Publications:

THE IMAGE OF WAR: 1861-1865

TOUCHED BY FIRE: A PHOTOGRAPHIC PORTRAIT OF THE CIVIL WAR

WAR OF THE REBELLION: OFFICIAL RECORDS
  OF THE UNION AND CONFEDERATE ARMIES

OFFICIAL RECORDS OF THE UNION AND CONFEDERATE NAVIES
  IN THE WAR OF THE REBELLION

HISTORICAL TIMES ILLUSTRATED ENCYCLOPEDIA OF THE CIVIL WAR

CONFEDERATE VETERAN

THE WEST POINT MILITARY HISTORY SERIES

IMPACT: THE ARMY AIR FORCES' CONFIDENTIAL HISTORY
  OF WORLD WAR II

HISTORY OF UNITED STATES NAVAL OPERATIONS IN WORLD WAR II
  by Samuel Eliot Morison

HISTORY OF THE ARMED FORCES IN WORLD WAR II
  by Janusz Piekalkiewicz

A TRAVELLER'S GUIDE TO GREAT BRITAIN SERIES

MAKING OF BRITAIN SERIES

THE ARCHITECTURAL TREASURES OF EARLY AMERICA

For information about National Historical Society Publications, write:

The National Historical Society, 2245 Kohn Road, Box 8200,
Harrisburg, Pa 17105

THE ELITE
The World's Crack Fighting Men

THE ARMY

Ashley Brown, Editor

Jonathan Reed, Editor

Editorial Board

Brigadier-General James L. Collins, Jr. (Retd.)
Former Chief of Military History, US Department of the Army

Ian V. Hogg
Authority on smallarms and modern weapons systems

Dr. John Pimlott
Senior Lecturer in the Department of War Studies,
Royal Military Academy, Sandhurst, England

Brigadier-General Edwin H. Simmons (Retd.)
US Marine Corps

Lisa Mullins, Managing Editor, NHS edition

A Publication of
THE NATIONAL HISTORICAL SOCIETY

Published in Great Britain in 1986 by Orbis Publishing

Special contents of this edition copyright © 1988 by the
National Historical Society

Library of Congress Cataloging-in-Publication Data
The Army / Ashley Brown, editor, Jonathan Reed, editor.
    p.   cm.—(The Elite: the world's crack fighting men ; v. 4)
  ISBN 0-918678-42-0
  1. Armies. 2. Military history, Modern—20th century.
I. Brown, Ashley. II. Reed, Jonathan. III. Series: Elite
(Harrisburg, Pa.) ; v. 4
U42.A77   1989
355.3′5—dc20   89-3313
                      CIP

CONTENTS

Introduction   7

1   **Blasting the Way**   Nigel de Lee   8

2   **Crowbar Action**   James Hooper   14

3   **Hell on the Kokoda Trail**   William Franklin   22

4   **Jungle Trackers**   F. A. Godfrey   28

5   **Tigers in the 'Nam**   Rod Paschall   35

6   **Victory at Vimy**   Adrian Gilbert   42

7   **Tank Slayers**   Barrie Pitt   48

8   **Death Trap**   R. G. Grant   54

9   **Jungle Marauders**   William Franklin   60

10   **Argyll Law**   Francis Toase   67

11   **Backs to the Wall**   J. S. Common   74

12   **Over the Top**   W. B. Brabiner   80

13   **Recondo**   F. Clifton Berry, Jr.   86

14   **Darby's Rangers**   R. G. Grant   94

15   **Colonial Firefight**   Keith Simpson   100

16   **The Cabanatuan Raid**   Leroy Thompson   107

17   **ANZACs**   Adrian Gilbert   114

18   **Hand to Hand Combat**   Adrian Gilbert   121

19   **Death Walkers**   Ian Beckett   132

20   **Storming the Heights**   James D. Ladd   138

21   **Into the Cauldron**   James Lucas   146

22   **Jackals in the Casbah**   Jean Mabire   155

23   **Giap's Gunners**   Ashley Brown   160

24   **Shock Army**   Terry Gander   166

Combat Skills of the Elite: Camouflage   173

INTRODUCTION

In times of strife, nations from around the world call upon their armies. From one conflict to another, the course of history rides, and has ridden, in the foot-soldier's knapsack— the destiny of nations decided on the blade of his bayonet and the steel of his nerve.

Even then, some special few outfits always stand out, either for what they have done, or what is demanded of them. These are THE ELITE. They might have been the Malta Independent Brigade Group, who not only stormed ashore on Gold Beach on D-Day, but also had behind them two previous amphibious assaults, something few other outfits in history could claim. They might be the Koevoet, the tribesmen of southwest Africa who manned units charged to hunt down the Swapo insurgents. They might be the Viet Minh's 351st Division who smashed the French defenses as Dien Bien Phu. Whoever they were or are, the armies' finest face and overcome the challenges that only the special few can meet.

Some of their stories have been told in books and even on film. Darby's Rangers and their intrepid leader Lieutenant Colonel William Darby took their lead from British commandos, training specially for their missions at Dieppe, in North Africa, Tunisia, Sicily, Salerno, and their biggest job of all, spearheading the January 1944 landings at Anzio. The famed ANZAC's, the Australian and New Zealand Army Corps, bore the brunt of the vicious, pointless fighting at Gallipoli in 1915, where their bravery in the face of hopeless assaults on Turkish positions was one of the few points in the campaign that high command could look at with pride.

The exciting—often unbelievable—stories of a host of these special outfits are all here in this volume, filled with the exploits of men who rise above themselves. They did it in World War I, in World War II, in Korea, in Viet Nam, in the Falklands, in North and South Africa, wherever they were called upon. Their bravery knew no limitations of cause or country—German, American, British, African, French, Vietnamese—when special men were needed, these men stepped forward.

That is why they are a part of THE ELITE.

BLASTING THE WAY

Top right: Field Marshal Montgomery with (on left) Sir Alexander Stanier, commander of 231 Brigade. Bottom right: Men of No.47(RM) Commando come ashore from their LCI. Below: The gun emplacement at Manvieux, with (bottom) a Sherman crew of the Sherwood Rangers and (bottom right) Private S. Knock of the 1st Dorsets.

Already a veteran of two major amphibious assaults, 231 (Malta) Independent Brigade Group landed at Gold Beach on D-day, tasked with the capture or destruction of key elements of the German defences

ON D-DAY, as part of the vast Allied invasion force pouring onto the Normandy beaches, 231 (Malta) Independent Brigade Group came ashore on the extreme right of the British 50th Division's assault area of Gold Beach. The men had a number of important tasks. They were to protect the open right flank of the British Second Army until it made firm contact with the US First Army landing on Omaha

Beach, 16km away. Arromanches, the intended site of the British Mulberry Harbour, was to be taken. as was Port-en-Bessin Huppain, which was to serve as a fuel port until PLUTO (an acronym for 'pipe-line under the ocean') was supplying fuel from England. Finally, they were to silence the Longues Battery, which menaced the whole area of the Normandy operation. Adverse circumstances and enemy action delayed the men's securing some of the objectives until D+2, but the brigade performed well and continued to function despite heavy casualties and unexpected difficulties.

In order to reinvigorate the battalions, half the soldiers were posted and replaced by fresh men

The success of 231 Brigade was due in large part to experience, preparation and training, and to good operational planning. The brigade had arrived back in England early in 1944, having taken part in the amphibious assaults on Sicily and Italy, and the troops were seasoned but weary. In order to reinvigorate the battalions, half the soldiers were posted and replaced by fresh men. In this way the brigade combined enthusiasm with experience. The new brigade commander, Sir Alexander Stanier, ordered a scheme of training that was vigorous and tough, with each exercise approached in the spirit of a rough game to maintain interest.

The confidence of the troops was raised by familiarisation training with the 'funnies' (specialist armoured engineer vehicles of the 79th Armoured Division) in East Anglia. Commanders and soldiers were sent to Inverary in Scotland for live-firing exercises at the Amphibious Battle School. This led on to joint training with artillery and armoured support. The culmination of the training process was a series of major rehearsal exercises; Smash I and Smash II were assault landings on the south coast of England, while Fabius tested the administrative

services. By June 1944 the units of the brigade were co-ordinated, fit and confident of their new skills.

In the meanwhile, the brigade and battalion staffs had been planning the assault. The brigade was one of four in 50th Division. The division ordered 231 Brigade to land east of Le Hamel, advance inland as far as Ryes, then swing westwards to take high ground above Arromanches, and continue moving in the same direction until it made contact with the Americans near Port-en-Bessin. The brigade would then hold firm, to protect the right flank of 16 Brigade to the east and provide a lodgement for 69 Brigade, which was to pass through 231 and go on to capture Bayeux. The brigade plan was made quickly; to a large extent it was dictated by the ground, and intelligence of the terrain and enemy positions was excellent. Assessments that the enemy, mainly from the static 716th Division, some of whom were Russians, would not fight hard, were less accurate. The

231 (MALTA) INDEPENDENT BRIGADE GROUP

Known at different times during its World War II career as the Malta Infantry Brigade, the Southern Infantry Brigade, 1st (Malta) Infantry Brigade, 231st Infantry Brigade and, finally, 231 (Malta) Independent Brigade Group, this formation always retained its link with Malta through its badge (above), a white Maltese cross on a scarlet shield.

The core of the formation throughout its several changes of identity consisted of three regular battalions. These were the 2nd Battalion, The Devonshire Regiment, the 1st Battalion, The Hampshire Regiment, and the 1st Battalion, The Dorsetshire Regiment. The Malta Infantry Brigade fought during the great siege that lasted from June 1940 until late 1942, withstanding air attacks of unprecedented ferocity and famine caused by an Axis blockade that all but succeeded in starving out the beleaguered island. The successful conclusion of the campaign in North Africa led to the end of the siege and in April 1943 the brigade was withdrawn to Egypt, where it underwent special training and became an independent brigade group.

When the British Eighth Army landed in Sicily in July, 231 Brigade Group was fully committed to the fighting advance across the island to Messina. It landed on the beaches at Pizzo on the Italian mainland and fought its way up the west coast until withdrawn to Britain later in the year. The Normandy invasion of 6 June 1944 was the brigade group's third amphibious assault landing, and it went on to fight in Northwest Europe until the end of 1944.

The 231 (Malta) Independent Brigade Group mustered seven major units, plus supporting detachments, for the Normandy landings, becoming a formidable formation of 7000 men. The British 50th Division, of which it was a part, contained four such brigade groups and had an overall strength of 38,000.

The heart of 231 Brigade Group was the infantry brigade of the 1st Hampshires, 1st Dorsets and 2nd Devons. No.47(RM) Commando was attached quite late, and had a special mission which took it beyond the control of the group. The infantry battalions were supported by the 90th Field Regiment, Royal Artillery, 147th Field Regiment and the Essex Yeomanry. Armoured support was supplied by a squadron of Royal Marine Centaurs (Cromwell tanks fitted with 75mm guns), and DD Sherman tanks of the Sherwood Rangers. In addition to a detachment from the Royal Engineers, the brigade had 'funnies' from the 79th Armoured Division, including flail, fascine, bridge and flame-thrower vehicles. The Royal Army Medical Corps provided a detachment to handle and evacuate casualties. Brigade group administration was the role of the 6th Battalion, The Border Regiment, which had been organised as No.10 Beach Group, but in fact this unit was occupied with mopping up snipers in the area of the beachhead, as well as handling supplies. Brigade HQ was split into three elements. Tactical HQ consisted of the brigadier, a liaison officer, a signaller, and two drivers equipped with a Bren carrier and a jeep. The Reserve Tactical HQ was under the brigade major, while Main HQ was run by the staff captain. All HQs were capable of command.

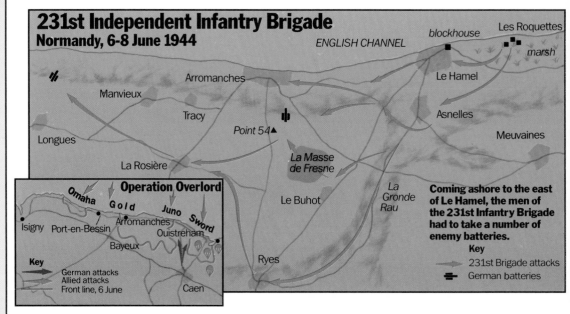

231st Independent Infantry Brigade
Normandy, 6-8 June 1944

ENGLISH CHANNEL

Operation Overlord

Coming ashore to the east of Le Hamel, the men of the 231st Infantry Brigade had to take a number of enemy batteries.

Key
→ 231st Brigade attacks
⊟ German batteries

Key
→ German attacks
→ Allied attacks
→ Front line, 6 June

brigadier decided on battalion objectives, attached artillery and tanks to the battalions, assigned tasks to the engineers, and vetted battalion plans.

The brigade major transformed the brigadier's wishes into formal orders. Specialist staffs produced plans and orders for the amphibious lift across the Channel. Liaison with the Royal Navy was good, for both transport and fire support planning, with the spirit of co-operation consolidated by joint exercises and frequent social contact. In contrast, the RAF remained remote and resisted attempts to establish contact. In consequence the brigade was not able to establish effective co-operation with the four squadrons of aircraft that were, in theory, on call to it.

As it was drawn up, the brigade tactical plan was as follows. The 1st Hampshires and 1st Dorsets, with their attached tanks and artillery, were to land as the first wave. The Hampshires were to be delivered opposite Le Hamel, assault the town, go on to take Asnelles, then move westwards to clear Arroman-ches, Tracy-sur-Mer and Manvieux. It was known that Le Hamel and Arromanches had been prepared for defence. In particular, there was a strong and well-protected blockhouse in Le Hamel which was masked towards the sea and could enfilade the beach to the east for at least a kilometre. The brigadier asked the Navy and RAF to pay special attention to the destruction of this fortification, but it survived to cause great disruption to the assault.

The Dorsets were to land about 900m to the east, at Les Roquettes, where an enemy platoon held a complex of pillboxes. They were to move directly inland, then wheel to the right and advance to take an enemy battery and entrenchments on Point 54, between Le Hamel and Arromanches. They were also to occupy the village of Ryes.

The 2nd Devons were to land near Le Hamel half an hour after the leading battalions, then advance up La Gronde Rau to capture Ryes, where there was known to be a German HQ. Having handed the village over to the Dorsets, they were to advance westwards, via La Rosière, to take the Longues Battery. Then they were to resume the westward movement until they met Americans coming east from Omaha Beach.

No.47(RM) Commando was to land behind the Devons, then move inland as swiftly as possible and make a forced march, evading the enemy, to seize Port-en-Bessin, a base for coastal motor boats. The commandos were to assault the defences on the east cliff with direct support from the Navy and RAF.

The brigade embarked at Southampton on 3 June. The crossing, on the night of the 5th, was rough, but all arrived safely off the Normandy coast by dawn. At sunrise the coastal panorama that appeared was recognised at once, due to the intense study of photographs and terrain models. Soon it vanished in smoke and dust as the bombardment commenced.

The shelling and bombing were impressive, but not entirely effective. The same was true of the 'Hedgerows', (landing craft fitted with rocket batter-

Below far left: An infantryman of 231 Brigade Group, armed with a 9mm Sten sub-machine gun, takes advantage of good cover to maintain a watch on the ground ahead. The scene is typical of the Normandy battlefield, where dense vegetation and deep ditches offered the Germans innumerable excellent sites for anti-tank gun emplacements and machine-gun nests. Below: A Bren-gunner of the 1st Hampshires, the 'TT' (Tyne and Tees) badge of the 50th (Northumbrian) Division on his shoulder, keeps an eye out for snipers. Inset below: Men of the 1st Dorsets bombard German positions at Hottot-les-Bagues with 3in mortars. Below right: Supporting the blockhouse-blasting operations of 231 Brigade were Churchill tanks of the 79th Armoured Division, equipped with the Petard spigot mortar. The Petard's round, a 40lb bomb (seen on the right), was nicknamed 'the Flying Dustbin'.

ies to give close support to the infantry), which could not fire accurately because the sea was too rough. Nor could the landing craft with gun armament. The heavy seas and strong currents wrought havoc with other parts of the plan too. Navy and Royal Engineer clearance teams were unable to demolish beach and offshore obstacles as planned, because the water was too deep. Those DD (Duplex Drive) amphibious tanks and Centaurs that were launched were swamped and sank, so the infantry arrived without any immediate armoured support. When the infantry did arrive, some were misplaced. The delay in the arrival of tanks, and of the 'funnies', especially the flails to clear paths through the minefields, kept the first wave of infantry on the beach for longer than expected. This led to congestion and confusion, a beach traffic jam, as subsequent waves arrived. The elaborate scheme for the arrival of a vanguard of specialists, armour, and self-propelled artillery to assist the infantry was wrecked by the weather. The assault and advance inland became an infantry battle with other arms in an auxiliary role.

The Hampshires had intended to assault Le Hamel straight over the beach with B and C Companies. A Company was to push directly inland to take Asnelles, and D Company was to act as reserve. Subsequently, they would make their way along the coast to take Arromanches and patrol out to Tracey and Manvieux. But their landing craft beached well to the east of Le Hamel at 0735 hours after a turbulent run-in lasting 90 minutes. B Company came ashore at Les Roquettes, rushed the pillboxes, then pushed on to swing into a left-flanking attack on Asnelles. They cleared the village by 1200. A and C Companies moved over the beach, through an uncleared minefield beyond, and tried to advance along the coast road into Le Hamel from the east. Enemy machine-gun and mortar fire from the fortified houses pinned them down. An anti-tank gun in the blockhouse knocked out tanks and flails which were coming over the beach in support. Some of these vehicles got stuck in patches of soft mud and made easy targets. Within a short time the Hampshires suffered so severely that A and C Companies were amalgamated. The commanding officer, second-in-command, the naval forward officer bombardment and the officer commanding the attached artillery battery were all hit.

The brigadier arrived to sort out the mess, and shifted the direction of the attack inland. B Company left Asnelles to ascend the high ground to the west and then move into Le Hamel from that direction. The amalgamated A and C Companies swung inland and advanced on the town from the southeast, while C Company of the Dorsets moved above Asnelles to give fire support. An AVRE (Armoured Vehicle Royal Engineers) moved up along the B Company axis, smashing open the fortified houses with Petards (large-calibre mortars). Eventually, after five Petard rounds had struck it, the blockhouse surrendered. The garrison of eight, all shocked by concussion, groped their way out with blood streaming from noses, ears and mouths. Le Hamel was secure by 1600, after every strengthened house had been broken open and combed out.

The Hampshires pushed on, with D Company pressing into Arromanches along the coast road, while A/C and B Companies advanced along the Manvieux Ridge. Arromanches was bombarded by destroyers and 147th Field Regiment, and was then assaulted by D Company at 1800. By 2100 the town was clear. The enemy in Arromanches, demoralised by the fall of Le Hamel, did not resist strongly. The Hampshires lost 182 casualties on D-day, mostly in Le Hamel. On D+1 they held their ground, patrolling the Manvieux Ridge to clear out the numerous and

Below left: Field Marshal Montgomery pins the Distinguished Conduct Medal onto the breast of Sergeant R.F. Curley, 1st Battalion, The Hampshire Regiment. The award was for gallantry in the field after the Normandy landings. Bottom left: Two infantrymen of the 2nd Battalion, The Dorsetshire Regiment, compare pistols captured from the retreating German forces in Normandy.

Below: An M4 Sherman tank of 147th Field Regiment hurtles down the road to Amaye-sur-Seulles at its top speed of 26 mph. The Sherman was the most widely deployed tank of World War II. Its armament consisted of a 75mm M3 gun, a co-axial 0.3in M1919A4 machine gun, another M1919A4 in a ball mounting in the bow, a 0.5in M2 machine gun mounted on the turret, and a 2in M3 smoke mortar.

active enemy snipers.

Like the Hampshires, the Dorsets arrived scattered and to the east of their destination. A and B Companies had to move westwards along the beach, under fire, to get into the brigade area. The drained marsh just inland was mined. C Company arrived at Les Roquettes, and cleared the area of enemy before going up to Asnelles to support the Hampshires. B Company stayed at Les Roquettes to guard against enemy counter-attacks on the beach. In the evening this company moved up to occupy Ryes. C and D Companies moved up the slope of the Meuvaines Ridge, then wheeled right to advance on Point 54. They encountered a strong enemy force posted in Le Buhot and La Masse de Fresne just beyond. C Company managed to take Le Buhot, but D was stopped in front of the woods. A Company, the reserve, came up to assault the enemy in the wood. The attack was supported by a concentration from 90th Field Regiment and tanks of the Sherwood Rangers. C and D Companies gave fire support. The enemy attempted a counter-attack on Le Buhot, but was forced back and beaten. The three companies moved forward to their objective, the battery at Point 54, to find that it had been silenced by naval bombardment and abandoned. They dug in on the high ground, with anti-tank weapons covering the line of La Gronde Rau. The Dorsets lost 128 casualties, including 14 officers, on D-day. On D+1 they mopped up their battalion area. But their rest was short, for on D+2 they were detached to act as motor infantry with 8th Armoured Brigade. The Dorsets fought hard on D-day; they took their objectives in sequence if not on schedule, and gave help to the Hampshires as well.

They were delayed by mortaring and sniping, and by machine-gun posts lodged in copses and hedgerows

The Devons had planned to land beside Le Hamel, form up in Asnelles, move up La Gronde Rau to take Ryes, then move directly westwards via La Rosière to capture the Longues Battery. In the event, only C Company landed close to Le Hamel, at 0815, and was drawn into the fighting there. A, B and D Companies were carried to Les Roquettes by the current. The beach was cluttered with men and materiel. The three companies moved inland in single file, avoided Asnelles where the Hampshires were fighting, and got into the declivity of La Gronde Rau. On the advance south to Ryes they were delayed by mortaring and sniping, and by machine-gun posts lodged in copses and hedgerows. B and D Companies moved to the right across higher ground to assault the village. Ryes was secured by 1600. The enemy HQ there proved to be the depot of a horse-drawn transport unit. C Company came up from Asnelles by 1900 and went on towards La Rosière, where it was held up by strong enemy posts. At nightfall, the Devons dug in and waited. They had lost 88 men, including eight officers.

On the 7th the Devons moved onto the Longues Battery, which was protected by an elaborate system of entrenchments. After a heavy bombardment by the Navy and artillery, two companies made the assault, supported by a platoon of medium machine guns of The Cheshire Regiment. The battery was still operational, despite high-altitude bombing by the RAF and naval bombardment, so its capture was of great importance. About 120 Germans were taken prisoner. One of these said that when the naval bombardment began he felt as if he was inside a cocktail-shaker. On the next day the Devons made a difficult attack, through an open park, on a château housing the local enemy naval HQ. The soldiers moved in steadily despite a great volume of automatic fire, and took the house.

No. 47(RM) Commando had orders to land after the Devons, get to Port-en-Bessin without involvement in combat, and assault the east cliff by 1400. Support would be provided by the RAF, and, in addition, 147th Field Regiment and two destroyers would be on call. The commandos were unable to keep to their plan. They landed on time, at 1000, but sustained losses because three of their landing craft sank. They also lost all their radios, so were unable to call up support. Their assembly area, near Le Hamel, was still partly under enemy control. They moved inland swiftly, but bumped into the enemy post at La Rosière, and lost time skirting round the village. As night fell they were still a distance from Port-en-Bessin, so dug in for the night. Next day they decided on a new plan; to seize Escures as a forward base, infiltrate into Port-en-Bessin in the early hours of the 8th, then take the port. This plan was executed, and the cliff was taken by 0400 on the 8th. But the commando attack was unsupported and incurred 200 casualties.

The infantry had to bear the brunt of the fighting, especially in the chaotic early stages on the beaches

The assault troops who invaded Normandy on 6 June have been accused of showing a lack of urgency. This accusation cannot be sustained. The tasks set for 231 Brigade Group would have been hard to accomplish even if all had been according to plan. But the elaborate plan of attack, with massive support for the infantry battalions at every stage, was wrecked by the weather. The infantrymen had to bear the brunt of the fighting, especially in the chaotic early stages on the beaches and just beyond them.

They did receive effective support from their attached artillery and tanks, and got quick and accurate fire support from the Navy. But the RAF took three hours to call up, far too long a delay in a fluid situation. The enemy proved to be very determined in some critical places, particularly Le Hamel, where the fighting was prolonged. The Germans also had very persistent and troublesome snipers; the brigade lost a disproportionate number of officers and NCOs to these marksmen. The brigade had not only to take ground, but to secure it against expected enemy counter-attacks. In the event, the Germans never made a major counter-attack into the brigade area, and only one minor effort, at Le Buhot. But the threat was a factor, and 231 Brigade had to cover the right flank of 69 Brigade and the rear of 16 Brigade. Although it was D+2 before Port-en-Bessin fell, by the end of D-day 231 Brigade had taken Le Hamel and Arromanches and was firmly ensconced on the ridge inland. In the face of great adversity, it was hard training and good instinctive co-operation between the units, particularly between the infantry battalions as they secured their objectives, that carried the brigade to success.

THE AUTHOR Nigel de Lee is a Senior Lecturer in the War Studies Department, RMA Sandhurst. He and the publishers would like to thank veterans of 231 Independent Brigade Group for their help in the preparation of this article.

CROWBAR ACTION

Scouring the bush lands of South West Africa for SWAPO insurgents, the hunter-killer combat groups of Koevoet operate on the principle of maximum firepower

THE COLUMN of four Casspirs and one Blesbok had broken from the heavy bush into an open pan spotted with trees and drooping thickets, a water hole at the centre. Suddenly it came...Boesman's voice crackled over the radio – 'Contact!' My eyes snapped to Du Rand, sitting across from me. There was one of those forever half-seconds before Jim spat 'Contact!' and grabbed for his weapon.

Following a week-long tour of the South West Africa/Namibia Operational Area, I stepped off the C-130 Hercules back at Ondangwa Air Force Base. The lieutenant meeting me looked as though he was attending a funeral. 'Authorisation finally came through an hour ago,' he intoned, shaking his head. 'You leave tomorrow for a week in the bush with Koevoet.'

'Koevoet' – pronounced 'koofoot' – is the old and now unofficial name for the South West Africa Police Counter-Insurgency (SWAPOLCOIN) unit. Little known outside the operational area, this predominantly black unit has accounted for almost 25 per cent of the 10,351 losses suffered by the Soviet-backed South West African People's Organisation (SWAPO) terrorists infiltrating across the border from Angola. Since its shaky beginning eight years ago, SWAPOLCOIN has killed over 2500 armed terrorists. Its own losses have been less than 90.

'I was sent up here in '78,' recalled Brigadier J.G. Dreyer, the commanding officer of SWAPOLCOIN, 'to see what role the police could play against terrorism.' Drawing on experience gained in the Rhodesian bush war, Dreyer at first envisaged a Selous Scout-type unit, employing blacks in the counter-insurgency role. 'I learned in Rhodesia,' Dreyer emphasised, 'that you must use the local people because of their knowlege of the language,

customs and terrain. An all-white force would be totally ineffective in this kind of war.'

As the Ovambo people comprise half the population of South West Africa/Namibia, Dreyer approached a senior Ovambo headman and discussed his ideas. The headman was impressed and, at Dreyer's request, recruited 60 Ovambos skilled in tracking and weapons handling. The new unit was given the letter 'K' as its designator. The K became Koevoet, Afrikaans for crowbar. Never was a unit more aptly dubbed.

Reporting to SWAPOLCOIN headquarters, I walked into Captain Bernie Ley's office. He got down to business. 'Blood group?' he asked. 'Next of kin? Your group leader will issue you with a weapon. Ever fired an R5?' Any thoughts that this might be a boy-scout-camping-trip-in-the-woods affair quickly evaporated. I asked if I needed to take any identification. Captain Maritz – who has the reputation of carrying around more shrapnel than the rest of 'Ops K' combined – walked in as I asked my question. He smirked as he replied: 'I don't think any "terr's" gonna be too impressed with your press cards.'

Outside, the Casspir armoured personnel carriers (APCs) and Blesbok mine-protected supply trucks pulling out that morning were being loaded. The cars' guns, which had been taken down when the groups had returned from a bush patrol the week before, were being remounted. Depending on the personal preferences of the group leaders, the cars carried a combination of two 0.3in Brownings or 7.62mm light machine guns (LMGs), or a 0.5in Browning with two of the lighter guns. At one time, a number of Casspirs carried Soviet 14.5mm guns. This practice ended, however, when supplies of captured ammunition ran out. Looking into the cars, I saw a bewildering array of foreign and domestic hardware. In addition to each man's Armscor R5 rifle with 50-round magazine, there were 60mm mortars, RPDs, PKMs, RPG-7s, single and six-shot 40mm grenade launchers, LMGs with bipods, an occasional R1, and enough belted and boxed ammunition to keep things hot for quite a spell. 'Maximum firepower,'

KOEVOET

During the first few months of Koevoet's existence, Colonel, now Major-General J. G. Dreyer's force operated on a shoestring budget. Dreyer had been allowed to take only four officers with him to the South West Africa/Namibia Operational Area, but he was determined that his concept for combatting the 'terrs' should succeed. After recruiting another two officers and 60 Ovambo tribesmen from the area, Dreyer put 'Ops K' through a rigorous training programme.

Koevoet's first major success came in 1979, after 12 SWAPO terrorists bayonetted four civilians to death and managed to elude the army. One 'Ops K' officer and 23 Ovambo trackers were flown to the scene and followed the spoor for the next seven days. In the contact that ensued, the SWAPO commander was killed. Koevoet was soon killing 50 to 80 terrorists a month.

Armed with combat statistics, Dreyer flew to Pretoria to argue his case. Money and equipment were soon on the way, including three Hippo armoured personnel carriers, the forerunners of the Casspirs. Dreyer was now convinced that highly mobile hunter-killer teams were the most effective way of dealing with terrorists in the dense bush. Each heavily armed Koevoet group was therefore organised into 40 Ovambo trackers, four officers and four Casspirs. Added to each group was one Blesbok supply vehicle. Above: The insignia of the South West Africa Police Counter-Insurgency unit.

said a voice. I looked around. It was Warrant Officer Marius Brand. I would be spending the next week with Brand and his group, Zulu Alpha. Brand is tall, lanky and moves with the loose-jointed swagger of a western gunslinger: 'In a contact, you gotta overwhelm the terrs, break them up and kill 'em now-now. Especially in an ambush...you drive straight into them with maximum firepower.' He smiled, but his eyes stayed as cold as those of the snake on Zulu Alpha's group insignia.

Once on the road, Brand noted: 'We're killing them faster than they can be replaced. The terrs are having to kidnap recruits and train them against their will.' Later in the week, I would follow the progress of a group tracking three SWAPO terrorists who had kidnapped 10 people. The radioed reports lasted two days before the civilians were rescued. The kidnappers never made it across the border either.

Once in the bush, every civilian becomes a possible source of information. At each kraal, the trackers dismount and question the local population. To my surprise, the trackers came back with reports that three terrorists had been seen or heard about in the last two days. My surprise must have been evident.' I can promise you, there are 10 to 15 terrs within 10 "klicks" of here,' volunteered Marius, answering my unasked question. 'The bad thing is that if they hear we're in the area they sit tight or get the hell out. They're really scared of us.' Working the area until late afternoon, it was obvious that these three were keeping a very low profile. With the sun low on the horizon, we joined up with Dean Viljeon who was temporarily ramrodding Zulu Mike's new Wolf Turbo APCs. Just before sunset, a suitable location for a temporary base (TB) was found. With the Casspirs and Wolf Turbos set around the TB, guns facing outward, food and bedding were unloaded. A dozen cooking fires were soon going strong. Being in the middle of 'indian' country with fires blazing seemed a touch unorthodox, I thought, but the guys explained that SWAPO was too frightened of Koevoet even to think about hitting us.

What they could tell from an imprint that I could hardly see was incredible

Late one afternoon a few days later, we were barrelling down the dirt road towards the army base at Eenhana. On either side was thick, heavy cover. More than a couple of groups had been hit along this stretch. Special Warrant Officer Otto Shivute, senior Ovambo of Zulu Alpha, was looking through an Oshivambo-Afrikaans-English dictionary. Finding the words he wanted, he turned to me with a smile: 'If we lucky, ambush!' From sunup to sundown, the radios in the cars were constantly in use. Groups operating from Opuwa in the west, to Rundu in the east, kept Zulu Base and each other advised of their progress and situations. Marius would keep me abreast of the Afrikaans transmissions, especially when a group was on a 'follow up' – chasing spoor. Everyone would be particularly attentive to the radio when a group reported closing on a hot spoor, finally calling for gunships when contact was imminent. Sometimes the attention-grabbing 'Contact' would come through unexpectedly, leaving everyone hanging in suspense until the outcome was relayed. The worst were calls for a casevac chopper to take out their own wounded. Ops K is a close, tightly-knit family – blacks and whites together – and a call for a casevac would keep each man holding his breath

Right: Carrying his favourite weapon – a 40mm grenade launcher – 'Eme' searches an area for signs of SWAPO insurgents. Below: Warrant Officer Lukas Kilino. Below right: After chasing a group of terrorists close to the Angolan border, Zulu Alpha becomes bogged down in one of Ovamboland's marshy oshanas. Note the 7.62mm GPMG and 0.5in Browning mounted in tandem. Bottom right: Heavy going for one of the group's Casspir armoured personnel carriers.

until the extent of the injuries was known.

The first good spoor the trackers found was soon lost on hard ground, found, lost, then found again. Side by side with Zulu Mike, we followed it most of the day. Although it had been described to me time and again, I was amazed at the aggression the trackers showed when they had the spoor. Cars flanking them, they would move at a dead run, often outstripping the Casspirs which could not keep pace through the thick bush. They would run until winded, drop back to their cars, and their places would be taken by others who would drop off the sides of the rolling cars and take the spoor. On hard ground, where the spoor became indistinct, the cars would stop and everyone debuss, fanning out in an attempt to pick it up further on. What they could tell from an imprint that I could barely see was incredible: 'This one old man – short steps', or 'this woman and child', or 'this one SWAPO – soldier with gun walks proud.'

The spoor of 30 to 40 terrorists was found and the groups fanned out, racing off in a cloud of dust

On the fifth morning, we received word that a small army base near the Angolan border had been mortared in the middle of the night. 'Saddling up', we headed for the scene of the crime. When we pulled up an hour later, three other groups were already there. I noted that half the mortar rounds had failed to detonate. The aim wasn't too good, either. All had impacted at least 150m short of the intended target. The spoor of 30 to 40 terrorists was found and all the groups fanned out, racing off in a cloud of dust to pick up the spoor further ahead. The dust came to an abrupt end as we ran into a series of oshanas, low marshy areas with a foot or more of water. The cars slowed to a crawl. Struggling through the 'shanas, it was accepted that the terrorists had probably already made it across the border to safety, but no-one was ready to give up the chase. By early afternoon, and 100m short of the border, it was obvious that Koevoet had lost this round. Zulu Base radioed to say intelligence sources indicated 58 SWAPO terrorists had crossed the border heading for the Popular Armed Forces for the Liberation of Angola (FAPLA) base at Namukunde, a few kilometres north of us. They had crossed to safety – SWAPOLCOIN's only operational limit is the Angolan border.

As sunset approached, the trackers started unloading bedrolls and weapons, wading to an island in the middle of the 'shana. As they began setting up mortars it finally started to dawn on me that we were there for the night. It also struck me that maybe we weren't exactly in the best of situations. We were stuck fast in the middle of a particularly soft-bottomed oshana. It was getting dark. No other group was near enough to get to us that night and render assistance. Not all that far away were 58 SWAPO holed up in a FAPLA base. And with another FAPLA border post less than five klicks to the east, they had to know where we were. But the night passed without incident, and late the next morning Dean Viljoen and the Wolf Turbos roared in and dragged us out of the quagmire.

On my last morning with Zulu Alpha, we responded to the scene of another mortaring. Again, spoor was found, this time eight of them, but lost on hard ground, found again – just as before. At least this time we had no 'shanas to wade through.

In the middle of a field of rumbling cars, Marius asked if I'd like to ride with the 'Brig', who had come

'Contact.' Only seconds after Zulu November catches sight of a group of SWAPO insurgents, the air is thick with the sound of gunfire. Bottom left: After breaking open his 'blooper' and feeding in a round, Eme takes aim (above left). Meanwhile, Ovambo trackers spray the area outside the Casspir with machine-gun bullets (top and bottom right). Right and far right: Changing a magazine in the heat of battle. Left: Sergeant Jim Du Rand.

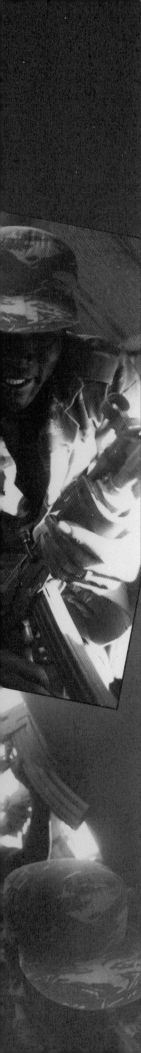

out for the hunt. He pointed to a Wolf Turbo. Grabbing my camera bag, I hopped out and ran to the Wolf. Climbing through the rear doors that hissed open for me, I thought maybe I had the wrong car. There was no sign of Brigadier Dreyer. Then I caught sight of a familiar figure in the driver's seat. 'If he has time, you can't keep him out of the field,' one of his staff volunteered with a barely suppressed grin.

The week with Zulu Alpha came to an end. SWAPO, through fortune or skill, had managed to keep out of our way. Groups working other areas of Ovamboland's 33,000 square miles, however, found what they were looking for. Seven more notches were added to Koevoet's guns.

The following morning, after being granted permission to stay for another week, I climbed aboard the number two car of Zulu November. At the last minute, Sergeant Jim Du Rand had been assigned to ride with me. I felt guilty as hell when he explained this was his last week with Ops K, but since my car commander spoke no English, they wanted someone with me who could translate. After six years with Koevoet, over 120 contacts and more than 300 kills, Du Rand was heading back to South Africa to take up somewhat quieter police duties. When he mentioned that it seemed guys always got hurt or killed just when they were ready to leave, I started feeling pretty rotten. 'No, no, it's okay,' he assured me. 'If I wasn't doing this, I'd be out setting up night ambushes anyway!'

The group leader of Zulu November is the stocky, barrel-chested Willem Boesman. Zulu November is a top-scorer – in 1985, Boesman's group claimed the lives of 50 terrorists. In February 1986, Zulu November hit a 40-man SWAPO detachment, killing 35 in a 12 and a half minute contact. It was a record for Ops K. As we rolled out of Zulu Base, Boesman's score for the first four months of 1986 already stood at 47.

'And then the crazy bastard casually told him to pick it up and bring it to the car'

My car commander for this second week with Koevoet was Warrant Officer Lukas Kilino, who had started soldiering at the age of 14 with Holden Roberto's National Liberation Front of Angola (FNLA). When the Soviet-backed Popular Movement for the Liberation of Angola (MPLA) seized power in Angola, Kilino made his way south and joined South Africa's little-publicised 32 Battalion. Later, he moved to Ops K. It was not difficult to spot him as a professional.

Boesman's uncanny sixth sense took us into an area where the trackers picked up fresh spoor almost immediately. At one point, they figured the spoor was no more than two hours old and Boesman radioed the air force, putting the gunships on standby.

The relationship between SWAPOLCOIN and the South African Air Force is first-rate. Both think highly of the other. As Marius told me the week before: 'They know we won't scramble them unless we're on a hot spoor and they have a good chance to get kills.'

Although a contact appeared imminent, this particular group of terrorists 'bombshelled' – each taking off in a separate direction – and 'anti-tracked' – backing up on their own spoor, staying on hard ground wherever possible and moving carefully from one tuft of tough grass to another. Anything and everything to make their tracks indistinguishable.

Setting up a TB that night, I listened to an inexhaustable repertoire of contact stories. Du Rand told of the time he found himself face to face with a 'terr' holding an RPG-7. Jim levelled his gun, only to discover it had jammed. The terrorist looked down at the RPG in his hands, looked up at the 20mm pointing at him and dropped the rocket launcher like a hot potato, raising his hands. Actually, I had heard the story a week earlier from someone who added: 'And then the crazy bastard casually told him to pick it up and bring it to the car!'

Mornings at a TB start before dawn, when the first sleepy risers stir last night's coals into life, sending sparks into the cold, dark air. There is the lonely sound of a cough here and there. The small, ruby glow of a first cigarette punctuates the camp. Sweaters are pulled on against the chill and dark figures begin to cluster round the first fire, palms towards the warmth. As light begins to filter through the bush, more figures slip from brown sleeping bags. Before the sun has made its appearance, there is the smell of coffee in the crisp air. Sleeping bags are rolled up and everything loaded on the Blesbok. Boesman, deeply religious and private, unwraps a small bible and sits alone, reading a passage. I wonder which it might be. When the sun is full-born on the horizon, we move out, another long and dusty day ahead of us. On this morning, a full moon still hangs large and white in the western sky.

The rhythmic ripple of *shh-klacks* is heard as bolts come back and fall on chambered rounds

The morning follows the pattern of all the others: stopping at kraals and questioning the locals, moving through the bush, everyone scanning the ground for spoor. We are sitting under a mopane tree during a noon coffee-break when, without preamble, comes that attention-grabbing word over the radio: 'Contact'. Behind the word, gunfire is heard. Coffee cups stop at lips, and are slowly lowered as ears strain to pull more from the air. Then the call comes for a casevac chopper. Silent looks pass between the men sitting cross-legged on the ground. Pierre goes to stand nearer the car, as though that will force more from the radio. Finally the story crackles through the speaker. A group has hit an ambush. Three terrorists have been killed, but one car commander has been seriously wounded. Nothing more is heard.

Flicking what is left of the coffee aside, we climb into the Casspirs. The mood is camouflaged with thin jokes. Diesels rumble, clutches are engaged and we move out. The routine continues. Later, with two hours of daylight left, we turn west towards Ohangwena. Du Rand and I are sitting inside, opposite each other. The interior of the Casspir brightens as we crash out of the thick bush into the open. It was then Boesman saw them...'Contact'...I came back from wherever I was, my eyes meeting Jim's for one of those interminable half-seconds. Du Rand spat 'Contact', and snatched his R5 from its vertical rack. Engine powering up and ahead I hear guns of at least one car already going...our car is veering hard left, the car ahead breaking right and everyone grabbing weapons. The rhythmic ripple of *shh-klacks* is heard as bolts come back and fall on chambered rounds, the firepower of a Koevoet group exploding like a burst water main...perhaps only the lead car having a positive target but no-one knowing where the main force might be and everyone laying down maximum suppressive fire. The high-pitched chatters of the R5s mingle with the deep-throated *thud-*

Once the spoor has been picked up, a Koevoet group will attempt to follow it at maximum speed. Unlike most other elements of the security forces, Ops K is not restricted by battalion, company or even sector boundaries. Indeed, its only operational limit is the Angolan border. If the spoor is lost at any point during the chase, men will debuss from the Casspirs and join the trackers in an attempt to find it again. If this proves unsuccessful, however, the search will be widened and information will be sought from the local civilian population. A contact with a single SWAPO insurgent or a small group is normally handled by the trackers, with the vehicles providing second-line support.

If the spoor is obviously one of a large group of insurgents, however, the trackers will be pulled back into the vehicles. The contact will then be handled as a mounted action. After the Blesbok logistic vehicles have pulled clear for their own safety, the Casspirs circle through the area of contact and lay down maximum firepower. The area is then divided into sections and the group spreads out, combing the bush for insurgents who may have fled from the battle. By using these tactics, Koevoet virtually eliminates the confusion that would usually occur during a bush firefight. Mobility, protection and firepower, in addition to a reservoir of combat experience, are the keystones of Koevoet's success in the counter-insurgency role.

thud-thud-thud of the Browning 'fifties' and everyone in the car is shouting, firing, looking left-right for targets: some standing and firing over the edge of the Casspir, others through the spring-loaded gun ports below the windows. Everyone shouting, the shouting drowned by the firing, hot brass on bare skin, the hollow *whunk!* of a 40mm grenade launcher to my left and seeing Eme, whose baby it is, breaking it open, dropping in another swollen round, firing, reloading, firing. The man to my right jams the short muzzle of his R5 through the gun port just as the 10-ton Casspir bounces hard over a bump, and the R5 comes back inside on full automatic, spraying the inside with hot splinters of 5.56mm rounds. Me jerking my legs away with a sharply expelled 'jeezus!', and then being trampled over by Eme who's run out of ammunition and is diving to the rear of the Casspir for more – bowling me over a second time as he comes back through the throng of unsteady legs: everyone trying to hold on, keep his balance, and fire from the shaking, twisting car that is careering from left to right to present as difficult target as possible for any RPG or Heatstrim, either one of which can take out a Casspir. Me trying to take photos of the chaos inside, and the air seeming solid with the firing, shouting, thin smoke, yelling, hot raining brass and bursts of excited Afrikaans over the radio. Engine racing and drive train screaming in pain as the driver jams up, down and through the gears...me yelling stupidly at Du Rand: 'How many are there! Where are they?' He yelling back: 'When you drive into them like this there's nothing else you can do!' I'm trying to stand to get shots of what's going on outside, only to be slammed down by Lukas' hand, then looking out the window and seeing the ground erupting zipper-like under the impact of the fifties racing towards the water hole, tree limbs splintering and shouts of '*komesho!*' (forward) '*kolomesho!*' (left), '*kolodio!*' (right),...*Shinga! Shinga!* (Go! Go!). I'm trying to get a shot of the one next to me who sprayed the inside, his hand laid open and bleeding badly, another whose leg is bleeding...I wonder if I'm bleeding as well,

Below: One of Zulu Alpha's Casspirs on patrol in the bush. By mounting the wheels and axles outside the vehicle's V-shaped hull, the designers have ensured a high degree of protection from land mines. Wheels or axles may be blown off, but very seldom do the occupants of a Casspir receive even minor injuries from SWAPO mines concealed on the road.

only I don't want anyone to see me looking a whatever it was that stung my legs. I stand again shaking off Kilino's hand to see Boesman's ca angling away from us and pouring fire into the area around the water hole. Du Rand is yelling: 'Unde the bush, under the bush' and suddenly we're stopped, the hydraulically-operated doors hissing open...I'm out and running behind the trackers who half-moon around a clump of low-hanging thicket their R5s erupting streams of empty brass, leaves trembling under the impact of the rounds. Du Rand is next to me, yelling: 'There's one in there!', and I'm wondering what the fuck I'm doing outside the Casspir...following the trackers in under the bran ches expecting to see a body but seeing only webbing and leather pouches, a gourd half-filled with local mahango beer...I realise the firing has stopped, replaced with hard, gasping laughter and the high-pitched giggles of excitement and relief.

'The bodies are over here,' I heard Du Rand say behind me. Turning and walking towards the wate hole, I saw the first one lying face up on a pile of deac branches. Bare feet protrude from camouflage trousers. Further on at the base of a tree was the second, face down, the right foot almost severed by a 50-calibre round. Both bodies with the limp heavi ness of new death. One of the trackers yanked the second body onto its back. He reached inside the

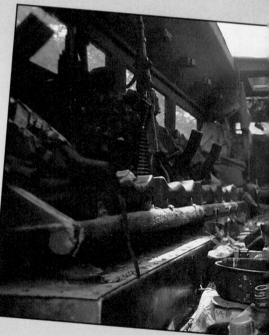

camouflage shirt and pulled a tan, checked collar into view. 'Civvie clothes, see?' he hissed, contemptuous of the deceit. An AK-47 lay alongside, the ballistic launcher for the nearby Heatstrims shot cleanly off the muzzle. The bodies were stripped of equipment and quickly searched for documents.

Back at the cars, Boesman explained that, as we came out of the bush, the two had broken from their hiding place next to the water hole. Had they stayed hidden, they could easily have taken out one of the Casspirs, or else gone entirely unnoticed. Such is fate. Jim Du Rand called the contact: 'A last one just for old time's sake.' Daubing at a blood smear on his leg, he admitted it was the worst injury he'd taken in his six years with Koevoet. I breathed a sigh of relief.

Lukas caught my eye. He nodded, raising his fist, thumb up. Thanks, I nodded back

That night, the contact was relived over and over again. The tape I had made of it brought everyone clustered around to hear, asking to have it rewound and listening again, recognising each other's voices amid the fury of the firing. Some re-enacted Lukas shoving me down whenever I tried to stand. Others howled with laughter as they described how Eme ran over me once, and then a second time. In the middle of it all, Lukas caught my eye. He nodded, raising his fist, thumb up. Thanks, I nodded back.

The morning after returning to Oshakati, I was scheduled on a Hercules 130 back to Pretoria. On the way to Ondangwa Air Force Base, I asked the army lieutenant to make a short detour. It was Wednesday, the beginning of a new week for half of Ops K. There was Zulu Alpha, loading up for another seven days in the bush, having spent a week in base. There was Marius, and Apie, Christo, Thys, Otto and Sandsak, Dean, Porky, Jack and the rest whose names I could never remember, just as I had seen them that first day two weeks before. Shaking hands, saying my goodbyes, I knew I was going to miss them. As the car pulled away, I turned to look back, watching until they disappeared from view. Facing forward, I suddenly felt more a deserter than a writer. You crazy bastards, I thought. Go safely.

THE AUTHOR James Hooper is a freelance photojournalist who accompanied Koevoet on several missions in the South West Africa/Namibia Operational Area during 1986-87.

HELL
ON THE
KOKODA TRAIL

In 1942 the relentless Japanese advance on Australia was finally halted by a desperate campaign in the jungle highlands of New Guinea

GENERAL SIR THOMAS BLAMEY

THE LITANY OF RUNAWAY Japanese victories that followed the devastating pre-emptive strike against the US Pacific Fleet at Pearl Harbor in December 1941 brought the Imperial Japanese armed forces almost within striking distance of the Australian mainland. In late January 1942, Japanese assault troops carried out successful attacks on Rabaul in New Britain and Kavieng in New Ireland, and the Japanese General Headquarters issued further orders to strengthen their defensive ring in the southwest Pacific. Advanced bases were to be created on Fiji, Samoa, New Caledonia and, most important of all, at Port Moresby on the southern coast of New Guinea.

As Japanese land and carrier-based bombers launched sorties against Darwin, the capital of Australia's Northern Territory, the first phase of the attack on New Guinea was launched. Virtually unopposed, Japanese forces took the towns of Lae and Salamaua on the island's northern coast in early March and pushed south along the Markham valley. Units of the Australian Imperial Force (AIF) Independent Companies and members of the New

The man who became the Australian Middle East Commander in World War II, General Sir Thomas Blamey, had been one of the outstanding Australian leaders of World War I. In 1914 Blamey was stationed in Britain in the War Office, but at the outbreak of hostilities he was appointed intelligence officer in the 1st Division. Blamey took part in the Gallipoli landings but spent most of the war carrying out staff duties. By 1918 he was General Sir John Monash's chief-of-staff and he was credited with originating the idea for the decisive Battle of Amiens. He left the army after the war to take up the post of Chief Commissioner of Police of Victoria in Australia, a position he held until forced to resign following an enquiry by a Royal Commission.

Left: Members of the Second Australian Imperial Force thread through the jungle before the attack on the Japanese-held town of Lae. Top far left: Diggers file out of a native village to reinforce the block on the Kokoda Trail. Top left: Aussie sappers improvise a rope and pulley 'flying fox' to ferry supplies over the Kanusi river.

Guinea Volunteer Rifles monitored, and clashed with, enemy patrols in the area. Activities in the north were, however, intended as a diversion. The Japanese intended to make their main attack on Port Moresby from the sea.

Despite the victories in the north, a number of reverses at sea in the following months forced the Japanese to replan the New Guinea strategy. In early May a naval task force escorting troopships bound for Port Moresby was forced back after losing a carrier during the Battle of the Coral Sea. In June, the US Navy sank three more carriers in the Battle of Midway. Taken together, these actions ended the immediate threat of large-scale Japanese naval involvement in the southwest Pacific campaign.

An amphibious assault on Port Moresby now out of the question, the main focus of the war in New Guinea became the Kokoda Trail. A native supply route running from Buna in the north to Port Moresby, it ran through dense tropical forests and across the precipitous ridges and valleys of the Owen Stanley Range. By any standards, the battlefield was one of the worst of the war. One Australian officer recorded its horrors:

'The track [was] a treacherous mass of moving mud interlaced with protruding roots that reached out [like] hidden hands to bring the laden troops heavily to the ground. Vines trapped

When the Second Australian Imperial Force was formed in 1939, Blamey was given its command and, after the outbreak of war, was placed in charge of the ANZAC Corps fighting in the Mediterranean. Once Greece had been overrun, Blamey returned to his position in the AIF and was also appointed Deputy Commander-in-Chief Middle East. When the Japanese began to bomb the Australian mainland in early 1941, Blamey was recalled from the Middle East. Although an admirer of General Douglas MacArthur, Blamey was far from a 'yes-man' and was often in conflict with him.

Above: General Blamey (left) inspects the fighting conditions in New Guinea with Lieutenant-General R.L. Eichelberger, the US commander in New Guinea.

them. Wet boughs slapped at them. Their breath came in gulps. Their eyes filled with perspiration.'

Elements of the Australian 30th Brigade, a militia force of volunteers and conscripts under Brigadier S. H. W. C. Porter, probed along the trail towards Buna during July, but the Japanese struck in force first. On the night of 21/22 July a 2000-strong seaborne assault group landed at Buna, easily dispersed a battalion of Papuan light infantry and began to move down the trail towards the airfield at Kokoda as more troops were put ashore. Porter was ordered to stall the Japanese.

The first clashes between the Australian advance guard, the understrength and untried 39th Battalion, and the Japanese were bloody. Prolonged engagements were fought out at close quarters with rifle, sub-machine gun and grenade. Unit cohesion was lost in the desperate struggle and the battle was fought between platoon-sized outfits. Men were lost in the jungle and casualties were often left behind – few were ever seen again. The fortunate faced an agonising trek back to the main Australian base at Uberi, carried by native stretcher-bearers who had been christened 'fuzzy-wuzzy angels' by the grateful wounded.

But the militiamen stood up well to the Japanese onslaught. At Kokoda on 9 August, the Japanese attempted their tried and trusted envelopment tactics to overcome the Australian defenders. They received a nasty, morale-shaking surprise that brought their headlong rush down the trail to a temporary halt. A veteran Japanese officer wrote of his dismay:

'... the enemy fire forced us to withdraw. The platoon was scattered and it was impossible to repeat our charge. The night attack ended in failure. Every day I am losing my men. I could not repress tears of bitterness. Rested, waiting for tomorrow, and struggled against cold and hunger.'

During the next night the Japanese returned to the fray with renewed vigour. After 90 minutes of sustained combat the warriors of the 39th Battalion were tipped out of their positions and fell back on Deniki, a few miles down the trail from Kokoda. Though their ranks had been thinned by death, injury and jungle diseases, they were still a fighting force.

Australian attempts to delay the enemy received a well-timed boost when a second militia unit, the 53rd Battalion, moved up to the front. For the weary men of the 39th, who had been in continuous contact with the Japanese for three gruelling weeks, the reinforcements arrived in the nick of time. The 39th's commanding officer, Lieutenant-Colonel Honner, described his men's condition:

'Physically, the pathetically young warriors of the 39th were in poor shape. Worn out by strenuous fighting and exhausting movement, and weakened by lack of food and shelter, many had literally come to a standstill. Practically every day torrential rains fell all through the afternoon and night, cascading into weapon pits and soaking the clothes they wore – the only clothes they had.'

The weeks of skirmishing along the muddy trail were only the opening gambit of the campaign, and both sides were steadily building up their forces for the main battles to come. The Japanese regional commander, Lieutenant-General Harukichi Hyakutake, despatched some 13,000 men to the island – most were war-hardened veterans of either China, the Philippines or Manchuria. The AIF's 7th Division, under Major-General 'Tubby' Allen, was on the south side of the Owen Stanley Range preparing to relieve the worn-out militia units. The Australian chain of command was also being formed. In the forthcoming weeks, Allen reported to General Rowell and later to General Blamey. Both reported directly to General Douglas MacArthur, who was increasingly impatient for a decisive, clear-cut victory.

The enemy were still losing heavily in the deadly game of ambush and counter-ambush

As the 7th Division moved forward from the advance base at Uberi, the militiamen were slowly giving ground under renewed Japanese pressure. Although forced on them by the ferocity and doggedness of the Japanese, the withdrawal was working to the advantage of the Australians. The enemy were still losing heavily in the deadly game of ambush and counter-ambush, and as they moved closer to Port Moresby their tenuous supply lines were becoming dangerously over-extended.

The Japanese tried to remedy this situation with an amphibious assault. In the southeast of the island, some 2000 men landed on the beaches at Milne Bay. The main assault began on the night of 25/26 August, well after the main battles for the island had begun in the north. Meeting unexpectedly stiff opposition from Australian militia units, the Japanese were fought to a standstill and forced to evacuate on 6 September.

Meanwhile Allen was marshalling his forces for a decisive encounter on ground of his own choosing. Under the not altogether welcome attention of MacArthur, two of the 7th Division regular units, the Second Australian Imperial Force's 14th and 16th Battalions (2/14th and 2/16th Battalions), took over from the decimated militiamen on the Kokoda Trail.

The regulars had little experience of jungle fighting but soon showed their mettle. On 29 August, Private B. S. Kingsbury earned a posthumous VC for singlehandedly defeating a Japanese charge. Firing his Bren gun from the hip, Kingsbury, leading other members of the 2/14th, was credited with inflicting close to 200 casualties on the enemy. The Australians were, however, fast running out of food and ammunition, despite the sterling efforts of their Melanesian porters. Retreating across Eora Creek back to Templeton's Crossing, which was held until 5 September, the regulars finally halted at Myola. Here the Australians fought skilfully and held the Japanese for six valuable days. To the rear, stores were being

Below: Australian troops, members of the New Guinea Volunteer Rifles and porters await the order to move out. Left: A casualty is borne away by New Guinea bearers, known to the troops as 'fuzzy-wuzzy angels'. Centre and far left: The hallowed Australian tradition of a 'smoko' is observed.

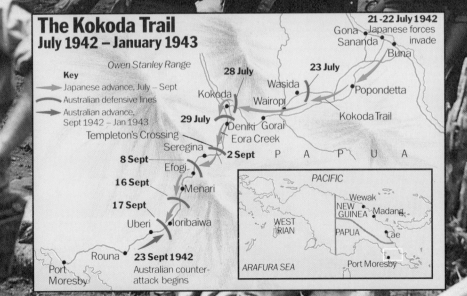

The Kokoda Trail
July 1942 – January 1943

Owen Stanley Range

Key
→ Japanese advance, July – Sept
⌒ Australian defensive lines
→ Australian advance, Sept 1942 – Jan 1943

21 -22 July 1942
Gona
Sananda
Japanese forces invade
Buna

28 July
Kokoda
Wasida
23 July
Wairopi
Popondetta
Kokoda Trail

29 July
Deniki Gorai
Eora Creek
Templeton's Crossing
Seregina
2 Sept
8 Sept
Efogi
16 Sept
Menari
17 Sept
Uberi Ioribaiwa

Rouna
23 Sept 1942
Australian counter-attack begins
Port Moresby

P A P U A

PACIFIC
Wewak
NEW GUINEA
Madang
WEST IRIAN
PAPUA
Lae
ARAFURA SEA
Port Moresby

Running roughly north to south from Buna to Port Moresby, the Kokoda Trail was little more than a mud track that ran through the mountains of the Owen Stanley Range. Cut through thick rain forest, the trail proper began at Uberi, a native village some 25 miles from Port Moresby. From Uberi, the trail rose some 1200ft in three miles. The path here was known as the 'Golden Staircase', a series of steps each between 10 and 18in in height. From the first 1200ft ridge the trail dropped dramatically by 1600ft. Porters then faced a second steep climb of some 2000ft up to the Imita Ridge.

From Imita there was a succession of ridges to be negotiated before the main ridge at Myola was reached. From this village, the track ran down a ledge, ending up at Templeton's Crossing on the Eora Creek. From the crossing, the route traversed a second run of ridges before finally descending to Kokoda itself, a former administrative centre roughly half-way to Buna. North from Kokoda the going was marginally easier, with the last 40 miles to Buna being downhill to the coast.

Nearly 100 miles long, the Kokoda Trail was the most direct, but difficult, route between Buna and Port Moresby, and as such it was recognised by both the Australians and the Japanese as the key to the outcome of the campaign in New Guinea. Much too hard going for heavy equipment, control of the trail could only be decided by the military skills of the individual soldiers on either side. As a battleground, it had little to offer the tactician.

Top: Operating in virgin jungle, the Australians had to contend with fast-flowing rivers and tracts of deep, clogging mud. Bridges and firm walkways were essential for the movement of large-scale parties. Above right: The submachine gun was an essential weapon for close-quarter contacts. Right: A combat patrol searches for pockets of Japanese troops.

brought up from Port Moresby and stockpiled at Uberi in preparation for the planned counter-attack.

As their frontline troops fell back, inflicting heavy losses on the Japanese, the Australian commanders made their final preparations. The position chosen for the stand was a short distance away from the village of Ioribaiwa, along the line of the Imita Ridge. The ridge, less than 30 miles from Port Moresby, was turned into a strong defence line. Trenches were dug and strongpoints were positioned to cover likely approach routes. Once the enemy had been decisively checked, the Australians would go over to the offensive with the aim of driving the Japanese back over the Owen Stanley mountains and out of Kokoda.

The 7th Division's 25th Brigade, led by Brigadier Eather, was moved up to the ridge. Eather's orders from Allen were bluntly unambiguous: 'There won't be any withdrawal from the Imita position. You'll die there if necessary. You understand?' The Japanese were also preparing for the final push on Port Moresby and, although short of food due to a chaotic supply system, they did receive 1000 reinforcements. In total, two full-strength infantry brigades, supported by a pair of mountain guns and engineers, were committed to the forthcoming battle for Imita Ridge.

Backed by two portable, short-barrelled 25-pounder mountain guns, the diggers fought the enemy to a standstill

Between 17 and 26 September the Japanese tried to cut a way through the Australian line. Both sides fought and jockeyed for position, seeking to gain a decisive advantage that would open the way to victory. Contacts were frequent and decided by small groups of men who battled ferociously for a few square yards of sodden ground. On the 19th, an Australian patrol dealt with a party of Japanese engineers as they built a carefully concealed strongpoint. Total Australian casualties in the campaign up to late September were 314 killed and 367 wounded. The enemy were losing men at a faster rate – 1000 dead and 1500 wounded – and many of those who had survived were cripplingly ill through disease and malnutrition. The campaign was swinging slowly but irreversibly in the Australians' favour.

Imita Ridge – a sound defensive position – shortages of supplies, exhaustion, growing Allied air superiority and, above all, the indomitable spirit of the ordinary Australian soldier, finally smashed the enemy drive on Port Moresby. Backed by two portable, short-barrelled 25-pounder mountain guns, the diggers fought the enemy to a standstill. As they recoiled from the ridge, the counter-attack was ordered.

On the 26th, Eather's men began the long haul back down the trail to Kokoda. Air supply was gradually improving but still too intermittent to be relied upon fully. The troops carried everything they needed: rations for five days, their personal kit, smallarms, extra ammunition and spare rounds for the support weapons.

Enemy resistance was everywhere stubborn but the brigade's three battalions made steady progress. By the first week of October, they were poised to cross Eora Creek at Templeton's Crossing. The rate of advance was much too slow for MacArthur, however, who wanted Kokoda airfield and a decisive victory in equal measure. But for the officers and

men on the ground, any careless moves against the enemy could spell disaster, and fighting against Japanese snipers and ambush parties was a time consuming, nerve-racking business. On 17 October Eather began to pull his exhausted, disease-ridden men out of the line. They were replaced by the AIF veteran 16th Brigade under Brigadier Lloyd. The three battalions, the 2/1st, 2/2nd and 2/3rd, were the first Australian units to see service in World War II, fighting with great distinction in the Western Desert. As the men moved towards the front, the signs of the bitter struggle were evident. One man recorded the scenes of death and destruction that clung to the trail.

'Along the route were skeletons picked clean by ants and other insects, and in the dark recesses of the forest came to our nostrils the stench of the dead, hastily buried or, perhaps, not buried at all.' Advancing by platoons and companies, the three battalions went into action on a narrow front in the vicinity of Eora Creek. Fighting through dense undergrowth with scouts thrown out in front to draw enemy fire, the diggers made painfully slow progress. The Japanese, though on the defensive, prove

to be masters of the arts of concealment and ambush. A handful of men or a lone fanatic could hold up an entire company for hours until winkled out. The creek was only five miles from Kokoda but every yard of ground was contested. It was a tense, edgy type of soldiering, but the Australians remained remarkably buoyant. The struggle to break through the enemy defences along the creek lasted for a week, but then a devastating flank attack by the 2/3rd Battalion rolled up the Japanese line. Australian casualties amounted to 92 dead and 200 wounded. Enemy losses were probably higher.

The Japanese forces on the island were at the end of their tether after the protracted slogging match in the Owen Stanley mountains

MacArthur was far from satisfied with the speed of the Australians' advance and he exhorted Blamey to redouble his efforts. He ordered: 'Press General Allen's advance. His extremely light casualties indicate no serious effort yet made to displace enemy. It is essential that the Kokoda airfield be taken.' Yet the Australians had taken only 35 days to advance from Ioribaiwa to the gates of Kokoda, while the Japanese had taken over 50 days to accomplish the same feat in the opposite direction. Allen kept his feelings to himself but was clearly unhappy with MacArthur's apprehension of the situation in New Guinea. In fact, Kokoda was about to fall. The Japanese forces on the island were at the end of their tether after the protracted slogging match in the Owen Stanley mountains and were under orders to stage a withdrawal back to the north coast, where they were to prepare to defend a number of important settlements, including Buna. As one Japanese correspondent wrote, the effects of the scarcely denied retreat were shattering:

'None of them had ever thought that a Japanese soldier would ever turn his back on the enemy- … The pursuit grew hotter every day until the enemy was close upon our heels. From time to time we came upon large fields extending over the side of a mountain, but we could not find a single piece of potato in them.'

Kokoda was finally entered on 1 November, and its fall marked a turning point in the war in the southwest Pacific. The fight for New Guinea was far from over and it would be many months before the Japanese were evicted from their enclaves on the northern coast, but Port Moresby and Australia were safe from the Japanese.

Sadly, Allen never enjoyed the fruits of victory. Five days before the first of his troops entered Kokoda, he was sacked by an impatient MacArthur. However, it was under his direct orders that the Japanese were defeated. The Australian victory was undoubtedly due to the stoical resistance of both the regular and militia troops under his command. Later in the Pacific War, battles would be decided by tens of thousands of men backed by massive resources. The fighting along the Kokoda Trail was fought at divisional level, yet it proved to be the beginning of the Allied riposte in the Pacific that would finally lead to the defeat of the Japanese. A desperate passage of arms, it was ultimately decided by the heroism of a few thousand dogged Australians.

THE AUTHOR William Franklin has contributed to a wide range of military publications and has a particular interest in the elite forces of World War II.

THE SUFFOLK REGIMENT

The history of the Suffolk Regiment began with a regiment raised and led by the Duke of Norfolk in 1685. It fought at Dettingen in 1743 and earned its most prized battle honour at Minden in 1759 when, with five other infantry regiments, it drove the French cavalry from the field.

In 1751 the regiment became the 12th of Foot, and from 1779 it grimly but successfully resisted a Spanish siege of Gibraltar for over five years. In 1781 it became the East Suffolk Regiment, thereby gaining a link with Suffolk for the first time.

The next century saw the regiment serving in campaigns in India, Africa, Australia and New Zealand. The Regimental Depot was established at Bury St Edmunds in 1878, and in 1881 it finally earned the title of the Suffolk Regiment (12th of Foot).

The Suffolks (whose cap badge is shown above) were expanded to 25 battalions in World War I, seeing service in France, Gallipoli, Egypt and Palestine. World War II saw Suffolk battalions in action both in Europe and the Far East. The 1st Battalion was driven from France via Dunkirk but returned in triumph landing on the Normandy beaches on D-day 1944. The 2nd Battalion saw active service in India and Burma, while the unfortunate Suffolk TA battalions were captured at the fall of Singapore after only one or two weeks' fighting.

Much reduced in size after World War II, the Suffolks saw action in Egypt and Palestine prior to sailing for Malaya in 1949.

During the Malayan Emergency, the 1st Battalion of the Suffolk Regiment became a deadly exponent of jungle warfare, with the highest score of terrorists killed of any British unit

THE ENTRY in the War Diary of the 1st Battalion, The Suffolk Regiment (1 Suffolk) for 6 July 1952 reads as follows:

'1330 hours: Kuala Langat Forest Reserve (South): Grid Reference VU 485440: 5 Platoon, B Company opened fire on a lone bandit seen running across their front: he escaped. In the follow-up to this incident the patrol entered a bandit camp in time to see three bandits leap out of a jungle shelter. Fire was brought to bear on them and one was killed outright. The other two were wounded but made off. The patrol commander pursued them and shot them both dead. One was immediately identified as Liew Kon Kim.'

This tersely-worded report scarcely gives an indication of the significance of the event it describes, but in fact the incident was to be the high

JUNGLE TRACKERS

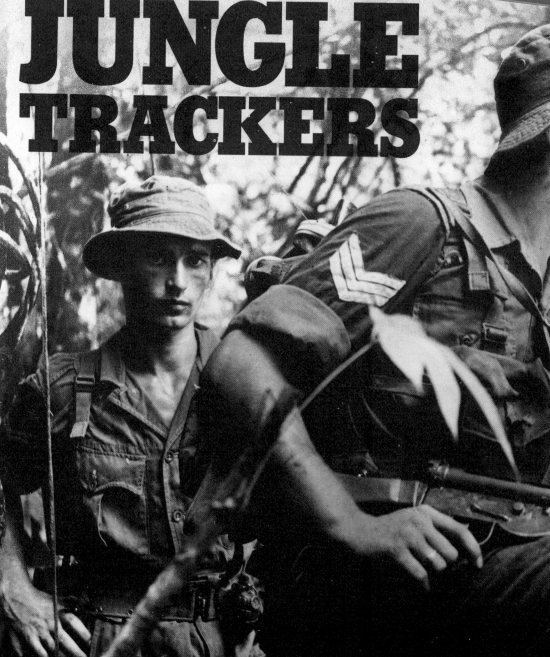

Left: British patrols were particularly vulnerable to sniper fire when crossing the wide Malayan water-courses. Below: An Iban tracker reports to Sergeant Lister of the 1st Suffolks. Bottom left: In the close jungle environment, vigilance was a matter of life or death. Bottom: Private Derek Hexter, a Bren gunner of B Company, 1 Suffolk, takes a rest from the slog.

point of a gruelling three-and-a-half year tour of duty served by 1 Suffolk during the Malayan Emergency, a political upheaval which lasted from 1948 to 1960.

The Suffolks arrived in Malaya in July 1949, just 12 months after the Malayan Communist Party (MCP) had ordered its military wing, the Malayan Races Liberation Army (MRLA) to launch an armed revolt to bring down the government. The action of 6 July 1952 took place, therefore, towards the end of the Suffolks' tour of duty. By that time, careful training and preparation followed by weeks, months and years of dogged patrols and ambushing had converted the unit from a battalion of infantry of the line into a well co-ordinated and highly efficient team of expert jungle fighters. It was capable of finding the enemy (no mean task in a country the size of England, four-fifths covered by dense and almost impenetrable tropical forest and swamp), then forcing him into battle and destroying him.

For most of its tour of duty in Malaya, 1 Suffolk was stationed in the central Malayan state of Selangor to the south of Kuala Lumpur, the capital city. By maintaining an active presence in their area of operations, the Suffolks came to know the ground and their enemy intimately. Day after day a steady stream of patrols was despatched to search the outlying rubber estates and beyond into the jungle to hunt down their prey.

Vigorous and prompt action by the Suffolks would almost invariably win the day

Despite the knowledge that groups of the MRLA in the area often numbered more than 100 terrorists, the battalion's technique was to deploy small patrol parties of 10 or 12 men. At first sight it might seem that such limited groups would meet disaster if confronted by a much larger body of the enemy, and very occasionally this did occur, with the Suffolks suffering some casualties. Experience taught, however, that in the dense vegetation of the jungle, where a man could be lost from view only five metres from the men following him, any group larger than a dozen or so would be of little use. Again, when contact was made with the enemy it was never clear how many of them there were, nor could the terrorists tell the size of the army patrol. Vigorous and prompt action by the Suffolk patrol, however small, would almost invariably win the day in such circumstances.

Another important advantage gained by patrolling in such small numbers lay in the Suffolks' consequent ability to put out large numbers of patrols and ambushes at any one time, thereby continually saturating their area. There was always a risk in pursuing such a policy, but the risk was accepted and it paid off.

In the first year or so of their tour in Malaya, the Suffolks planned their patrolling and ambushing operations very much on a random basis. The aim was to build up a familiarity with the area for which they were responsible, and to accustom the men to living and working in the extremely hostile and unhealthy environment of the swampy jungle. Initially, contacts with the enemy were largely a matter of chance, but as patrol commanders became more experienced and jungle expertise was developed, the men of the Suffolks became adept at sensing tell-tale signs of the presence of bandits.

Malaya, 1949 – 1953

In July 1949, a year after the outbreak of the Malayan Emergency, the 1st Battalion, The Suffolk Regiment, was deployed in the central Malayan state of Selangor. For the next three years the Suffolks hunted the MRLA insurgents in their jungle and swamp hideouts.

Gradually, as platoon and section commanders became skilled in relating their maps to the impossible jungle terrain through which they cautiously made their way, patrols became less haphazard and the task of locating the enemy was pursued far more systematically. It was no longer a case of bumping into a group of bandits totally unexpectedly. The men had developed ways of seeing, hearing and smelling signs of enemy activity, and finally tracking him down with considerable stealth and cunning.

This transition from what in jungle-fighting terms might best be described as amateur status to that of the professional seems all the more remarkable when it is remembered that the vast majority of the men of the Suffolks in Malaya were National Service recruits who came, not from rural Suffolk, where they might have been expected to know something about hunting or even poaching, and thus be able the more easily to adapt to Malayan conditions, but from the towns of East Anglia and the sprawling urban encroachments of northeast London.

When the Emergency broke out in June 1948, the government and police forces were caught virtually unprepared and were initially unable to respond effectively to the challenge. Intelligence of the enemy's strengths, weapons and locations is an essential prerequisite of successful warfare against guerrilla forces, and scarcely anything was known about the MRLA when the terrorist campaign began. Slowly but surely the Special Branch of the Malayan police was built up, and information about the enemy was soon being sifted and collated. By the time the Suffolks arrived in South Selangor Police Circle in 1949 the Special Branch there could provide fairly detailed knowledge of the order of battle of the MRLA units in the area.

The Suffolks' commanding officers (there were two in Malaya) knew that their men, however well trained they were, however diligently they patrolled, and however expert their patrol commanders were in seeking out the enemy, would find their task immeasurably easier if they were in possession of the latest information held by the Special Branch. Consequently, a close relationship was established with the police, and throughout its tour in Malaya the Battalion HQ was actually located inside the Police Headquarters building. In this way the information provided by the police could be communicated directly to the commanders of the Suffolk patrols. The Suffolks' jungle expertise, dogged determination and fearless action, now coupled with first-rate intelligence, was to prove an unstoppable combination and the battalion went from success to success.

As the conflict in Malaya progressed, the men of the Suffolks came to see their enemy in very individual terms, and the personal nature of the conflict was emphasised by the very fact that when seeking out their adversaries they were working in small close-knit groups bound together by a friendship forged during months of shared dangerous experiences. This type of warfare was far removed from the impersonal nature of modern conventional war, when bombs and shells do most of the killing and close contact with the enemy is infrequent and anonymous.

The MRLA lived and moved in the jungle with an expertise born of many years' experience

For the Suffolks, then, the jungle war became a very personal matter. As police intelligence about the enemy approached completion, almost everything about him was known except his exact whereabouts at any given moment. The terrorists that made up the forces of the MRLA lived and moved in the jungle with an expertise born of many years' experience. They were led by harsh and in many cases highly capable leaders. Their campaign of terror led them not only into conflict with the security forces but into a brutal round of murder, destruction and intimidation of those among the civilian population who either did not or would not support them in their aims.

The action reported in the War Diary on 6 July 1952, quoted earlier, was not significant in terms of the number of terrorists killed nor in the manner in which the action was executed. In both these re-

Left: A Suffolk patrol creeps forward in an area previously devastated by an RAF bomb attack. Top left: The radio set was a vital link between small patrols carrying out co-ordinated jungle sweeps. Far left: The Sten Gun carried by the corporal was one of the most common weapons in Malaya, although many preferred the Owen sub-machine gun because its vertical magazine did not impede movement.

BRITISH STRATEGY

During the course of the 12-year Malayan Emergency a great many British and Commonwealth formations served in the war against communist insurgency. Regiments of the line, the Guards, artillery regiments, the Gurkhas, the Royal Marines and the SAS were all represented, together with battalions from Africa, Australia, New Zealand, Fiji, Singapore and Malaya itself.

At the start of the Emergency, the MRLA's jungle bases were situated within a few hours' walking distance of the Chinese settlements which provided most of their food and recruits. When the Briggs Plan (see page 854) began to be put into effect, however, most of the government forces were deployed on the village outskirts, saturating the jungle fringes and patrolling the roads to end all communication with the bases. The supply of food to the MRLA steadily dwindled and the guerrillas were forced to raise their own in jungle clearings. Retreating into the interior, they were pursued by army units aided by Iban trackers from Borneo.

The withdrawal of the MRLA created a need for deep-penetration patrols which could remain for long periods in the jungle until contact was made. Accordingly, the SAS was reformed and small teams were inserted by parachute into the primary jungle, where they were maintained with airdropped supplies. Eventually, nine forts were established in key positions all over Malaya, and landing facilities for aircraft were created. Co-ordinating with the forces on the fringe and with indigenous tribes, the forts' garrisons drew a closing net around the MRLA.

31

spects it was typical of the countless short, sharp battles which preceded it during three years of relentless slog. Its importance lay in the fact that one of the terrorists killed was Liew Kon Kim.

Liew Kon Kim was, at the time he met his death, still only a young man in his early thirties and yet he already had a wealth of military experience. His first taste of action came when he joined the Malayan People's Anti-Japanese Army (MPAJA) during World War II. This force, formed by the Malayan Communist Party, was a resistance group against the Japanese. It was ultimately supported by the British and personnel, together with weapons and supplies, were delivered to the MPAJA both by air and from submarines.

After the war the MPAJA temporarily disbanded, but in 1948 its veterans became the nucleus of the MRLA and they used their experience during World War II to aid them in creating a military force which, though not capable of confronting the British Army in large-scale battle, was able to terrorise the civilian population and tie down large numbers of troops and police.

Liew Kon Kim was the commander of the most important MRLA unit in South Selangor, and from the arrival of the Suffolks he was the main target of all their efforts. He was recognised as a ruthless and courageous adversary. His reputation had·been enhanced through his own efforts at personal image-building. For example, few Chinese choose to grow beards, but he sported a fully-grown, strong black beard, nurtured, no doubt, to add to the charismatic aura he developed around himself. To the Suffolks he was known simply as 'the Bearded Wonder,' a nickname which nicely demonstrated the Suffolks' attitude towards him – a certain respect tinged with derision.

By the spring of 1952 the Suffolks' relentless pursuit of the Bearded Wonder and his Independent

Company of the MRLA (more frequently and contemptuously referred to as the Kajang Gang) had led to his being driven out of the areas of operation where he could most easily terrorise the civilian population and ambush the security forces. Seeking to lie low and gain a breathing space, he moved the majority of his men to one of the more inaccessible areas within south Selangor, the Kuala Langat Forest Reserve (South). This particular forest reserve measured roughly 30km by 25km and consisted of dense, jungle-covered swampland. Here he established his base. Jungle shelters (commonly known as bashas) were built, supported by platforms erected above the level of the muddy swamp waters. Supplies of food had been stored in caches near the camp over the previous months, and he hoped thus to cut down the need for his men to leave the hideout to go in search of food.

Liew Kon Kim's respite was, however, to be short-lived. Special Branch information pointed to the fact that he was currently based somewhere in the Kuala Langat Forest Reserve (South), deep in the swamp. The Suffolks designed plans to flush him out of hiding, and on 28 June 1952 orders were issued for the commencement of Operation Churchman.

The aim of the operation was to search the forest reserve systematically, sector by sector. Ambush parties were to be deployed to block enemy movement out of the sector through which a large number of patrols was to move. Additional troops were made available and put under command of the Suffolks: they included a company of men from Kuala Lumpur Garrison; two companies of the 1st Battalion, The Royal West Kent Regiment and two squadrons of the 22nd Special Air Service Regiment.

The Suffolks moved into the Kuala Langat Forest Reserve (South) to take up ambush positions

Large-scale operations of this kind had been tried before and the concentration of resources had rarely proved to be worthwhile, but on this occasion Special Branch information was graded as very reliable. Among both the police and military forces there was a feeling of confidence that Operation Churchman would achieve success. By the end of June companies had been withdrawn from other patrolling and ambushing activities, and 30 June and 1 July were devoted to preparing for this major operation.

At 1930 hours on 1 July the SAS squadrons, the Royal West Kent companies and A Company of the Suffolks moved into the Kuala Langat Forest Reserve (South) to take up ambush positions. The move into the area was made initially along a disused logging track, which made penetration of the swamp relatively easy. However, as most of the move took place after nightfall it was a nerve-racking, slow and somewhat hazardous business. Nevertheless, all ambush parties were finally reported to be in position by 0900 hours the following morning, 2 July. Meanwhile, B Company of 1 Suffolk with elements of D Company under command had moved out at 0600 the same morning to position their patrols for the sweep through the swamps towards the companies waiting in ambush.

The sweep commenced at 0930, and slowly the patrols moved forward through the daunting terrain. Movement was extremely difficult as they slithered and clambered over the swampy ground covered by thick tangles of vegetation. Often men found them-

Private, the Suffolks, Malaya 1950

This National Serviceman wears jungle green trousers and shirt with canvas and leather boots. His hat carries a yellow recognition device. A canvas pouch for ammunition, possibly of local manufacture, and a waterbottle hang from a 1944-pattern web belt. He carries an Owen sub-machine gun.

Top left: Members of B Company, 1st Suffolks, receive praise for their successful elimination of Liew Kon Kim, known as 'the Bearded Wonder' (shown far left). The Malayan government had offered $20,000 for his capture. Left: A typical Suffolk patrol group: the Bren on the right provided fire support, while Owen sub-machine guns and grenades were used on first contact.

THE BRIGGS PLAN

In April 1950, only months after the arrival of the 1st Suffolks, Lieutenant-General Sir Harold Briggs was appointed Director of Operations in Malaya. A veteran of jungle warfare, Briggs had commanded the 5th Indian Division in Burma from 1942 to 1945, and he was soon to demonstrate a keen insight into counter-insurgency warfare.

Briggs' intention was to clear the country systematically from south to north, forcing the insurgents into the open. Ethnic Chinese squatters, who would be expected to support the predominantly Chinese MRLA, were to be forcibly moved from areas where their activities could counter the war effort. The task of clearing the jungle of terrorists became the exclusive responsibility of the army, while the police were detailed to keep cleared areas secure and maintain order in the areas of Malaya still unchallenged by the insurgents. Briggs insisted on close co-operation between civil police and military authorities at all levels.

Briggs left Malaya a disillusioned man, stating that his lack of executive power had minimised the effectiveness of his programme. However, the Briggs Plan, as his scheme became known, remained the blueprint for the security forces until the end of the Emergency, and it was within this context that the Suffolks operated.

selves up to their waists in slimy, filthy water as they struggled to climb over rotten tree-trunks lying beneath the surface. The rate of advance was seldom more than a few hundred metres an hour and it was made even slower because the greatest care had to be taken not to disturb the bandits before they could be seen and dealt with. Ideally, in any jungle patrol the noise of movement has to be kept inaudible beyond the distance visible to the leading scout. Such an ideal is rarely if ever achieved, of course, given that the limit of visibility was usually no more than four to five metres, and evidence of this came within half an hour of the commencement of the sweep. Shortly before 1000, 10 Platoon of D Company reported that one of their patrols had come across a camp for 20 men which had just been vacated: food was still cooking over the bandits' camp fires!

Even if they had not been keyed up before now, all the men on the operation grew tense in the knowledge that action must surely be imminent. During the next hour and a half no less than five fleeting contacts were reported with groups of bandits. At least seven were reported to have been wounded in the various brief firefights that ensued, but none was killed or captured, though five personal packs were recovered. All bandit parties were reported as fleeing southwards towards the ambush positions.

No further contacts were reported during the day and the sweep was called to a halt at 1800. As darkness fell early under the dense jungle canopy, the patrols were ordered to make their way out towards the jungle fringes. All ambush parties remained in position throughout the night, and on the morning of 3 July they commenced patrolling northwards to cover the ground up to where the previous day's patrols had ended. However, no contacts were made during that day, though several old camps were located. All patrols were ordered to withdraw from the jungle that evening, and the following day was set aside for administration and rest while the next phase of Operation Churchman, sweeping and ambushing the next sector, was planned.

During 3 July information had been received from

Below: Men of the 1st Suffolks raise a resounding cheer for General Sir Gerald Templer, who had just congratulated them on completing their tour.

Special Branch that Liew Kon Kim had been seen on the southwest side of the Kuala Langat Forest Reserve (South), outside the area of the sector designated for searching during Operation Churchman Phase II. The information seemed reliable and the operation was delayed to allow for investigation. The commander of B Company, 1 Suffolk, was briefed to send a patrol into the area on the next day (4 July). A guide, a terrorist who had surrendered, was provided to assist the patrol in locating the right place. Once on the ground he indicated that Liew's camp was just inside the jungle edge in an area that had, many months before, been bombed by the RAF. The vicinity was searched very thoroughly but no contact was made. However, there were many signs of recent movement by bandits through the area and it was decided that a further patrol should continue the search the following day.

It was this patrol, led by Second Lieutenant Raymond Hands, a National Service subaltern due for release in August, that came across the camp and succeeded in eliminating Liew Kon Kim.

Further to the north, Phase II of Operation Churchman began on the same day and successive phases went ahead until the operation was finally concluded on 26 July. A number of contacts with the enemy were reported and numerous camps and food dumps were located, but perhaps inevitably after the earlier huge success there was a sense of anticlimax.

The Suffolks continued on operations in Malaya for a further six months, adding to their already considerable successes. They finally sailed from Singapore for the UK in January 1953, having built up a reputation second to none. Indeed, no other British infantry battalion ever came anywhere near achieving the same results during the long conflict in Malaya.

THE AUTHOR Major F. A. Godfrey, MC, served in Malaya, Cyprus, Malta, Libya, Aden and Berlin before retiring from the British Army in 1969. From 1973 to 1982 he was on the lecturing staff at RMA Sandhurst, and he is now serving in the Territorial Army.

TIGERS

IN THE 'NAM

CAPITAL DIVISION

The first direct expression of the Republic of Korea's willingness to make a firm commitment to the ground war in South Vietnam was the deployment of the Capital 'Tiger' Division to Qui Nhon in September 1965. By April 1966, the entire unit was in action in the coastal and highland regions of central South Vietnam.

At its greatest strength, the Tiger Division consisted of a well-balanced all-arms combat force. Its heart consisted of two infantry units: the 1st and 26th Infantry Regiments. These were backed by the Cavalry Regiment. For fire support the division could call on the 10th, 60th and 61st Field Artillery Battalions, equipped with 105mm howitzers, and the 628th Field Artillery Battalion, a unit operating 155mm howitzers. A reconnaissance company completed the division's order of battle.

Like most of the allied forces in South Vietnam, the Tiger Division was part of, but separate from, the American forces. The division had its own distinctive chain of command and local priorities, but under a young and capable commander, General Lew Byong Hion, it often played a central role in joint operations. One of the division's most renowned and successful missions was an action against Phu Cat Mountain in September 1966. Working in conjunction with US forces, the division overran positions occupied by two North Vietnamese battalions, capturing over 600 weapons and inflicting severe casualties.
Above: The shoulder patch worn by members of the ROK Capital 'Tiger' Division.

First deployed to Vietnam in 1965, the Korean 'Tiger' Division soon demonstrated its power to inflict savage maulings on the NVA

SOME OF THE American leadership in Vietnam claimed the unit was difficult to get along with; others said it had a limited set of tactics and needed a more sophisticated approach to the war. The Viet Cong (VC) and North Vietnamese called it a brutal tool of the Saigon regime. The Republic of Korea's (ROK) Capital 'Tiger' Division was controversial. But, to one group of observers, those of us who fought alongside this unique organisation, there was no ambiguity. We – all of us – thought it was just fine. In the slang of the American infantryman, the view was: 'Hey... that Tiger outfit knows where it's at.' The South Vietnamese rifleman expressed it in a different way: 'ROK... Number One!'

There was a reason for this difference of opinion. The American generals in the US Military Assistance Command, Vietnam (MACV) found that the Koreans were not always agreeable to proposals involving the employment of the Tiger Division. The division often had its own agenda, its own area, and its own war. The disagreements usually centred on whether the division could be rapidly moved for individual operations at some distance from its normal area of

Previous page: The men of the South Korean Tiger Division became renowned for their cold and professional approach to combat. Right: On watch with a 0.3in Browning M1919A6 machine gun.

Above: Hueys bring in Tiger Division troops after the area has been sprayed with defoliants. Bottom: Korean infantrymen run from their Hueys to form a perimeter around the LZ.

Trooper, ROK Capital Division, Vietnam

This soldier is wearing a version manufactured in the Republic of Korea of the camouflage uniform issued to the US Marines in World War II. His torso is protected by a US M1955 flak vest, and both his World War II M1 steel helmet and its cover are American. His weapon is the US 5.56mm M16 rifle.

operations in Binh Dinh Province.

General Westmoreland, MACV commander in Saigon, had been told by Korea's President Park that ROK troops would be under his command. Unfortunately, an acrimonious debate in Seoul had placed a burden on the Korean commanders in Vietnam. Korea was not to be seen as a 'vassal' of the United States but as a co-equal partner. The first Korean commander, General Chae, arrived at a face-saving arrangement. He told Westmoreland to give his orders as 'requests'. Throughout the more than six years of Tiger Divisions service in Vietnam, there is no record of the commander of the unit ever turning down a 'request' from the American commander. There were honest differences of opinion in planning conferences, but Korean generals well recognised the principle of unity of command.

Captured documents clearly indicated that Hanoi's strategy was to split the country in half

There were a number of factors that influenced Westmoreland's decision on where to employ the Tiger Division. The chief factor was the enemy. The North Vietnamese were rushing as many of their divisions and regiments as they could support into the central part of South Vietnam. Captured documents clearly indicated that Hanoi's overall strategy was to split the country in half. North Vietnam's southern allies, the Viet Cong, had been assigned the role of securing as much of the populated region of central South Vietnam as possible. During 1965, the VC had all but succeeded in conquering the heavily populated coastal province of Binh Dinh, the eastern terminus of the ill-famed Route 19. Westmoreland knew that the Koreans would not be able to achieve the mobility of his US helicopter-borne units and did not want to put the combat forces of an Asian ally of the United States on the border of another Asian state. He correctly suspected that 1966 would see major battles in the high plateau regions of central South Vietnam and badly needed a secure port facility in the area so that he could build a logistical base. After consulting with the South Vietnamese leaders, he made his decision.

The Tiger Division's initial missions were to secure the growing logistical base at the port of Qui Nhon, assist the Vietnamese government in the pacification of Binh Dinh, and subsequently conduct operations against North Vietnamese combat elements to the west. With a safe port, US units could be located closer to the Cambodian border. But there was no time to secure the base first. Everything was to be done simultaneously. The last of the division's units arrived in South Vietnam during November 1965, while others had already been fighting for several weeks.

A few months later, I was in Vietnam with the 27th Infantry Regiment (the Wolfhounds), and I began hearing stories about the Koreans. We were very interested in their performance because, like the Tiger Division, we had been placed in a heavily populated, VC-controlled province, Hau Nghia northwest of Saigon. There were three remarkable observations about the division: the quality of its soldiers, the thoroughness of its operations, and the terrible effect it had on the enemy.

In the jungle, the Koreans looked much the same as us. A small towel around the neck to keep the brow dry and weapons clean. Unshaven, dirty, a wary look, boots caked with mud, and a constant thirst. The

ROK Tiger Division
South Vietnam, 1965-73

KONTUM

Kontum

BINH DINH

Pleiku

Route 19

An Khe

Phu Cat
Mtn

PLEIKU

Tiger
Division HQ

Qui
Nhon

SOUTH VIETNAM

CAMBODIA

PHU
YEN

PHU
BON

Tuy Hoa

Southeast Asia

THAILAND

Hue

Da
Nang

LAOS

Route 21

Route 1

Qui
Nhon

Ninh Hoa

CAMBODIA

KHANH
HOA

Phnom Penh

SOUTH
VIETNAM

Nha Trang

Saigon

Da
Lat

Cam
Ranh

SOUTH
CHINA
SEA

NINH THUAN

difference between us was that within a few hours back at base camp the Koreans were all spit and polish. They looked as though they had just stepped off the plane. In their base camps they made themselves comfortable, like all soldiers, but the Tiger Division did it with a bit of style that we seemed to lack. The soldiers would use wooden ammunition boxes to erect a quick hut that was topped by a unique roof. The Koreans found that the tar-impregnated cardboard of our ration cartons could be made into shingles. Somehow, the Koreans always seemed at home.

Route 19 and Route 1 had a number of bridges in Binh Dinh Province, some guarded by South Vietnamese, some by Americans, and others by the Tiger Division. You were lucky to see the Vietnamese guards, the Americans took the duty somewhat casually, but the Koreans invariably discharged their responsibilities with fervour. Their machine guns were tightly bunkered, the foliage was cleared, and the guards were fully uniformed,

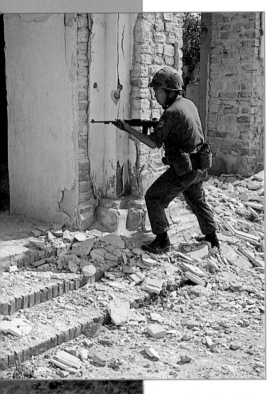

Left: Two members of the ROK Tiger Division, armed with M1 carbines, warily approach the doorway of a church suspected to contain Viet Cong guerrillas in Bong Son, a town lying to the north of Qui Nhon in Binh Dinh Province. Below: A Tiger Division 105mm howitzer supplies close support for an infantry assault near Ninh Binh. Below left: Viet Cong guerrillas are kept under close guard during ROK Tiger Division clearing operations north of Bong Son.

ches were far more thorough. Our operations lasted from four to six hours; the Tiger Division units would take as long as three days. An American search would involve a single sweep of the village, but the Koreans often conducted one search and then put in an entirely new unit to do it all over again. In some instances they would withdraw their units from the village itself, retain some innocent villagers and let some of the known VC spouses return. This ruse could result in domestic discussion and the surrender of the VC half of the family. The Tiger Division was slower but far more successful than we were at this work.

In a cordon operation against a North Vietnamese or VC main-force unit, the Tiger Division's technique was little different from our own. We both piled in troops as quickly as possible to prevent the escape of enemy personnel. Normally, we both held still at night and then tightened our cordon during the day, using artillery to keep the enemy on the defensive. The difference came in the final search. The Koreans were simply more painstaking than we were; the proof was in the number of weapons captured. Their count always exceeded ours. The division did not carry out as many large-scale operations as we did, and we were in contact with more enemy elements than they were per battalion, but they often had a greater impact on individual enemy units.

In the summer of 1967, enemy main-force units largely withdrew from South Vietnam to the security of Laos and Cambodia and would return only for brief, specific operations. The enemy did not relish battle with American units, but there is every reason to believe they particularly dreaded contact with the Tiger Division.

armed and alert. It gave one a sense of well-justified security. A senior American colonel expressed it best: 'The Korean soldier is the closest to perfection that I've ever seen . . . he's almost faultless.'

The Tiger Division became noted for two types of operation: village searches against local VC units, and cordoning off battalion-sized main-force elements. The village search looked like a standard American operation. A village with a known VC contingent was quickly sealed and all the inhabitants were moved to a nearby area where interrogation took place and medical assistance was given. On some occasions, entertainment was staged. Meanwhile, a search of the village was being conducted. The difference was that the Korean operations were more carefully planned, lasted longer, and the sear-

American tank crews fired canister rounds and the Koreans began triggering off their claymore mines

Perhaps an incident that occurred during this period of the war would explain the enemy's view of the Koreans. After much discussion, the Tiger Division was persuaded to assist the US 4th Division on the Cambodian border, far from its normal coastal area of operation. The idea was to establish widely scattered, reinforced company-sized patrolling bases in the hope of finding enemy elements or luring the famed North Vietnamese Army (NVA) 101st Regiment out of Cambodia. One Tiger Division company was given three US tanks and their crews for support and this tiny combined force settled in to their assigned area. The North Vietnamese regiment took the bait and decided to test the Koreans.

In the dead of night, supported by a simultaneous barrage of mortar rounds, a North Vietnamese battalion suddenly rushed the Korean position. It was met by an interlocking band of machine-gun fire placed just forward of carefully laid barbed wire. The American tank crews fired canister rounds at prearranged targets and the Koreans began triggering off a number of their claymore mines. The enemy battalion faltered just as US artillery rounds began to arrive on the pre-planned final protective targets. The game North Vietnamese withdrew, licked their wounds, and conducted another assault with the same results. Two more attacks also failed before the Vietnamese began dragging away their dead and wounded. As dawn broke, the Korean company commander counted five of his soldiers dead. No Americans were hurt, but the growing light revealed 182 bodies of enemy soldiers that had not been taken

KOREA ENTERS THE VIETNAM WAR

In the first months of 1954, the leader of the Republic of Korea, Syngman Rhee, offered to despatch a force from the Korean Army to assist in the war against the North Vietnamese. The offer was turned down, but 10 years later, after further discussions, six Koreans and five US officers left for South Vietnam. From this small initial commitment, the South Koreans gradually expanded their role in South Vietnam.

The forces sent were initially non-combat personnel who were skilled in winning over the support of the local population, but in June 1965 the Korean minister of national defence agreed to send a division-sized combat force.

The first Republic of Korea (ROK) combat unit deployed to South Vietnam was the Capital Division, known as the 'Tiger' Division because of its insignia. The division was based at Qui Nhon and soon gained the reputation of a hard-fighting unit. By June 1966 the Capital Division was operating on the main coastal road through South Vietnam, Highway 1, and several victories were scored over the local enemy forces. Other Korean units sent to South Vietnam consisted of the ROK Marine Corps' 2nd 'Blue Dragon' Brigade, based at Hui An from October 1965, and the ROK 9th 'White Horse' Division, which began to arrive in September and operated out of Ninh Hoa near Cam Ranh Bay. The Koreans had responsibility for the central coastal area of Vietnam, stretching from Phan Rang in Ninh Thuan Province to the north of Qui Nhon in Binh Dinh Province. Although their main role was to provide security for the ports and logistical bases in the region, the units were also deployed to keep major roads open and curtail the enemy's activities. The Koreans quickly gained a fearsome reputation, not all of it favourable, but their fighting skills earned them widespread admiration. Some 4400 Koreans lost their lives in the war before the last ROK units left in March 1973.

away. The 101st NVA Regiment returned to Cambodia, minus at least one of its three battalions. It never took on a unit of the Tiger Division again.

A hallmark of the Tiger Division was its favourable kill ratio, that is, the numbers of enemy dead compared to its own deaths. In Operation Flying Tiger during January 1966, the division accounted for 192 enemy killed while losing only 11 of its own soldiers. During Operation Hong Kil Dong in mid-1967, the division scoured the villages and outlying districts of Binh Dinh, hunting the most elusive of the enemy forces, the local VC guerrillas. By the time of the elections in that province, the Koreans had killed 638 VC and captured some 457 weapons, suffering only 27 battle deaths. Just prior to the Tet Offensive of 1968, the Tiger Division completed Operation Maeng Ho 9, a toe-to-toe, stand-up battle with a main-force battalion that had been trapped by the

Koreans in the dense jungle terrain of Phu Cat Mountain. After a six-day ordeal, the Koreans killed 278 of the enemy for a loss of 11 men. In terms of the grim and grisly statistics of war, the Tiger Division was a rather efficient machine.

In comparison with other major military logistical centres, the port city of Qui Nhon was rather quiet in 1968. Some infiltrators managed to enter the city and there was some fighting but, on the whole, it remained a relatively trouble-free area. The reason was that the Tiger Division's successful pacification operations had made the South Vietnamese government's control of the province more effective than it had been for the past six years. The Vietnamese authorities were therefore able to execute a plan that previously they had feared to undertake. Two days prior to the launching of the Tet Offensive on 31 January 1968, South Vietnamese police raided a house and made 11 arrests. The prisoners were VC

agents whose mission it was to broadcast a victory message after the Binh Dinh public radio station had been captured. Their audio tapes were seized, the police listened to them and appropriate precautionary measures were taken.

After the Tet Offensive, the character of the Vietnam War changed dramatically. In the first half of 1968, the enemy had been easy to find and his forces were being systematically destroyed. But eventually Hanoi changed its strategy and the battered units resumed their previous method of operation by returning to safe areas in Laos and Cambodia and making forays into South Vietnam only when opportunities were highly favourable. With America beginning to withdraw from the war, Hanoi no longer depended on victory on the battlefields; battle was only used to enhance the negotiation position. The professional competence of the Tiger Division, the Americans and other supporters of the Republic of South Vietnam meant little to the final outcome of the war.

By the middle of 1969, the Tiger Division had killed 12,365 enemy soldiers, captured over 3000 more and taken over 6500 weapons. Although the division was to fight on with its sister unit, the ROK 9th 'White Horse' Division, the burden of the war was rapidly being passed over to the South Vietnamese Army. Many units were asking for and receiving withdrawal instructions, but not the Koreans, who stayed with the Americans until the last.

The Tiger Division did not finally depart from Vietnam until March 1973. The Vietnamese will remember it as a military organisation of unquestioned professionalism and one with superb fighting skills. Many will also remember it as the military force that came from another rice culture and brought new agricultural techniques into the country. The division may also be credited with building

Below left: A South Korean trooper attempts to calm a terrified Vietnamese woman caught up with her children in operations against the Viet Cong. Bottom left: Amid a jumble of equipment, Korean infantrymen await the order to resume operations. Below: Although the Tiger Division was primarily in Vietnam to wage war against the enemies of the South Vietnamese government, the men also had an important role in winning the 'hearts and minds' of local people, supplying such benefits as medical aid. Bottom: ROK troops receive their farewell speech from General Westmoreland at Ninh Binh.

over 1300 houses, 136 bridges, 25 temples and 260 classrooms for the Vietnamese peasants.

As a nation, the Republic of Korea proved in Vietnam that it was an enemy to be feared and a friend to be trusted. The young nation actually improved its own security and its own economy during the war in Southeast Asia. Many present-day commanders of Korean battalions, brigades and divisions are battle-tested veterans of that war. While the historian may find these facts of interest, what really matters to the infantryman in combat is the quality of the men on his flank. For many of the American foot soldiers in Vietnam, the hands-down favourite was the Tiger Division. The accolade 'ROK . . . Number One!' was well earned.

THE AUTHOR Colonel Rod Paschall served six years in Laos, Vietnam and Cambodia during the Vietnam War. He was later the commander of Delta Force, the main anti-terrorist unit in the United States.

VICTORY AT VIMY

In April 1917, the German High Command boasted that Vimy Ridge was impregnable – the Canadian Corps proved otherwise

DURING THE EARLY hours of 9 April 1917, the infantry of the Canadian Corps moved up the communication trenches and chalk tunnels towards the front line and forward saps that would be the jumping-off point for the assault on the notorious Vimy Ridge. The Germans had occupied the hogs-back of Vimy Ridge in October 1914, and, over the years, had built a vast complex of emplacements and trenches beneath which were vast underground cellars and miles of tunnels. As a fortification, it was comparable to the Rock of Gibraltar, and in 1915 the French had

Canadian Infantryman, Vimy Ridge April 1917

This soldier from the 4th Division wears standard British Army Service dress and a leather jerkin for extra protection against the cold. A gas respirator is carried around his neck, and a British 0.303in calibre rifle on his shoulder.

suffered 150,000 casualties in a series of brave but unsuccessful attempts to wrest the ridge from the German Army. Now it was the turn of the Canadians. In the hours before the signal to attack, the men prepared themselves for the coming ordeal: they had their tots of rum, checked their weapons and fixed bayonets in anticipation of the most chilling order of them all – to be sent 'over the top'.

The weather was atrocious and the frozen men watched the sleet and snow gust across the cratered landscape of 'no-man's-land' until, at 0530 hours precisely, the pre-dawn silence was shattered by the thunder of 1000 guns. The suddenness and shock of the bombardment was felt by all present, and one infantryman's comment was typical: 'the whole atmosphere was rent by screaming shells passing overhead, every gun seemingly having been fired by clockwork. The German line was erupting along its entire length and seemed to be enveloped in sheet lightning.' The Canadians clambered out of their trenches into 'no-man's-land', while stunned German front-line troops sent up a fire-work display of SOS rockets in a desperate call for fire support from their own guns. The battle for Vimy Ridge had begun.

The assault on Vimy Ridge was part of the larger Battle of Arras, an attack by the British First and Third Armies that was intended to act as a large-scale diversion for the main French offensive of 1917 under General Robert Nivelle. Vimy Ridge was not an imposing geographical feature; it rose to a maximum height of only 145m (Hill 145), and stretched in a southeasterly direction from the village of Givenchy-en-Gohelle for a little more than four miles to Farbus Wood. The front line at Vimy followed a direct north-south axis and the Canadians began to occupy the 7000yd frontage below the ridge from December 1916 into the New Year. One of the three corps in the British First Army, the Canadian Corps was commanded by Lieutenant-General Sir Julian

At Vimy Ridge, British artillery (below left and main picture) created a rolling barrage, laying down a curtain of fire 100yds in front of the infantry; every three minutes it would advance a further 100yds, enabling the infantry to follow in its wake. A private of the 2nd Canadian Mounted Rifles recalled: 'it was the most perfect barrage of war, as it was so perfectly synchronised.' Below: Heavy rains prior to the assault created daunting problems for an ammunition convoy.

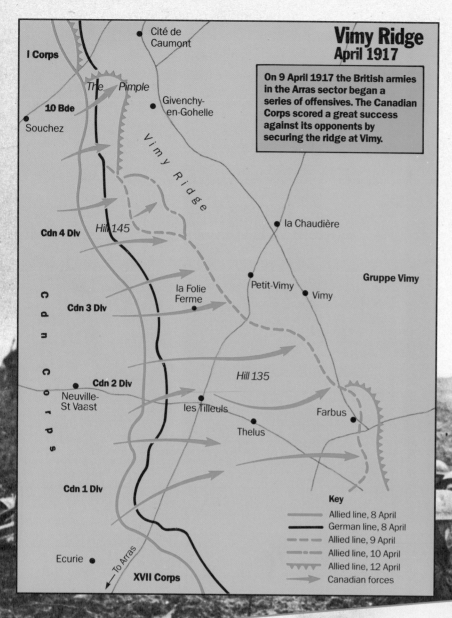

Vimy Ridge
April 1917

On 9 April 1917 the British armies in the Arras sector began a series of offensives. The Canadian Corps scored a great success against its opponents by securing the ridge at Vimy.

I Corps

Cité de Caumont

The Pimple

Givenchy-en-Gohelle

10 Bde

Souchez

Vimy Ridge

Cdn 4 Div   *Hill 145*

la Chaudière

Gruppe Vimy

Cdn 3 Div   la Folie Ferme

Petit-Vimy   Vimy

C d n   C o r p s

Hill 135

Cdn 2 Div

Neuville-St Vaast

les Tilleuls

Farbus

Thelus

Cdn 1 Div

Ecurie

To Arras

XVII Corps

Key

— Allied line, 8 April
— German line, 8 April
--- Allied line, 9 April
—·— Allied line, 10 April
∿∿∿ Allied line, 12 April
→ Canadian forces

Byng, and comprised four full-strength divisions which for the coming operation would be supplemented by the British 5th Division (in reserve), and extra British heavy guns and howitzers from the neighbouring I Corps in support of the Canadians' own artillery. These and other reinforcements (engineers and labour units) brought the strength of the Canadian Corps to a massive 170,000 men, of whom just under 100,000 were Canadians. Among those 100,000 were the 12 brigades of Canadian infantry whose task it was to secure the ridge.

The Canadians had already proved themselves first-class soldiers when, during the Second Battle of Ypres, they had held the line during the surprise German gas attack of April 1915. The grinding struggle of attrition that became known as the Battle of the Somme (from July to November 1916), gave the Canadians further experience of trench warfare, so that by 1917 they were fully battle-hardened. Surprisingly, the heavy casualties sustained on the Somme did not lower the Canadians' morale and there was no loss of enthusiasm nor any decline in their effectiveness, even during the latter stages of the war. Along with the Australian and New Zealand Army

Corps (ANZAC) divisions, the Canadians were generally acknowledged to be the best infantry on the Western Front: Vimy Ridge secured them this reputation, and, in the battles that followed, they maintained the accolade. The Canadians prided themselves on the initiative displayed by all their troops; the other ranks could operate effectively without officers, showing an independence of spirit that made them ideal soldiers in offensive action. This contrasted to the British rank and file who excelled in the defensive but lacked the dash and confidence of the Dominion troops in the attack.

The plan of action for the four infantry divisions (running from the 1st on the right flank to the 4th on the left) was very simple: to advance behind the barrage and occupy an allotted section of the ridge. Four lines (black, red, blue and brown) represented intermediate stages in the advance, the aim being to gain each successive colour line at a fixed time in order to keep pace with the barrage.

A two-week bombardment had combined with the weather to ensure that Vimy Ridge was a moonscape of craters and mud. Each shell hole was full of water, presenting a fatal trap to the wounded should

Although the Canadian assault was part of the larger Battle of Arras, Vimy Ridge was an important objective in its own right: it overlooked Douai and the surrounding plain – a key communications centre for the Germans – and acted as a linchpin in linking the northern section of the new Hindenburg defence system to the main German front line. Far left: With a dense cloud of smoke obscuring much of the battlefield, Canadian troops advance across 'no man's land'. Below left: Their objective secured, Canadians of the 19th Infantry Battalion construct trenches in anticipation of a German counter-attack.

they fall in; a number of men drowned in this way. Heavily laden, the Canadian infantry staggered up the slope. On the right flank, progress was so rapid that a number of over-enthusiastic troops ran into their own barrage.

The intensity of the bombardment and speed of the attack caught the Germans by surprise: many of the dazed front-line troops meekly surrendered to the advancing Canadians, while those Germans who had retreated into their shell-proof underground bunkers found themselves overrun. A British officer working alongside the Canadian 2nd Division noted the advantage of such a rapid advance:

'By 10am the Canadians were in possession of the village of Thelus. Nearby we descended a deep shaft and to our surprise found that it led to a vast underground system of dug-outs and tunnels. So unexpected and rapid had been the advance that the inhabitants were blissfully cooking or awaiting their breakfasts. They offered no resistance. Among them was an artillery colonel, who owned a nicely papered bedroom and a feather bed with sheets. Above ground in the village itself, the troops captured several guns and then continued the attack towards the crest of the ridge – a distance of about 4000yds.'

Much of the fighting was at close-quarters, with grenades and bayonets the favoured weapons

While many of the Germans encountered by the Canadians were content to surrender, more resolute troops carried on the fight, even though they were completely cut off. A number of machine-gun emplacements that had survived the bombardment proved particularly troublesome, and most of the Canadian casualties were the result of their fire. The only way to neutralise these emplacements was to creep up on them and throw grenades into the machine-gun slits – a perilous task, calling for resolute nerve.

At centre left of the advance, the Canadian 3rd Division met some spirited resistance from the defenders and a number of tough firefights broke out. Inevitably, much of the fighting was at close-quarters, with grenades and bayonets the favoured weapons. Private Parsons of the 2nd Canadian Mounted Rifles joined up with a group of Canadians led by Sergeant Al Swamby – well-known as a 'fire-eater' – in an unscheduled attack on La Folie Farm. Parsons recalled:

'There we engaged eight Jerries. They gave us a bad time and we gave them a bad time, but it ended up that Sergeant Swamby and I were the only two alive. Our group bumbled into a machine-gun crew, and three of our men were killed. With Mills bombs [grenades] we stirred them up, and made another try; two fell dead. We separated to about 30yds and came at them from two directions with bombs flying. There were three live Huns in that trench when we jumped in. When we left there were eight dead ones. I might add, they were good soldiers, they made no attempt to surrender.'

By 0730 hours the 3rd Division had reached the edge of La Folie wood – attaining its main objective after a series of fierce engagements lasting just two hours. But while the first three divisions had been remarkably successful, the 4th Division (on the left flank) suffered a major setback. The division's objectives included Hill 145, the most heavily defended part of the complex, but a serious mistake was made by the commanding officer of the 87th Infantry Battalion in asking for a section of the German trench line, in the centre of the division's advance, to be spared artillery bombardment. His plan was to use the undamaged trench as a defensive line from which to repel any German counter-attacks. However, unharassed by shelling, the enemy was able to put up a coherent defence, and machine-gun positions poured fire down on the advancing lines of Canadian infantry. On the 4th Division's flanks, although the advance went well during the early stages, the attack was dislocated by the failure in the centre. Encouraged, the defenders even began to prepare counter-attacks against the Canadians. Faced by greater resistance overall, the attackers found German troops that had been overrun in their dug-outs more likely to fight back, and considerable nerve had to be shown to get them to surrender. One such instance won an officer of the 38th Infantry Battalion, Captain T.W. Macdowell, a Victoria Cross. Macdowell, on reaching the German line, found himself separated from his own men until he spotted two Canadian infantrymen, and together they knocked out two German machine-gun outposts. Finding a tunnel entrance, Macdowell climbed down alone, leaving the other two men at the top, only to discover a cellar packed with 75 German soldiers. Reacting with great speed Macdowell turned to shout back orders to a large, if completely fictitious, force above ground and then persuaded the Germans to surrender and throw down their arms. He sent them up out of the cellar in batches of 12 men, where they discovered, too late, that Macdowell's 'force' consisted of only two infantrymen, who then handled them back to the rear.

By the late afternoon, some progress had been made but Hill 145 remained firmly in German hands. A decision was made to resume the attack the following day, using the fresh 10th Infantry Brigade. A heavy bombardment was laid down on Hill 145, while two battalions charged the German position. Although suffering heavy casualties in the rush across the shell craters, the Canadians broke into the enemy defences and by 1315 hours this key part of the German defence had fallen. The Canadians rooted out the remaining defenders on Vimy Ridge and began to dig in as a precaution against a German counter-attack.

By 12 April, the commanding officer of the 4th Division had reorganised his forces sufficiently to launch the concluding phase of the operation, to

Below: German prisoners carry wounded Canadians across the battlefield. Right: Canadians examine a captured gun emplacement. Far right: Lieutenant-General Julian Byng (right of picture) and Sir Arthur Currie (centre). Centre right: German prisoners of war. Centre left: Captain T.W. Mcdowell (right of picture).

secure the high ground on the northern tip of Vimy Ridge known as 'the Pimple'. Over 100 field guns were brought to bear, and, after a short but intense bombardment, the Canadian infantry advanced on the Pimple – a driving snow-storm at their backs. By nightfall the Germans were either Canadian prisoners or dead. The ridge was finally in Canadian hands, a fact accepted by the German commanders who made no attempt to launch a counter-attack, instead withdrawing their troops two miles eastwards.

The Canadian Official History notes that:

'The Canadian Corps had advanced some 4500yds and seized 54 guns, 104 trench mortars and 124 machine guns. It had inflicted severe losses on the enemy, capturing more than 4000 prisoners. The victory had been gained at a cost in Canadian casualties of 10,602 all ranks.'

Although the capture of Vimy Ridge was only a part of the overall Arras offensive, which was to bog down in rising casualty figures, it proved its worth in the following year when the German offensive against Arras, in March 1918, foundered on the British defences on Vimy Ridge.

The Canadian victory at Vimy heralded their arrival as a true, national fighting force, capable of mounting their own operations. In recognition of this fact, a Canadian soldier, Sir Arthur Currie, was given command of the Corps. The French Army was greatly impressed by the Canadian performance and sent officers to study how they had fought the battle. A new standard had been set: the Dominion troops had demonstrated that they were a match for anyone and that they were capable of mounting successful offensive operations with a level of professionalism equal to that of their German opponents. In honour of the Canadian sacrifice, in 1922 the French government ceded Hill 145 to Canada 'in perpetuity', and there the 125-foot Canadian War Memorial stands as a tribute to the 60,000 Canadians killed in World War I.

THE AUTHOR Adrian Gilbert has edited and contributed to a number of military and naval publications and is co-author of *Vietnam: The History and the Tactics*.

THE CANADIAN CORPS

When Canada joined Britain in declaring war on Germany in 1914, her 'Permanent Force' consisted of a mere 3000 men organised into a battalion of infantry, a battery of artillery and two squadrons of cavalry. Alongside the Permanent Force, however, was the 'Non-Permanent Active Militia' (NPAM). The mobilisation of Canada's partially-trained militia had earlier been rejected by the Canadian government. Instead, a call for volunteers was made. By early September 1914, over 30,000 volunteers had come forward, many of them members of the militia, and they formed the nucleus of the Canadian Expeditionary Force (CEF). The first commander of the Canadian Corps (badge above) was a British soldier, Lieutenant-General Sir Julian Byng, who led the Corps at Vimy and afterwards went on to command the British Third Army. As volunteers flooded in from all over Canada, a divisional level organisation began to take shape. A special feature of the Canadian system was the decision to limit the CEF to a single corps of four divisions which would always be at full strength and which would have generous artillery and machine-gun support at corps level. The 1st Canadian Division took up its position in the line on the Western Front in March 1915, to be joined by the other three divisions over the following 15 months. From September 1916, the Canadian Corps fought on the Western Front until the German surrender on 11 November 1918.

Left: A Canadian artillery crew uses a captured German howitzer against enemy lines.

THE RIFLE BRIGADE

From its beginnings as 'An Experimental Corps of Riflemen' in 1800, the Rifle Brigade was unique. While other regiments were armed with the musket and wore red tunics, the new unit carried rifles and was clad in green. In 1803 it became known as the 95th Regiment, or the Rifle Corps, and the 2nd Battalion was raised two years later. The regiment won acclaim under the command of the Duke of Wellington, and, following the Battle of Waterloo, the 2nd Battalion led the triumphant entry into Paris. In 1816 the formation was renamed The Rifle Brigade and later saw action in the Boer and Crimean wars. During World War I, a number of the brigade's battalions served in France.

During World War II, the Rifle Brigade was tasked to operate as motor battalions in support of tanks in the armoured divisions. The 2nd Battalion served in the Western Desert, and from March 1944 it fought in Italy as part of the 61st Infantry Brigade.

From 1946 to 1948 the 2nd Battalion served in the Army of the Rhine, where it was merged with the 1st Battalion. In 1966 the battalion handed over its responsibilities to the Royal Green Jackets.

During the Battle of Alamein, the courageous gunners of The Rifle Brigade defended 'Snipe' position against Axis heavy armour

BY NIGHTFALL on 24 October 1942, approximately 24 hours after the start of the Battle of Alamein, two aspects of the fighting were becoming obvious. Although the infantry of General Oliver Leese's XXX Corps had borne the brunt of the advance and reached their main objective – the Oxalic Line – the armour of X Corps was finding it difficult to close up behind. Large concentrations of enemy 88mm anti-tank guns were making it suicidal for the armour of X Corps, commanded by Lieutenant-General Brian Horrocks, to show itself. An alternative strategy was called for.

With the 9th Australian Division wearing down enemy resistance on the flanks of the northern advance, and the 51st Highland Division holding the front line to the south, Major-General R. Briggs, commander of the 1st Armoured Division, sought to break the deadlock. He decided to send out two rifle battalions of his 7th Motor Brigade, one on each side of Kidney Ridge, to take and occupy positions from which they could dominate the enemy anti-tank posts to the west. If successful, the two battalions would create a passage through which the British armour could pass.

Shortly after dark, on the night of 26 October 1942, advance parties of both battalions – the 2nd Battalion, The King's Royal Rifle Corps in the north, heading for 'Woodcock', and the 2nd Battalion, The Rifle Brigade, heading for 'Snipe' – set out. Although their advance was preceded by an artillery barrage concentrated on the Axis defences, both commanders were convinced that the shells were falling in the wrong direction. In the case of the northern drive towards Woodcock, this belief was confirmed with the first streaks of daylight. In some haste, the commanding officer withdrew his force back towards its starting point under fire from an unexpected anti-tank post.

Lieutenant-Colonel Victor Turner, commanding the 2nd Battalion, The Rifle Brigade, experienced similar problems to those of his colleague to the north, and his men were delayed by a dummy minefield. However, encouraged by the groups of enemy soldiers scattering before his advancing Bren carriers, Turner continued forward. Crossing a ridge and proceeding another 1500yds, he decided that his force, while not on Snipe, was far enough forward to carry out its allotted task. Ordering deployment for all-round defence, Turner fired the Success Signal and dug in, awaiting the arrival of the heavy weapons and ammunition trucks.

These had been left on the startline, in the charge of Major Pearson, the battalion's second-in-command. When the Success Signal was sighted, Pearson led the trucks and guns forward over what was to prove extremely heavy going; long ridges of sand sucked the wheels down to hub level, and only prodigious effort and sweat kept the column moving.

Nevertheless, by 0345 hours, 19 6-pounder anti-tank guns had reached their destination. They were promptly manoeuvred into positions designated by Turner himself, and, when the ammunition had been off-loaded, the empty trucks began their journey back to the startline. Behind them could be heard the clatter of a small but confused battle.

Hampered by darkness, Lieutenant-Colonel Turner had halted his force in the centre of what later proved to be a German engineers' dump, only half a mile northeast of a leaguer of enemy tanks. Shortly after their arrival, a number of Rifle Brigade Bren carriers had probed cautiously down into the leaguer, taking prisoners in the process. However, when the enemy guns sprang to life they were confronted by a bruising storm of fire and in the confusion the prisoners escaped. The Bren carriers swiftly retired to the Snipe position and the protection of the newly arrived 6-pounders. The battalion's sortie had alerted the German commander of enemy presence in the area, and he decided to retreat to the protection of a larger concentration of panzers to the north. However, as the German tanks began their move, they ran into the southern flank of Snipe. In the fracas that followed, one German panzer and a Semovente self-propelled gun were destroyed.

Dawn broke at 0545 hours, and it revealed to the 300 embattled riflemen the precariousness of their position. They were dispersed inside an oval of scrub-covered desert, 1000yds long and 500yds wide. An old German dug-out provided Turner with his headquarters and a number of small dips gave cover for the battalion's guns. Five of these were deployed in the southeasterly sector, four in the southwest and a further four facing north and northwest. The positioning of his artillery in this manner provided Lieutenant-Colonel Turner with an unrestricted line of fire. Alongside the Rifle Brigade's guns in the northern sector were another six from 239 Battery, 76th Anti-Tank Regiment, under the command of Lieutenant Alan Bauer. Bauer's commander had released him on detachment with the cryptic comment: 'From all the signs, I should think it highly

Below: British infantry advance at the double towards a ridge that lies beyond a disabled enemy tank. Left inset: Sergeant Henry Ayris and Rifleman Dennis Chard, who together destroyed 14 Axis tanks during the battle at 'Snipe'. Above: A shell explodes perilously close to a 6-pounder guncrew, blasting a dense cloud of dust into the air.

TANK SLAYERS

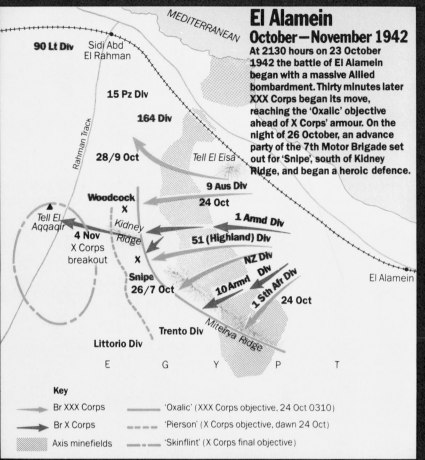

El Alamein
October — November 1942

At 2130 hours on 23 October 1942 the battle of El Alamein began with a massive Allied bombardment. Thirty minutes later XXX Corps began its move, reaching the 'Oxalic' objective ahead of X Corps' armour. On the night of 26 October, an advance party of the 7th Motor Brigade set out for 'Snipe', south of Kidney Ridge, and began a heroic defence.

MEDITERRANEAN

90 Lt Div
Sidi Abd El Rahman
15 Pz Div
164 Div
Rahman Track
28/9 Oct
Tell El Eisa
9 Aus Div
Woodcock
24 Oct
1 Armd Div
Tell El Aqqaqir
Kidney Ridge
51 (Highland) Div
4 Nov
X Corps breakout
NZ Div
Snipe
26/7 Oct
10 Armd Div
1 Sth Afr Div
24 Oct
El Alamein
Trento Div
Miteirya Ridge
Littorio Div

E G Y P T

Key
→ Br XXX Corps
→ Br X Corps
▨ Axis minefields
— 'Oxalic' (XXX Corps objective, 24 Oct 0310)
--- 'Pierson' (X Corps objective, dawn 24 Oct)
-·- 'Skinflint' (X Corps final objective)

---

probable that you are in for a death or glory affair!' As dawn came, Bauer started to appreciate the significance of his commander's parting words.

The concentration of German armour to which the enemy panzers had fled during the night lay about 1000yds to the north of the Snipe position. As dawn broke, the rumbling of enemy tanks on the move could be heard. However, to the astonishment of the watching riflemen, the entire assembly began trundling off to the west, ignoring the opportunity to advance on the Snipe position. In doing so, they exposed the more vulnerable sides of their armoured vehicles; it was a temptation that Snipe could not resist – the gunners sprang into action and opened the day's fighting.

The panzers responded immediately and, within minutes of the first exchange, the whole of Snipe's northern sector was blanketed by a layer of smoke, blown sand and explosions which lasted for over half

an hour. Eventually, the panzers withdrew out of range and the chaos subsided. As the smoke of battle lifted, the excited riflemen surveyed the area around them: the wrecks of six German panzers, eight Italian tanks and two Semovente guns were visible, with an additional two panzers being hastily towed away by German recovery teams. It was an astonishing debut in battle for the 6-pounder guncrews, though casualties had been taken. Three anti-tank guns were out of action, while a fourth was almost buried in soft sand by the effect of its own recoil.

The next phase of the fighting shifted to the southern section. Shermans of the 24th Armoured Brigade, moving rapidly to support the riflemen, reached the crest of the ridge behind Snipe at 0800 hours on 27 October. Opening fire on the only activity they could see in front of them, the British tanks were quickly informed of their true position and firing ceased – fortunately Snipe suffered no great damage

When the 7th Motor Brigade had attempted a daylight advance on Kidney Ridge, at dawn on 26 October, it was met by fierce resistance. Below left: Using a knocked out tank as cover, an infantryman aligns the sights of his Bren gun before firing. With the Sherman tanks (below) stranded behind the ridge, it was left to the 6-pounders to fend off the enemy advance. Above: The only gun that survived the action. It did not cease firing until the last round had been used. Right: A night barrage lights up the desert sky.

6-pounder was proving a most effective weapon if well dug in and manned by strong-nerved gun-crews.

By this time, it was becoming increasingly obvious that a powerful offensive would soon be launched against Snipe. At 1000 hours, Italian infantry were spotted massing to the west and Turner ordered the Bren carrier platoon to 'see them off', which it accomplished by charging straight for the enemy with rifles and Bren guns blazing. When 13 Italian M13s attempted to advance where their infantry had failed, they ran into a concentrated blast from every 6-pounder along Snipe's southern axis. Four 'brewed up', while the rest scuttled towards the safety of the western ridge. A devastating example of crossfire, which Turner described as 'cross-trumping', then occurred. A force of panzers drove out of their cover to the south, intent on attacking the Shermans of the 24th Armoured which were hull-down on the eastern ridge. However, again their flanks were exposed – this time to the uncanny eye of Sergeant Charles Callistan. Two Panzer Mk IIIs were accounted for within 200yds of their advance. The German tank commander then made a fatal error: by detaching part of his force to attack Snipe, he exposed its flank to the 24th Armoured, whose crews were intent on equalling the deeds of the riflemen. The range was long, but the situation clear; if the gunners kept their nerve and fired only at the panzers crossing their sight-lines, rather than those heading straight towards them, they could not fail. Soon, eight more enemy tanks were set ablaze while the rest hurried back behind their ridge.

Six Rifle Brigade carriers were hit in a burst of shelling just after noon

Despite the gunners' success, conditions inside the perimeter of Snipe were now becoming serious. The number of casualties was increasing, while the medical teams remained stranded on the startline, greeted by a storm of fire each time they showed themselves over the ridge. As the heat became more intense, the lack of water and medical attention added to the sufferings of the wounded, as did the increasing enemy bombardments.

Six Rifle Brigade carriers were hit in a burst of shelling just after noon, their gunners blinded by a combination of sand and smoke. Each time danger threatened, crews from less vulnerable positions, or from the disabled guns, raced across to bolster Snipe's defences. Turner was becoming increasingly anxious as to whether ammunition would hold out. Attempts by Major Pearson to send ammunition

as a result of the mistake. The Shermans then advanced down the ridge, but were spotted by a force of panzers to the south which moved out of cover to attack. In doing so, the German tanks had once again exposed their flanks; three were immediately taken out by 6-pounder fire, and, as the panzers withdrew, the Shermans drove down into Snipe and took up defensive positions. However, the German response was brutal and the subsequent barrage from enemy 88mm guns destroyed seven of the Shermans. To the relief of Turner's men, the brigade commander ordered a withdrawal and by 0900 hours the riflemen were once again on their own.

As the Shermans were withdrawing, however, Sergeant Binks of 239 Battery opened fire on a group of panzers some 2000yds to the north. To his joy and amazement Binks knocked out one enemy tank, and he then proceeded to harass another as it attempted to retrieve the disabled tank from the battlefield. The

6-POUNDER ANTI-TANK GUN

The 6-pounder anti-tank gun was designed in 1938 as a replacement for the existing 2-pounder. By late 1941, after successful trials, issue to units began and by April 1942 production had reached 1500 guns per month.

There were five variants, the most effective being the Mark 4. This had a 117in barrel which was fitted with a counter-weight and produced a muzzle velocity of 3020ft per second. The original armour-piercing (AP) shot was replaced by armour-piercing capped, ballistic-capped (APCBC) explosive rounds for use against the face-hardened armour plate of the German panzers.

Intended as the armament for the Royal Artillery anti-tank regiments, a small number of 6-pounders were also issued to infantry units once the Royal Artillery was up to full strength. They were popular with guncrews, being compact and manoeuvrable, as well as possessing a respectable range.

Their most spectacular engagement was at Snipe, with the 2nd Battalion, The Rifle Brigade. In action, the 6-pounder's weight was 252lb and the gun could traverse 45 degrees each side of the centreline. After the Mark 2, the traversing mechanism was removed to allow the gun to be freely traversed by the gun-layer as he pushed and pulled on the breech. The maximum range of the 6lb 4oz shot was 5550yds, though the 74mm armour of the panzers could be penetrated only by guns at a range of 1000yds or less. Above: Sergeant Charles Callistan.

trucks to the beleaguered riflemen had all failed, as had an attempt by one of Turner's officers to fetch more shells in two of the company carriers. Two jeeps, driven by a company commander and a corporal, darted around the Snipe perimeter under a torrent of machine-gun fire, shelling and thick smoke, collecting ammunition from the disabled guns and redistributing it. However, supplies were visibly sinking and no-one knew when the next heavy demand would fall, nor on which section.

Shortly before 1300 hours, the shelling and machine-gun fire increased still further. Over the ridge to the southwest appeared eight M13s and a Semovente self-propelled gun, doubtless encouraged by the fact that all but one of the guns in the southern sector had been silenced. Unfortunately, for the Italians, the remaining 6-pounder was that of Sergeant Callistan. As the enemy tanks advanced, only Callistan was manning the gun, his crew engaged in scrounging ammunition from nearby wrecks. Realising the danger, Turner and Lieutenant Toms raced to Callistan's assistance, Turner taking post as loader and observer, and Toms as No. 1. With the sergeant as layer, the three men waited until the M13s were within 600yds.

Callistan's expertise, combined with their own thin armour, proved fatal to the Italian tanks. The Semovente and five M13s were knocked out before they had closed to 400yds, and only a lack of ammunition prevented a clean sweep. Three tanks were left and Callistan had only two rounds. If he used them now, his gun would be at the mercy of the enemy. With machine guns still pouring fire on the defiant gun-post, Lieutenant Toms raced for a jeep some 100yds behind him and drove to the nearest wrecked gun. It required the strength of desperation to throw aboard every round he could find, before driving back to his colleagues under a hail of machine-gun fire. Turner lifted the vital ammunition clear and flung it towards Callistan's gun. Turning for the last time, a shell fragment pierced the Lieutenant-Colonel's helmet and cut into his head. Blood poured from the wound, temporarily blinding him.

The remaining three tanks were now within 300yds and bullets were streaking dangerously close to their targets, denting the 6-pounder's thin gun-shield. Success or failure now rested firmly in the hands and eyes of the gun-layer, but Sergeant Callistan refused to be hurried. In an astonishing display of his prowess, he took aim, fired and scored

Above: Lieutenant-Colonel Victor Turner, awarded the Victoria Cross for gallantry at Snipe. With his battalion isolated and coming under fierce enemy attack, Turner's leadership contributed to one of the finest actions of the war

Left: Its turret devastated by British artillery, a panzer Mark III lies abandoned on the battlefield. Beyond salvage, the tank has been set ablaze by a German recovery team.

a hat-trick. As the shells found their mark, all three tanks brewed up, their crews perishing to a man. 'Hardly miss 'em at that range', Callistan is reputed to have said later. 'Poor bastards.'

In late afternoon, an attempt by General Briggs to discourage another panzer attack miscarried with dreadful results. His artillery barrage crashed down on the Snipe positions and Turner later recalled, 'During an unpleasant day, this was the most unpleasant thing that happened.'

By now aware of his opponent's weaknesses, the German commander sent out 15 panzers to attack the northwest face of Snipe – held by only two guns. As the enemy advanced, frantic attempts were made by a lone officer to turn a third gun around into a firing position, while Lieutenant-Colonel Turner, by this time only semi-conscious, had to be forcibly held in his dug-out. It seemed to be only a matter of time before the end came for the riflemen. Making good use of cover, the panzers crept forward, sweeping each gun position with machine-gun fire and forcing the crews to back away. One crew was completely wiped out. Racing from the dug-out, Sergeant Swann loaded one of the 6-pounders and promptly knocked out the leading panzer. Sergeant Hine, commanding the other remaining gun, waited until the second panzer was within 100yds before firing. His remarkable patience was rewarded by the sight of his shell going clean through the first tank, and hitting a Mk III just behind. Not surprisingly, the panzers backed off, contenting themselves with laying a tapestry of machine-gun fire across the whole position.

One month later, a committee of enquiry counted the wrecks of 34 tanks or self-propelled guns

A stalemate had been reached, but there were two factors that ran in the riflemen's favour; darkness would soon fall, and the panzers were obviously running out of ammunition. By 1900 hours the light began to drain out of the sky, and the survivors of the remaining posts crawled back towards the dug-out. Lieutenant Holt-Wilson toured each position to ensure that every gun was either destroyed, or the breech-block removed. Under cover of darkness, the wounded were loaded onto jeeps and driven off. At 2230 hours the men who remained moved out, marching back to the ridge from behind which their comrades, and the armour, had witnessed their truly amazing performance.

One month later, a committee of enquiry counted the wrecks of 34 tanks or self-propelled guns – no-one has ever been able to establish how many disabled tanks were towed away from the battlefield by the Germans. Over 100 riflemen had been killed or wounded, though many of the wounded recovered to fight another day, including Lieutenant-Colonel Turner, who was awarded the Victoria Cross. Sergeant Callistan received the Distinguished Conduct Medal, and several Distinguished Service Orders and lesser awards were also given to the gallant defenders of Snipe. Perhaps the highest accolade to the riflemen came from Rommel himself, when he later wrote of the 'murderous fire' which 'struck into our ranks', bringing his heaviest counter-attack against the XXX Corps salient to a halt.

THE AUTHOR Barrie Pitt is well known as a military historian and edited Purnell's *History of the Second World War* and *History of the First World War*.

Right and below: Smiles all round. In the aftermath of Snipe, men of The Rifle Brigade enjoy a well-deserved rest, while a company commander (above) makes out his report of the battle. It had taken the gunners four hours, under heavy enemy fire, to reach the comparative safety of British lines.

DEATH TRAP

In the face of almost impregnable German defences, the Poles of General Anders' II Corps won through to plant their flag in the ruins of Monte Cassino

ON THE corpse-strewn mountains around Monte Cassino in late April 1944, the veterans of the British 78th Infantry Division, well used to the oddities of their various foreign allies in the Italian campaign, were nonetheless startled by the behaviour of the newest Allied force to come to their notice – II Polish Corps. As the Poles relieved the British troops in their precarious sangars dotted across slopes exposed to German fire, they exhibited a bravado and enthusiasm for battle that the hardened British viewed with a mixture of amusement and admiration. According to British accounts, the Poles 'exposed themselves with the most cheerful abandon' to enemy fire, and their officers, 'staggering from one sangar to another, beleaguering the Germans with foul oaths,...seemed to know no fear.' A British infantry officer later recalled that the Poles 'hated the Germans, and their military outlook was dominated by their hate. Their one idea was to find out where the nearest Germans were and go after them....'

This passionate hatred and keeness for a fight were perfectly comprehensible to anyone who knew the tragic recent history of Poland and the extraordinary background to the creation of II Polish Corps. In September 1939 the German Blitzkrieg had

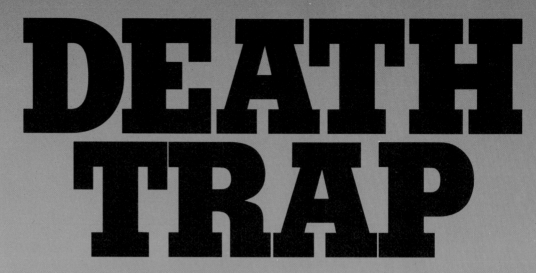

Below left: An infantryman, sprawling awkwardly in the mass of rubble left by the Allied bombing of Cassino town, lies ready to check any German movement within his fire zone. Below right: Soldiers of the 5th Kresowa Infantry Division beat their way forward on Phantom Ridge. At Cassino the grenade came into its own in flushing the enemy from his slit trenches in the broken terrain.

THE CHALLENGE OF CASSINO

II Polish Corps took part in the Italian campaign as part of the Eighth Army, which in turn was part of 15th Army Group. Since mid-January, all the Allied forces had been bogged down in front of the Gustav Line, the formidable set of defensive positions established by Field Marshal Albert Kesselring to block the path to Rome by exploiting the mountainous terrain.

Monte Cassino, with the famous abbey at its summit, was the centre-piece of the German positions. It towered 1700ft above Route 6, the main highway north, and had resisted three separate offensives by the Allies, attacking from the high ground to the west and north. Each time, the Allies had been repulsed with heavy losses. The abbey and the town had been reduced to rubble by air and artillery bombardments, but well-sited German artillery observers and experienced troops, especially the 1st Parachute Division, had survived everything the Allies had so far thrown at them when Anders was asked to lead a fourth attempt to break through the defences.

crushed the Polish Army, and Hitler and Stalin had proceeded to divide the Polish state between them as Soviet forces occupied the east of the country. Some 200,000 Polish soldiers were carried off to the Soviet Union as prisoners of war, along with countless civilians deported to Stalin's camps. The bitterness of the Poles at the loss of their country was compounded by the personal loss of friends and relatives, and by the experience of captivity.

Eventually, after Hitler's invasion of the Soviet Union, the Poles were allowed to form fighting units, and in autumn 1942, some 20,000 civilians and 40,000 military personnel under Lieutenant-General Wladyslaw Anders crossed over to the British-controlled sector of Iran. These refugees were turned into II Polish Corps after months of training in the Middle East. 50,000 strong, the corps consisted of the 5th Kresowa Infantry Division, the 3rd Carpathian Rifle Division (each of two brigades) and the 2nd Warsaw Armoured Brigade.

The Poles were now thirsting to take on the Germans. They were attached to the British Eighth Army in Italy, and in March 1944 Anders was asked if his men would attack the Monte Cassino position – a notorious death trap – to secure the Allied right flank as part of a general offensive to outflank this linchpin of the German defences on the Gustav Line.

There were good reasons why Anders might have refused a proposal to throw his men against the almost impregnable German positions around Monte Cassino. Casualties would undoubtedly be severe, and were arguably unjustified in taking on an objective that could be outflanked. Yet the Polish general accepted almost without hesitation. Like all the Poles, his overwhelming desire was to secure the independence of his homeland, and the highest immediate contribution he could make to that goal would be to achieve an outstanding feat of arms. Monte Cassino was known throughout the world, its significance almost mystical to the troops themselves – 'an idea and an obsession, as well as a sombre reality of rock and steel', as it has been described. If Polish soldiers took Monte Cassino, the

The commander of II Polish Corps in Italy, Wladyslaw Anders, was a man dedicated to the Polish nation. Born near Warsaw in 1892, he had served as an ensign in the Russian 3rd Dragoon Regiment during World War I. When Poland became independent in 1918, the Polish army units were reorganised, and when war broke out between Russia and Poland in 1919-1921 he commanded the 15th Lancer Regiment. He went on to command a cavalry brigade against the Germans in 1939, and then opposed Poland's invasion by the Red Army. He was taken prisoner and held until 1941, when he assisted in the formation of the new Polish Army.

The powerful challenge of Monte Cassino gave Anders a perfect opportunity to demonstrate the Polish fighting spirit to the Allies and thus stake a claim for Poland in the postwar world. Following that victory, the corps took Piedmonte in the Hitler Line and then fought steadily up the Adriatic coast. It played a prominent part in the Eighth Army's breaking of the Gothic Line. Partly due to its politically complex position, the Polish Corps received scant recognition of its sacrifices. It was denied a place in both the triumphal entry into Rome and in the London Victory Parade. Then Poland's postwar government, mindful of the staunch support Anders and his corps had given to the anti-communist government-in-exile in London, forbade them to return to Poland. Anders died in exile in 1970.

effect on world opinion could be sufficient to influence the future of Poland. More simply, it would certainly give the Poles their chance to have a go at the hated Germans.

No-one doubted that the German defences were a hard nut to crack – in the last attempt to clear the massif, in mid-March 1944, 4th Indian Division had suffered appalling casualties without achieving any notable gains. Before the Allied forces had arrived at Cassino, the Germans had had time to construct an extensive network of bunkers and shelters, all heavily camouflaged and almost indestructible, commanding broad arcs of fire across the maze of gullies, ridges and ravines. Even if an attacking force succeeded in taking one German strongpoint, it would come under withering fire from any number of other positions.

Anders' solution to this problem was to launch two simultaneous thrusts, hoping to saturate the enemy defences. A brigade of the Carpathian Division was to advance along Snakeshead Ridge against the German-held Point 593, while a brigade of the Kresowa Division moved forward from Monte Castellone to assault Phantom Ridge and Colle Sant' Angelo. After taking Point 593, the Carpathians would ignore the monastery, instead striking towards the German strongpoint at Albaneta Farm and breaking through to link up with British troops attacking along Route 6. After some vigorous debate, the operation was entrusted to 1 Carpathian Brigade and 5 Wilenska Brigade; 2 Carpathian and 6 Lwowska Brigades were to remain in reserve.

They were extraordinarily close to the enemy – a mere 70 yards distant in some places – and were often overlooked from three sides

Late in April, the Polish Corps moved forward to relieve the British 78th Infantry Division on the mountain salient, in preparation for the offensive, scheduled for the night of 11/12 May. The British troops were not sorry to see the Poles arrive, for conditions on Snakeshead Ridge and Castellone were, to say the least, unpleasant. Unlike the Germans, the Allied troops had never had the chance to construct proper shelters. The Poles found themselves huddled in hastily improvised sangars – small hollows in the rocky slopes protected from enemy fire by a parapet of stones, boulders and tins, and sheltered from the sun by a blanket erected as an awning. They were extraordinarily close to the enemy – a mere 70 yards distant in places – and were often overlooked from three sides. Almost no movement was possible unobserved.

The men lived off bully beef, biscuits and bacon, since preparing hot food was virtually impossible, and water was restricted to one pint a day for all purposes. Many of the sangars were surrounded by rotting corpses, the human wastage of the last three months of combat. The stench of rotting flesh was nauseating, mingling strangely with the irrepressible evidence of a Mediterranean spring – expanses of red poppies and, at night, a chorus of nightingales which made sleep still more difficult. In the most exposed sangars, it was impossible for the men to

move even to perform their natural functions. Forced to relieve themselves into their ration tins, Polish soldiers are reported to have launched the excrement-filled receptacles towards the German positions in a gesture of contempt and defiance.

As dawn broke on the grey, overcast morning of 11 May, the men knew the waiting was almost over. General Anders' Order of the Day opened with a stirring exhortation: 'Soldiers! The moment for battle has arrived. We have long awaited the moment for revenge and retribution over our hereditary enemy.' Undoubtedly, his sentiment was shared by the Polish rank and file, who had little need of rhetoric to fuel their passionate hatred of the Germans. Tension mounted through the day, and towards nightfall an unaccustomed silence fell over the battle-torn landscape, as the British artillery was ordered to hold fire and the Germans, by pure coincidence, also halted their bombardments. The clouds lifted, uncovering a starlit sky.

At 2300 hours, half-an-hour before moonrise, 1600 artillery pieces opened up in a numbing barrage of sound along the whole length of the front. The Poles still had 90 nerve-racking minutes to wait. Then, at 0100 hours, they moved into the attack. The initial assault by the 2nd Battalion, 1 Carpathian Brigade, met with immediate success. Closing swiftly on Point 593 as their supporting artillery barrage lifted, they caught the Germans out of position – they had moved to reinforced shelters during the artillery bombardment and were not given time to reoccupy their defensive posts. After 30 minutes of close combat, Point 593 was in Polish hands. But this provided only a momentary taste of victory, for all the Polish units engaged that night were soon to meet disaster.

They picked their way across the exposed slopes in the darkness, stumbling over the rocky ground and through the tough thorn scrub

The 13th and 15th Battalions, 5 Wilenska Brigade, advanced on Phantom Ridge with courage and determination, but as they picked their way across the exposed slopes in the darkness, stumbling over the rocky ground and through the tough thorn scrub, artillery and mortar fire rained down on them, killing and maiming many long before they even approached their objectives. Those platoons that did find their way in among the German bunkers were too few in number to drive off the enemy. Most of the attackers were soon pinned down in whatever scant shelters they could find, as machine-gun fire and shell splinters filled the air about them. Radio communications had broken down, denying the Polish commanders any chance to co-ordinate operations. By dawn, the 13th and 15th Battalions had been virtually wiped out and two other battalions committed to Phantom Ridge were sustaining heavy losses.

The advance on the strongpoint at Albaneta Farm met with a similar fate. The Poles put great faith in the tanks of 2 Armoured Brigade which were committed in support of the Carpathian infantry, but few got

Above: Soldiers attempt the highly dangerous task of wiping out the determined opposition entrenched in the strong positions inadvertently created for the Germans by the bombing of Cassino. Top left: In the foreground a soldier carries a Thompson M1928A1 sub-machine gun with pistol fore-grip. Top right: Poles armed with an SMLE Mark III* rifle and the later Thompson M1A1 with simple fore-grip, a model also seen above.

Taking Cassino
II Polish Corps, May 1944

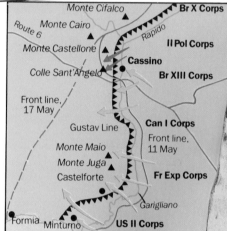

On the night of **11/12 May 1944** the Allies renewed their offensive along the Gustav Line between Cassino and the sea. From their positions on Snakeshead Ridge and Monte Castellone, II Polish Corps pushed forward, taking Point 593. But the enemy fought fiercely and the Poles paid a heavy cost.

Key

II Polish Corps
Other Allied Forces

Assault on Snakeshead Ridge

12 May 0100 1 Carpathian Bde pushes along Snakeshead Ridge against heavy resistance, taking Point 593. As 6 Lwowska Bde launches a feint attack further to the rear and 5 Wilenska Bde moves along Phantom Ridge, 1 Carpathian Bde attempts to advance as far as Albaneta Farm and Point 569. They meet fierce resistance and the attack grinds to a halt. Successive German counter-attacks are driven off and Point 593 is held temporarily.

Phantom Ridge

0200 5 Wilenska Bde attacks along Phantom Ridge towards Colle Sant'Angelo and Point 575. The attack is called off finally in the late afternoon.

16 May 2230 The assault on the German positions around Cassino is renewed, with 6 Lwowska Bde spearheading the Polish attack.

18 May 0950 A patrol from the Carpathian Division reaches the monastery on Monte Cassino and hoists the Polish flag.

anywhere near Albaneta. A combination of mines and anti-tank guns took a fearsome toll of the Polish armour. An infantryman later recalled how he had watched with horror as tank crewmen, their hair and clothing on fire, leapt from their burning vehicles and rolled on the ground in an agonised effort to extinguish the flames. Meanwhile, on Point 593 the situation had rapidly worsened after the Carpathians' initial success. Their efforts to advance against the next German position, Point 569, ground to a halt in the face of concentrated machine-gun fire. As German paratroopers began to counter-attack, Point 593 became a killing ground.

When dawn broke, the full scale of the Polish losses became clear to their commanders. Anders hoped the men could hold on until the following night and then renew their advance, but the position was hopeless. With little cover, in broad daylight, the Poles were dreadfully vulnerable to German snipers and machine-gunners. By late afternoon on 12 May, when Anders finally gave the order to retreat, Point 593 was being held by one officer and seven men.

Yet astonishingly, this carnage had not quelled the Poles' fighting spirit. A doctor treating casualties that day recorded that: 'The wounded and dying were all in a state of excitement… There was no fear to be seen in them, only a kind of fury and rage…' Nonetheless, the experience had been a waking

nightmare for all who had taken part, and General Harold Alexander, C-in-C Allied Forces in Italy, wisely decided the Poles should not be called upon to renew their efforts until they had had time to reorganise.

Despite finding themselves back at their start-lines, the Poles had in fact contributed immensely to the overall Allied operation, for they had tied down a considerable German force and inflicted heavy losses upon it. By 16 May the Allied plan to outflank Cassino was well under way, and that night the Polish Corps resumed its attack. This time the Lwowska Brigade took on Phantom Ridge. A probe against the northern extremity of the ridge met only light resistance and by dawn on 17 May the brigade had exploited this weakness to occupy neighbouring Colle Sant'Angelo. On the other flank Point 593 was once more captured after heavy fighting at close quarters, Polish soldiers using their grenades to deadly effect against the German positions.

But the story of 12 May threatened to repeat itself. German mortars, artillery and machine guns took their toll as counter-attack succeeded counter-

Far left: In the aftermath of the final battle for Cassino, Polish troops search for the bodies of their dead comrades in the shadow of Monte Cassino monastery. Wrapped in canvas, one is being carried away for burial. Left: A German paratrooper is led to captivity by the Poles. Right: The proudest moment of II Polish Corps in World War II – the flag of Poland (together with that of their British ally) waves high above the hard-won monastery.

attack. A Polish soldier later described that day, as ammunition ran out in forward positions: 'The Poles, deprived of their weapons, unable to move back, crouched beneath the German bunkers. They threw themselves flat and dared not change position or move at all…. And then, incredibly, someone began to sing the Polish national anthem…. All the soldiers joined in the chorus, on the summit of Colle Sant'Angelo, the mountain of death.'

Short of water, food and sleep, as well as of ammunition, the troops holding Point 593 and Colle Sant' Angelo were in a parlous condition on the night of 17/18 May. But relief was at hand, for the progress of the Allied offensive was now threatening to cut off the German forces on the massif and Field Marshal Albert Kesselring, C-in-C South, gave the order for withdrawal.

After dawn, guessing that the monastery had now been left undefended, a detachment of the 12th Podolski Lancers was sent to reconnoitre the position. Picking their way through a minefield, six men under Lieutenant Gurbiel approached the monastery and entered the ruins. They found only 16 wounded Germans, left behind in the withdrawal. Improvising a regimental pennant from a Red Cross flag and a blue handkerchief, the lancers raised their emblem and a bugler played the *Hejnal*, a traditional Polish bugle call. An eye-witness remembered that 'the hardened soldiers… cried like children' on hearing that evocative sound emerge from the previously impregnable German fortress.

Few would deny that the Polish Corps, which had lost 3799 dead in the week's fighting, had earned the historic honour of taking Monte Cassino.

THE AUTHOR R. G. Grant graduated in Modern History from Trinity College, Oxford. He has written extensively on recent military campaigns.

JUNGLE MARAUDERS

MERRILL'S MARAUDERS

During August 1943, US infantry units stationed in the Pacific, Caribbean and America received a request calling for volunteers from experienced jungle troops to form a long-range penetration group under the code-name 'Galahad'. Over the next few weeks, some 3000 men answered the call, and by the middle of September the last batch of recruits left San Francisco for India.

They arrived at Bombay on 31 October, and the men were then sent on two intensive jungle-training courses which were completed in early 1944. Despite these preparations, Galahad force still lacked an official title and a commanding officer. In January 1944 the unit became known as the 5307th Composit Unit (Provisional), and a senior officer, Brigadier-General Frank Merrill, was put in command of the force.

The 5307th, soon to be known as Merrill's Marauders (their badge is shown above) consisted of three battalions, numbered from one to three. In turn, each battalion was sub-divided into two combat teams: the 1st Battalion had Red and White Combat Teams; the 2nd had Blue and Green; and the 3rd had Khaki and Orange.

Each team consisted of 16 Officers and 456 men. Before its disbandment on 4 August 1944, the unit fought five major and 30 minor battles against the Japanese.

The Marauders actions were a fitting tribute to the first US ground troops to be committed to the Asian mainland in World War II.

Sweltering in the heat and humidity of the Burmese jungle, the men of Merrill's Marauders fought a grim and bloody battle against a fanatical Japanese adversary

IN THE EARLY morning light of 28 March 1944, Blue Combat Team of the 2nd Battalion, Merrill's Marauders began to withdraw from the Burmese village of Auche toward Nhpum Ga. Ahead lay a march over 5km of dense, leech-infested jungle. The men were already exhausted: in the last five days, they had covered over 112km, crossed 110 rivers and had fought one fierce, close-quarters battle against the Japanese. Although only a short distance away, it took five hours to reach their objective. The trail was steep, ankle-deep in glutinous mud and very slippery in places. One of the Marauders present later remembered the agony of the forced march:

'It was mostly a matter of waiting while they [the advance guard] slashed away up front. Pack, weapons, ammunition, knives, canteens; all grew heavier. The straps they were strung on cut into the flesh. You could sit down and lean back on your pack to rest your shoulders, but holding your head at a 45 degree angle was hard on your neck, and anyhow you might have to struggle to your feet immediately. So usually you just stood, leaning slightly forward.'

The heavy going, however, was the least of their problems. A few hundred metres out of Auche, the Japanese opened up with 76mm guns deployed at Warong, a native village lying 3km to the south. The gunners soon found their range and embarked on a

sustained bombardment. One of the first shells to land scored a direct hit on one soldier, blowing him to pieces, and another exploded against a nearby tree, unleashing deadly wooden splinters against the column. The planned orderly withdrawal was turning into a rout.

The Marauders, a 3000-strong American deep-penetration unit, was a key part in the Allied strategy to push the Japanese out of Burma, which they had occupied in 1942. Before a major offensive was launched, the Marauders, part of Lieutenant-General Joseph Stilwell's command, were ordered to strike at the enemy's supply lines. The force's first raid in February 1944 was a success, and Stilwell ordered the Marauders to carry out a simultaneous attack against Shaduzup and Inkangahtawng in March. Both raids met fierce resistance and the Marauders were forced to make a fighting withdrawal to the village of Hsamshinyang. The Japanese, however, caught up with the rear guard of the Marauders' 2nd Battalion on 28 March.

By 1030 hours, most of the 2nd Battalion had reached Nhpum Ga, a 900m-high saddle ridge which overlooked the Marauders' advance airbase at Hsamshingyang. The battalion's medical officer, Major Bernard Rogoff, set up his aid post and received his first casualty. He remembered his first case in particular:

'One man, a big burly fellow with a tommy-gun, was shaking violently all over, tears streaming down his face. He cried "Major, I'm not afraid damn it, I tell you I'm not afraid. I just can't stop shaking." Others, in worse shape, jumped and screamed each time a shell went off, and the shells were getting closer all the time.'

Knowing that the bombardment was a preliminary to

above: A weary mule troop of Merrill's Marauders takes a welcome break on the trail from Auche to Nhpum Ga in northern Burma. Below: head, a patrol, armed with M1 carbines, an M1 rifle and a Thompson sub-machine gun, talks the jungle for signs of the advancing Japanese.

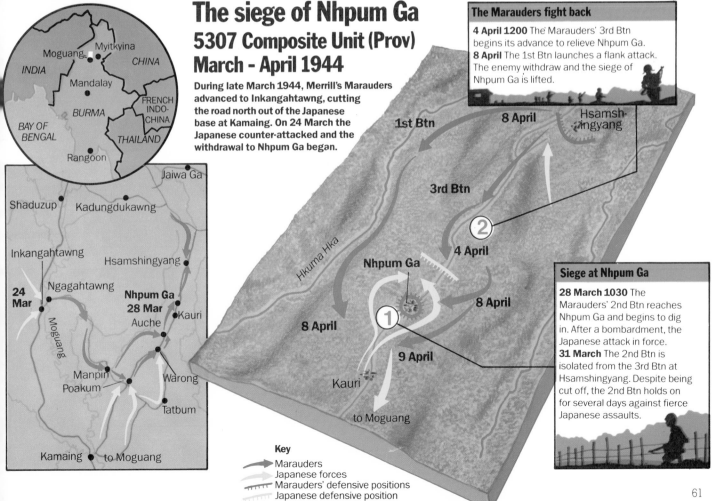

The siege of Nhpum Ga
5307 Composite Unit (Prov)
March - April 1944

During late March 1944, Merrill's Marauders advanced to Inkangahtawng, cutting the road north out of the Japanese base at Kamaing. On 24 March the Japanese counter-attacked and the withdrawal to Nhpum Ga began.

The Marauders fight back

4 April 1200 The Marauders' 3rd Btn begins its advance to relieve Nhpum Ga.
8 April The 1st Btn launches a flank attack. The enemy withdraw and the siege of Nhpum Ga is lifted.

Siege at Nhpum Ga

28 March 1030 The Marauders' 2nd Btn reaches Nhpum Ga and begins to dig in. After a bombardment, the Japanese attack in force.
31 March The 2nd Btn is isolated from the 3rd Btn at Hsamshingyang. Despite being cut off, the 2nd Btn holds on for several days against fierce Japanese assaults.

Key
→ Marauders
→ Japanese forces
Marauders' defensive positions
Japanese defensive position

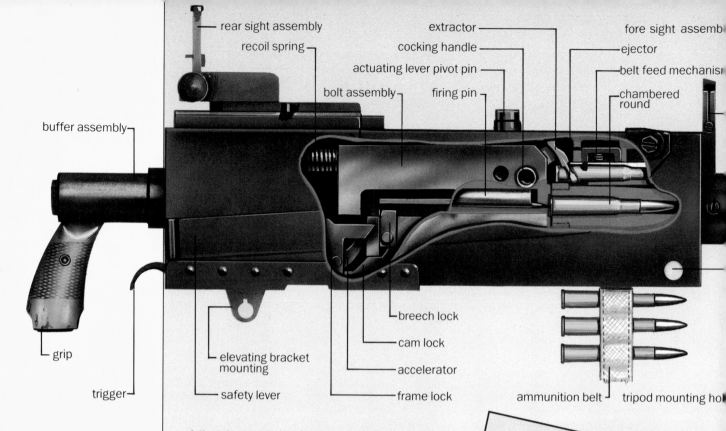

rear sight assembly

recoil spring

extractor

cocking handle

fore sight assemb

ejector

actuating lever pivot pin

belt feed mechanism

bolt assembly

firing pin

chambered round

buffer assembly

grip

trigger

elevating bracket mounting

safety lever

breech lock

cam lock

accelerator

frame lock

ammunition belt

tripod mounting ho

The Browning Model 1919, was the work of an arms' manufacturer, John Browning, who produced a weapon that was robust, easy to handle and reliable.

At normal operating temperatures, the Browning could fire up to 60rpm for up to 30 minutes without the barrel overheating, and stoppages were easily dealt with. Light, weighing 45lb (including tripod), and very portable, it was an ideal infantry weapon, and the A4 version, used throughout World War II, was standard to most combat companies.

When deployed with infantry in the ground role, the gun was mounted on the M2 tripod and its two-man crew depressed or elevated the barrel by turning a wheel positioned between the two rear legs of the tripod.

The feed mechanism for the Browning consisted of a woven fabric belt designed to hold up to 150 rounds of .30in calibre M1906 ammunition.

Although the Browning was undoubtedly a first-rate weapon, it underwent a series of modifications during the war: the original pistol-type grip was changed to a rifle-type stock, and an adjustable bipod was fitted, together with a carrying handle and flash hider.

The Browning light machine gun saw service in every theatre of the war.

a full-scale assault, the 2nd Battalion's commanding officer, Lieutenant-Colonel McGee, immediately set his men to constructing makeshift defensive positions. Within a few hours, the Marauders had built a perimeter about 400m long, and between 100 and 250m wide. Seen from above, it resembled a figure of eight. McGee, aware that he might have to defend the saddle for some days, had chosen his position well: it occupied all the available high ground and surrounded the only local well.

The Japanese launched their assault against the battalion's perimeter almost immediately. Their commander, Colonel Maruyama of the 18th Division, had recently received reinforcements from the 1st

M1919A4 MG

Calibre 0.3in
Length 104.4cm
Weight (gun) 14.1kg
Feed belt

System of operation recoil
Rate of fire (practical) 120rpm
Muzzle velocity 860mps
Maximum effective range 1000m

barrel

barrel jacket

Above: The Browning M1919A4 machine gun. Used during the Marauders' campaign in northern Burma, its ruggedness and firepower made it a firm favourite with the troops, who used it with devastating effect against the Japanese.

Battalion, 55th Regiment and, assured of overwhelming strength, had ordered his men to crush the Marauders' rearguard as quickly as possible. Despite enemy thrusts against patrols operating between Nhpum Ga and Hsamshingyang, communications between McGee's force and the 3rd Battalion, Merrill's Marauders at Hsamshingyang were maintained for the next two days. However, on 31 March, the Japanese ambushed, and inflicted heavy casualties on a patrol from the 2nd Battalion and the two

Left: Marauders and local Kachin tribesmen, who helped them in their jungle war against the Japanese, pose for the camera. Below left: Frank Merrill and two of his Japanese-American interpreters plan their next move. Below: Chow time. Using a steel helmet as a cooking pot, three Marauders supplement their rations with captured rice.

forces became isolated from each other.

The Marauders' position was hazardous in the extreme: the 3rd Battalion was having great difficulty in containing enemy patrols probing to the north of Hsamshingyang and would not be able to support the men at Nhpum Ga in the foreseeable future.

The Japanese attacked Nhpum Ga with suicidal ferocity from the end of March until the siege was lifted some 10 days later. Every day, each sector of the Marauders' perimeter faced a succession of charges and, on occasion, a series of well co-ordinated simultaneous assaults. The enemy troops were supported by howitzers and 75mm mountain guns that, with their high muzzle velocities, were ideal for blasting away at earthworks. Fired from the village of Kauri, a mere 900m from Nhpum Ga, their shells struck home before the Marauders could take cover.

Japanese snipers, hidden in the dense undergrowth kept up a continuous fusillade

Japanese snipers, hidden in the dense undergrowth that surrounded the hill, also kept up a continuous, nerve-racking fusillade during the day, and after nightfall, shot in the direction of the sounds made by men shovelling earth to deepen their foxholes or bury the putrifying remains of dead pack mules. The accuracy of the snipers' fire kept the Marauders in the shelter of their flimsy trenches and a serious sanitation problem soon developed. Men were forced to bury their waste around their foxholes, but the stench remained, worsened by the carcasses of the 75 mules which had been killed and, after 36 hours in the humid heat of the Burmese jungle, were grossly bloated and fly-ridden.

Just after dawn on the 31st, the enemy's artillery and mortars opened up in preparation for a co-ordinated assault on three sides of the Marauders' position. The largest party was directed at, and succeeded in, isolating the battalion's water supply. Its loss was keenly felt: the men were soon reduced to drinking the muddy water which had drained into holes dug by the unit's Pioneer and Demolition Platoon. Although the ration was small, only half a water-bottle per day, many were loath to drink it as several rotting mules lay in the water. The shortage became so severe that McGee requested resupply by air. The water drop took place on 3 April: some 500 gallons in heavy plastic bags were flown in.

After the Japanese invasion of Burma in January 1942 and the Allied retreat to the northeast frontier of India, the key task of the Allies was the reopening of the overland supply route through northern Burma to China.

The first counter-offensive took place in the Arakan in late 1942 and its failure threatened a reappraisal of Allied strategy. However, a deep penetration raid by Major-General Orde Wingate's Chindits a few months later was a notable success.

The performance of the Chindits rekindled Allied plans for the reconquest of northern Burma, and at the Casablanca conference in January 1943 and the Trident conference in Washington in May senior commanders discussed the fine details of future operations in Burma. Wingate was present at the Washington conference and his persuasive arguments in support of a more extensive role for his Chindits won the favour of senior US commanders. In detail, Wingate proposed that his troops push deep into enemy-held territory to establish a series of strongpoints that could be resupplied from the air. The Chindits could then launch attacks against Japanese convoys, railways and airfields.

His views fired the Americans into action and they suggested that a US combat team should support the Chindits' campaign. This force, which was to become Merrill's Marauders, would be under the command of Lieutenant-General Joseph 'Vinegar Joe' Stilwell, the officer in charge of Chinese troops operating along the Burmese frontier.

In October some of Stilwell's Chinese troops opened the offensive against the Japanese in northern Burma, and in January 1944 the Marauders went out on their first penetration raid.

BRIGADIER-GENERAL FRANK MERRILL

After graduating from West Point in the late 1920s, Merrill spent some time with a cavalry unit before attending the Massachusetts Institute of Technology.

Merrill had already been marked as a first-rate officer, and in 1938 he became Assistant Military Attache in Japan, acquiring a good knowledge of Japanese and observing the Japanese Army on manoeuvres.

When the Japanese attacked Pearl Harbor in early December 1942, Merrill was flying from the Philippines to Rangoon, and he remained in the Burmese capital until he joined the staff of Lieutenant-General Joseph Stilwell, commander of the Chinese troops in northern Burma. In this capacity, Merrill took part in the early jungle campaigns against the advancing Japanese, and accompanied Stilwell on the now famous retreat from Burma in May 1942.

During the next eighteen months, Merrill remained as an aide to Stilwell, rising from the rank of major to brigadier-general. At the beginning of January 1944, Merrill was given command of the Marauders and then led them in their first clashes with the Japanese. Over the next few months, both Merrill and his men were constantly in action. The strain of jungle warfare, however, seriously weakened Merrill's health and in late March he suffered the first of several heart attacks. After rejoining the Marauders in late April, Merrill led them to their final encounter of the war, the battle of Myityina.

Jungle scenes. Above: Mule skinners clean their weapons while waiting for an airdrop. Above right: Firing an 81mm mortar. Below right: Stalking an enemy bunker.

Despite being under constant bombardment and attack, the Marauders had given a good account of themselves in the battles with the Japanese. Until 1 April, their losses had been light: seven dead and 25 wounded. However, over 100 animals had been killed and lay rotting within the defences. The smell from their carcasses mingled with the stench rising from the decomposing bodies of over 200 Japanese who had died trying to pierce the perimeter.

Conditions were made even more unbearable by blood-sucking leeches. One man later remembered the effect:

'On everyone's uniform there were dark stiff patches. These were dried blood, from leech bites. The country was infested by these repulsive little rubbery monsters, black worms with suction cups at both ends able to contract to pea-sized balls or elongate themselves to a couple of inches.

'Unfortunately, mother nature had endowed the pests with the capacity of clamping on and opening up a lesion without you feeling anything, especially if you were asleep. Then, after you had found one of them on you and got him off, you were liable to have difficulty in stopping the flow of blood, for their saliva contained an anti-coagulant.

'All of us were more or less bloody all the time, and the mules suffered worse than we; their fetlocks were generally dark red and slimy with blood. In addition, eggs deposited in legions by a kind of fly, hatched into screw worms.'

Although McGee's men suffered untold agonies under these harsh conditions, they continued to sustain an aggressive defence of Nhpum Ga. One of the most successful actions was led by Sergeant Roy Matsumoto. Every evening he crept into the jungle to snipe at the enemy and gather useful intelligence and after one such mission, he reported that the Japanese were massing to launch a full-scale attack against an exposed section of the perimeter. The

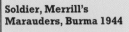

trenches at this point were held by 20 men under Lieutenant McLogan, and had already proved difficult to defend. Acting on Matsumoto's information, McLogan decided to booby-trap his position and then withdraw his men to the crest of a hill overlooking the exposed spur.

At dawn, the Japanese attacked: a reinforced platoon opened the charge, hurling a barrage of grenades at the deserted trenches. Bewildered by the apparent success of their attack, an officer wielding a sword rallied his men and pushed them further up the hill. On the crest, McLogan's men were ready and waiting: when the enemy were within 15m of his position, he gave the order to open fire.

Forty weapons – M1 rifles, tommy-guns and Browning automatic rifles – responded, cutting swathes through the advancing Japanese. Worse was to follow: another group, following in the footsteps of the first, was tricked into attacking by the Japanese-speaking Matsumoto and suffered a similar fate. In all, 45 Japanese soldiers, including two officers, were left for dead. In recognition of his bravery and devotion to duty, Matsumoto was later awarded both the Legion of Merit and the Bronze Star.

While the 2nd Battalion was maintaining its stubborn defence of Nhpum Ga, the Marauders' 3rd Battalion at Hsamshingyang was attempting to break through the Japanese ring. Before 2 April they were unable to make any significant progress beside forcing the enemy to withdraw their outposts from around the base, but on that day they received much-needed reinforcements in the shape of two 75mm pack howitzers and 400 rounds of ammunition. Arriving at 0930 hours, the guns and their crews were ready for action by 1100.

Howitzers were to be used for close-range fire support against enemy bunkers

On the following day, Colonel Charles Hunter, who took control of the Marauders after Merrill had suffered a heart attack on 28 March, felt confident enough to brief his officers on his plan for the relief of the 2nd Battalion. The 3rd Battalion would attack on the 4th with its Orange Combat Team along the trail to Nhpum Ga while its Khaki Combat Team made an outflanking move. The howitzers were to be used for close-range fire support against enemy bunkers. The attack was to begin at 1200 hours, and Hunter expected McGee to be relieved within three days.

Despite these preparations, the Marauders made only slow progress toward their objectives in the face of stubborn Japanese resistance. Radio reports between Major Lew, Orange Combat Team's senior officer, and Lieutenant-Colonel Beach, the commander of the 3rd Battalion, highlighted the beginning of a bitter struggle:

'The "fat boys" [75mm howitzers] are raising hell with the pill-boxes on the right slope of the hill – a direct hit on one – the Japanese ran from another. Have the fat boys hit that machine gun firing 200 yards west of their present target, then swing their barrage up the slope of the hill. We are preparing to push off.'

Later, as the battle developed into a bloody stalemate, Captain Burch, leader of the battalion's Assault Company reported the resilience of the Japanese defences:

'I am pinned down by heavy machine-gun fire from the west side of the hill. Artillery is hitting too high on the hill to do any good. My flamethrower is way round on my right flank trying to knock out that gun, but I doubt if he can get close enough. Am going to push up to a little knoll ahead and dig in as it's almost dark.'

Darkness put an end to all thoughts of reaching Nhpum Ga, but the Marauders had made significant progress: the Japanese had been blasted or burnt out of several bunkers and elements of the 3rd Battalion were within 1000m of the 2nd Battalion.

The overall situation changed little during the next two days, with the Japanese continuing to mount assaults against McGee's force and resisting the advance of the relief force. Only heavy air support enabled the Marauders to move forward across ground, which was, according to one man:

'Blasted bare along the trail. Every tree was either down or chipped all over with fragments or bullets, and the bamboo was cut as if with a huge knife. Japanese bodies were found in trees, where a 500lb bomb had blasted them yesterday afternoon.'

By 6 April, McGee's position was critical: his battalion had lost 17 men killed, four missing and over 100 wounded. Food and water were in short supply, and most of the men were too weak to resist any further Japanese attacks. On the following day, however, McGee received the welcome news that the Marauders' 1st Battalion had arrived from Shaduzup and that the relief force was 500m from his position.

Above: A crude bamboo cross marks the last resting place of one of the Marauders killed during the ten-day fight at Nhpum Ga. Below: Some of the lucky survivors are airlifted out of Burma for a well-earned rest in India. The strain of constant action was to lead to the disbandment of the unit a few months later.

That evening at Hsamshingyang, Hunter ordered those troops of the 1st Battalion fit for service, some 250 men, to prepare for a flank attack to the west and south of the Japanese forces surrounding Nhpum Ga, in support of the 3rd Battalion fighting along the trail.

The assault got under way during the morning of the 8th and, despite heavy enemy attacks against the 3rd Battalion, the flanking force was able to reach its objective by nightfall. After a tense night spent in fear of a surprise attack, the 1st Battalion began its advance against the village of Kauri in the early-morning light. Although expecting to meet the same fanatical resistance that had thwarted other attempts to push the Japanese out of their bunkers, the troops encountered little opposition, and as they advanced they came across the signs of a hurried retreat: equipment scattered on the floor, fires unattended and half-cooked meals. It was clear to all that the enemy had given up the struggle, allowing the 3rd Battalion to march into Nhpum Ga at midday.

The siege lasted for ten days, and the Marauders' 2nd Battalion had fought a valiant rear-guard action against a fierce and dogged foe. Remarkably, the battalion had lost only 25 men killed, and had accounted for over 400 Japanese.

THE AUTHOR William Franklin is a military historian who has contributed to numerous publications. His particular interest is the history of elite forces of World War II.

ARGYLL
LAW

Previous page: Incidents in a tough anti-terrorist campaign. After the retaking of the Crater district of Aden by men of the Argyll and Sutherland Highlanders on the night of 3/4 July 1967, their commander, Lieutenant-Colonel Colin 'Mad Mitch' Mitchell, imposed a martial regime. Known as 'Argyll Law', it effectively ended the attacks by the National Liberation Front (NLF). Clockwise from top: Suspected members of the NLF were rounded up (here, by a fusilier) and sent for interrogation at Mitchell's HQ in a local bank. Continuously manned roadblocks were set up at key points in the town and anyone leaving or entering was subjected to a vigorous body search. Mobile units patrolled the streets, stopping any suspicious vehicles to question their occupants. This page: An aerial view of Crater, with (inset) one of Mitchell's highlanders taking a break from the fighting.

When the Argyll and Sutherland Highlanders moved into the Crater district of Aden in 1967, they used tough tactics to gain the initiative and control the situation

DURING THE EVENING of 4 July 1967, the commanding officer of the 1st Battalion, the Argyll and Sutherland Highlanders, Lieutenant-Colonel Colin 'Mad Mitch' Mitchell, made Mohammed Ibrahim, the Superintendent of the Aden Armed Police, an offer that neither he nor his rebellious men could afford to refuse. In his usual tough, no-nonsense way, 'Mad Mitch' calmly informed the superintendent that unless his police immediately and unconditionally surrendered both their weapons and barracks, the wild hillmen (Mitchell's highlanders) would wipe out the mutineers at the first sign of trouble. Wisely, Ibrahim accepted the ultimatum, and over the next few hours the Argylls completed their re-occupation of the town of Crater. In less than 48 hours, Mitch and his fiercely loyal men had cleared out a den of unrest which had been a thorn in the side of the British Army for four long and bloody years.

Aden had always been an unpopular posting with the army and, even at the best of times, was commonly referred to as 'Arabia's arsehole'. The reasons for its unpopularity were not hard to find: the country was a wild, inhospitable place which offered few attractions to the army's young recruits. Its people held little affection for soldiers who often used heavy-handed methods in quelling the frequent and usually violent demonstrations against the British government's decision to include Aden in the Federation of South Arabia. If the troops disliked Aden in general, they reserved their greatest hatred for Crater; for it was in this teeming town that most of the terrorist attacks by the National Liberation Front (NLF) and their rivals, the Front for the Liberation of Occupied South Yemen (FLOSY), took place.

Crater, surrounded by the jagged cliffs of an extinct volcano, known as the Jebel Shamson, on all but the seaward side, was probably the most godforsaken town patrolled by the British Army during the 1960s. It was excruciatingly hot by day and bitterly cold by night; the surrounding cliffs only served to accentuate these contrasts, and contain the numerous smells rising from the open sewers which ran down many of the town's narrow streets. Except at two points, the fortress-like walls of the volcano denied access to, or exit from, Crater. To the east of the town, Marine Drive ran between the rocks and the sea, before passing along the waterfront. On the harbour side to the west, another road climbed to a break in the cliffs known as Main Pass. After the pass, this route descended into Crater, to become Queen Arwa Road.

The town was ideal ground for waging a protracted terrorist campaign: a rabbit warren of tortuous streets and small huts, it provided a perfect base from which the NLF and FLOSY could launch their attacks and a safe haven from British security sweeps. Using bazookas, grenades, smallarms, mortars and mines, the terrorists directed their main efforts against the frequent, and all too vulnerable, patrols carried out by foot soldiers accompanied by armoured cars. Often, the terrorists orchestrated riots to draw the troops within range of snipers.

After the NLF began its urban terror campaign in late 1963, it became increasingly difficult for the security forces to maintain their grip on Aden, and the number of terrorist attacks grew to almost unmanageable proportions. In 1966, British troops were called on to deal with 480 incidents, while in 1967, the last year of British presence, there were nearly 3000 similar outrages.

Undoubtedly, 1967 was a black year for the British Army in Aden, and the Argylls began their tour of duty at the worst possible time. On 20 June, just five days before they were due to replace the 1st Batta-

FIGHTING FOR INDEPENDENCE

Aden, a natural deep-water harbour, and an important staging post on the route to India, had been under British control since 1839, and ruled from Britain as a crown colony since 1937.

In February 1959, six of the nominally independent 'states', emirates, sheikhdoms and sultanates of the Western and Eastern Aden Protectorates came together to form the Federation of South Arabia (FSA) under the auspices of the British government. By the end of 1963, another 10, and the British crown colony of Aden, had joined.

The states joining the federation between 1959 and 1963 had done so on the understanding that the British presence in the region would be maintained after full independence, scheduled for some time before 1968. However, by the early 1960s,

the balance of both moral and political authority in the area had shifted away from the British and the states' traditional rulers in favour of nationalist movements.

The original threat to the stability of the FSA came from Yemen, which had claims to some of its territory, but the menace became serious only after 1962, when the Yemenis started to back openly the insurgent movement. There were two main but mutually antagonistic nationalist groups: the National Liberation Front (NLF) and the Front for the Liberation of Occupied South Yemen. (FLOSY).

On 10 December 1963 the federal authorities were forced to declare a state of emergency and call on the British government for aid. Initially the NLF focused its attentions on the hinterland, but in late 1964 they switched the main effort of their terror campaign to Aden.

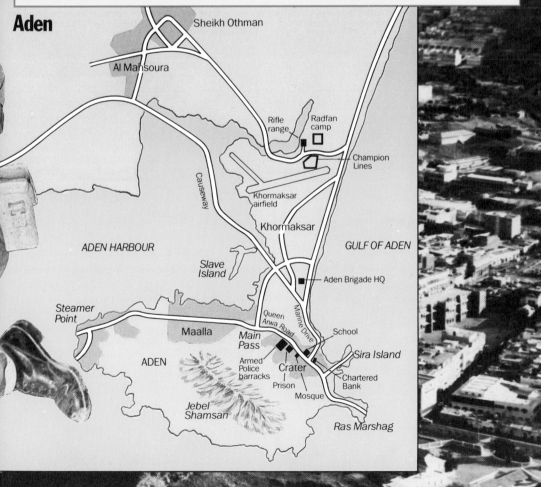

Aden

Sheikh Othman
Al Mansoura
Rifle range
Radfan camp
Champion Lines
Causeway
Khormaksar airfield
Khormaksar
ADEN HARBOUR
GULF OF ADEN
Slave Island
Aden Brigade HQ
Steamer Point
Queen Arwa Road
Marine Drive
School
Maalla
Main Pass
ADEN
Armed Police barracks
Crater
Sira Island
Chartered Bank
Prison
Mosque
Jebel Shamsan
Ras Marshag

lion, Royal Northumberland Fusiliers in Crater, the British forces suffered their heaviest losses of the entire campaign, losing 22 men killed and 31 wounded in a series of ambushes. Most of the casualties were inflicted during two mutinies by local security forces, whose morale, after persistent threats against them and their families, was understandably low.

The first mutiny occurred in Champion Lines, a training centre for members of the South Arabian Police (formerly the Federal National Guard). Hearing rumours to the effect that their comrades in the Federal Regular Army stationed at Lake Lines were being attacked by British troops, the police seized their weapons and then ambushed a passing truck, killing eight and wounding eight other men from 60 Squadron, Royal Corps of Transport. Later, the same rebels inflicted casualties on a relief force, and on British troops in the nearby Radfan barracks.

The example of the South Arabian Police was quickly followed by members of the Aden Armed Police, after they had heard rumours of the British turning on their Arab comrades in Champion Lines. As two land rovers carrying nine British soldiers passed their barracks on Queen Arwa Road, the mutineers opened up with rifles and machine guns, killing eight of the men. Three of the dead were Argylls, part of the battalion's advance party that had arrived in Aden on 7 June. However, worse was to follow: a four-man patrol sent out to investigate the incident failed to return (its members were never seen again), and three attempts to send in rescue parties were driven off by heavy fire. In one case, smallarms fire shot down a Sioux helicopter as it was lifting a group of men onto Temple Cliff on the western edge of the town, wounding all the occupants.

The failure of the rescue parties effectively ended the army's attempts to regain control of Crater and, as dusk fell, all troops were withdrawn from the im-

mediate area. Inside the town, the Armed Police issued 400 rifles to all comers, including criminals from the local gaols and members of the NLF and FLOSY. During the night a rejoicing mob subjected the bodies of several Britons to a grisly mock trial, following which the remains were mutilated and ritually hanged.

Under the circumstances, swift, decisive action might have ended the rebellion before it spread. However, the British commander, Major-General Philip Tower, decided to seal off Crater, thereby containing the mob in an easily held area. Tower felt that any large-scale operations might cause heavy British and civilian casualties, provoke armed retaliation against service families still in South Arabia, and lead to disintegration of the government.

On 21 June the British made two successful attempts to seal the only exits from Crater: simultaneously, both Marine Drive and Main Pass were attacked. At the pass, the Fusiliers and a party of Royal Marine Commandos were pinned down by heavy fire from the Turkish fort, but a round fired from an armoured car of the Queen's Dragoon Guards burst among the defenders and broke their will to resist. Emboldened by the ease with which his men had blocked off the two exits from Crater, Tower allowed his troops to tighten their grip on the town over the next 10 days. Snipers, working among the crags of the Jebel Shamsan, killed 10 rebels, all of whom were armed with British weapons captured on the 20th. By night, small patrols harassed the rebel positions, and the pipers taunted the enemy.

Main picture: Argylls armed with 7.62mm SLRs dive for cover from a terrorist grenade and (below right) the suspected perpetrator is dragged away. Below: Police Chief, Colonel Mohammed Ibrahim (right) looks suitably glum having been informed that either his men toe the line or the 'wild hillmen' would shoot them.

Despite these successes, the days after the rebellion were very frustrating for the troops. Limiting the trouble to Crater was no real compensation for seeing the terrorists strut around the town defiantly brandishing rifles and running up NLF flags in what was supposedly a British colony. The situation was particularly galling for the Northumberland Fusiliers, who were still responsible for Crater, and for Mitchell's highlanders, who were due to relieve the fusiliers on 25 June.

'Mad Mitch' was already in Aden when the mutinies took place, and could barely conceal his disgust at Tower's 'softly-softly' approach to the problem. Despite official objections, Mitchell was soon making it clear to all and sundry that he intended to avenge the humiliation of 20 June at the earliest opportunity and, without further delay, he drew up a bold aggressive plan for the retaking of Crater. Mitchell's strategy, codenamed Stirling Castle after his regiment's home headquarters, called for simultaneous attacks in which the north and west sides of the town were to be covered from hill-top positions, before the main thrusts along Marine Drive and from the Ras Marshag peninsula were launched. He also suggested that the Argylls mount the attack, and that it take place at night to catch the enemy off-guard.

The strains of the pipers changed to *Monymusk*, which had preceded every Argyll attack for generations

Mitchell submitted his ideas to the senior officers in Aden and, although Tower wanted the Crater retaken, he considered that the plan might cause heavy Arab casualties and lead to another mutiny by Federal forces. Tower argued that a piecemeal, 'nibbling' approach would reduce the risk of strong resistance and heavy casualties. Mitchell could barely disguise his horror at the suggestion; he argued that such a course of action would merely allow the enemy to prepare each position, forcing his men to fight a succession of bitter house-to-house and street-to-street battles.

As the discussion progressed, Mitchell put forward a series of arguments which supported his method; patrols by his own men and SAS teams had discovered that a night attack might meet little opposition. After several heated exchanges, Tower

71

'MAD MITCH'

The commander of the Argyll and Sutherland Highlanders during their 1967 tour of duty in Aden, Lieutenant-Colonel Colin Campbell Mitchell, was an officer of the old school with a touch of flair and a great deal of panache.

Mitchell had joined the Home Guard during World War II at the age of 14. He joined the Argylls late in the war in 1945 and served in the Po sector during the closing stages of the Italian campaign. Subsequently, he was wounded by Jewish terrorists in Palestine, fought in Korea, and served in Cyprus, Kenya and Borneo.

Mitchell lived and breathed the military life, and none of his officers and the men he led would hear a word said against him. On the other hand, he had a flair for self-publicity which many officers in other units or in senior positions found hard to take.

After Aden, Mitchell found his promotion prospects blocked and, unlike the other senior officers who served in Aden, he was not awarded the DSO. Despite the lack of official recognition, Mitchell was immensely popular with British servicemen who had been in Aden, and reports of his exploits caught the imagination of the British public who dubbed him 'Mad Mitch'.

relented, giving Mitchell permission to proceed. but with the proviso that the Argylls did not advance beyond the first Report Line without seeking further orders. The operation was to begin at 1900 on 3 July.

During the afternoon of the 3rd, one of Mitchell's companies was lifted by helicopter on to the Ras Marshag peninsula. Its men were to move into Crater from the southeast and link up with the main force. another company of the Argylls supported by armoured cars, which was to advance from a point on Marine Drive. Mitchell also planned to recapture Sira Island, by sending men along the causeway running through Aden harbour, and place a platoon on Aidrus Hill to identify rebel positions and give fire support. He hoped to reach the first Report Line by 2200, and then push on to occupy most of the town.

To the terrorists all seemed routine enough, and they would not have noticed the pipers' subtle change to *Monymusk* (the strains of which had preceded every Argyll attack for generations) at 1900. From their start positions, Mitchell's men moved off in darkness. In a tribute to their comrades killed on 20 June, one of their company officers

Line was soon reached and, having been given the go-ahead to continue, Mitchell urged his men deeper into the silent warren of streets and houses.

By 0300 hours on 4 July, the Argylls had secured all their objectives. Mitchell, up with the front runners, took control of the Chartered Bank and turned the building into his command post, which he christened Stirling Castle. At 0530 the citizens of Crater were roused by an unexpected, yet familiar sound, the massed pipes and drums of the Argylls playing reveille. The British were back, and the Queen's Dragoon Guards sent a triumphant signal to the Fusiliers: 'Your hackles fly again in Crater.'

Having recovered half of Crater without a single loss, the Argylls were straining at the leash to complete the job. Mitchell argued for and won, from Tower, the right to polish off the rebels. During the evening, his men advanced another 300 yards, meeting minimal opposition and taking the town's civil police barracks. Only the barracks of the Aden Armed Police remained outside British control but, after 'Mad Mitch' made the force's superintendent see the error of his ways, these too fell under the Argylls' care. Over the following hours, the police scoured Crater, collecting the rifles they had given to the rebels and re-arresting the criminals they had freed. Operation Stirling Castle was over, completed in two days without a single British casualty.

Mitchell and his men did not rest on their laurels; having recaptured Crater, they then set about pacifying it. In his own inimitable way, Mitchell eschewed the conventional wisdom, that his battalion should base itself outside the town, and opted to keep his men inside the district and control future operations from his headquarters at Stirling Castle in the heart of the town. Maintaining the aggressive spirit displayed in the initial operation, he rejected the usual practice of relying on the local police and adopting a 'low-profile' approach, in favour of maintaining a strong presence in the town.

'Argyll Law' produced the right results: never again did the terrorists flaunt their banners in Crater

Over the next few days, the Argylls established observation posts on rooftops and mounted continuous patrols, searches and round-ups of terrorist suspects. Mitchell also posted snipers outside the town's mosques, used as refuges by the terrorists, with orders to shoot anyone seen holding a weapon. After a score of terrorists had been disposed of in this way, Crater became one of the most peaceful areas in Aden. 'Argyll Law', as 'Mad Mitch' called his methods, produced the intended results: never again did the terrorists flaunt their banners in Crater. On 25 November 1967, four days before the British left Aden for good, the Argylls left the town as neatly as they had entered it.

The Argyll and Sutherland Highlanders had defeated an extremely dangerous insurrection with skill, flair and a large measure of raw courage. In doing so, they became a household name in Britain and wrote themselves into the annals of British military history.

Above left: A rude awakening for the inhabitants of Aden's most violent town. Heavily guarded, the massed pipes and drums of the Argylls herald the reoccupation of Crater. Above: A patrol moves down one of the district's main streets under the protection of a Ferret armoured car. Left: Two Northumberland Fusiliers. The return of their hackles to Crater on 4 July symbolised the British triumph.

carried with him a *cromaach,* a shepherd's crook, which had belonged to one of the victims. Every armoured car belonging to the Queen's Dragoon Guards had a red and white hackle of the Northumberland Fusiliers tied to its wireless aerial.

The attack went according to plan. Both main assault parties moved into Crater, keeping watch for enemy snipers and mines. Near the sultan's waterfront palace, there was a brief exchange of shots in which two terrorists died but, in the majority of cases, the opposition melted away into the night, fearful of meeting 'Mad Mitch's' wild hillmen. The first Report

THE AUTHOR Francis Toase is Senior Lecturer in the Department of War Studies and International Affairs at the Royal Military Academy, Sandhurst and has contributed to *British Military Operations 1945-1984, Armed Forces and Modern Counter-Insurgency* and the forthcoming *Modern Guerrilla Warfare*.

The formation that eventually became the 13th Guards Division started out as the 3rd Airborne Corps, and after sustaining heavy losses was reformed as the 87th Infantry Division. By May 1942, when it again lost heavily during the failed Soviet spring offensive, it had been awarded the coveted 'Guards' title. Losses in this offensive meant that the 13th Guards at Stalingrad was not composed of seasoned troops, for it was the practice of the Soviet high command to keep a unit in the front line until it was almost exhausted. In the battle of Stalingrad, there was, in any case, little choice. The 13th Guards was thrown into a desperate struggle to halt the juggernaut of the German advance.

In spite of relative lack of experience and the poor level of training in the Red Army, the 13th Guards performed heroically at Stalingrad. In part, no doubt, this was because they could expect little clemency from the enemy if they were captured (Nazi attitudes of racial superiority had soon alienated any Russians who might have welcomed the Germans as liberators from Stalin's totalitarian system), but the force of patriotism in the Red Army during this period cannot be denied. In addition, the high rate of losses meant that junior officers often got to command quite large units – commands which they might well keep should they prove successful at the front. It might be said that a combination of fear, patriotism and ambition made the 13th Guards such a vital element in the defence of Stalingrad. (The Guards badge is shown above.)

As the German Sixth Army closed on Stalingrad in 1942, the Red Army's 13th Guards Division was thrown in to block the German advance, and lived up to the highest standards of military achievement

ON THE evening of 15 September 1942, at the height of the most critical stage of the Battle of Stalingrad, General Vasili Ivanovich Chuikov, commander of the Soviet Sixty-second Army, left his headquarters, (known as the Tsaritsyn bunker), to get a first-hand impression of the course of the fighting. In Pushkinskaya Street, or rather what was left of it after several weeks of constant action, Chuikov encountered a red-headed young officer. 'Lieutenant, where are your men?' he asked. 'Ah, here, there's a job for you. The Germans need to be cleared out of the station. Is that clear?'

The young officer, Lieutenant Anton Kuzmich Dragan collected his men together and set off towards the central railway station to carry out Chuikov's order. As his unit, the 1st Company, 1st Battalion, 42nd Infantry Regiment of the 13th Guards Division, disappeared into the dust and smoke of the ruined city, it lost all contact with Chuikov's HQ, and it was only long after the end of the war that Chuikov discovered that the unit had not simply been annihilated in the vicious battle for control of the railway station during those crucial days of mid-September.

The station had already changed hands several times since the German Army entered Stalingrad on 23 August, and as Dragan's men stormed across the rubble, its German defenders withdrew, apparently under the impression that a much larger Soviet force was attacking. Realising their mistake, the Germans counter-attacked several times during the night, but Dragan's company threw them back on each occasion. With the first light of 16 September, the sky began to fill with deadly German Stuka dive-bombers, and the railway station was hit by hundreds of bombs, followed by a heavy artillery bombardment. The shell of the station was transformed into an inferno, but the German infantry were still unable to eject the Russians from their positions in the rubble.

The Germans used a building known to Dragan's men as the 'nail factory', because of the large stocks of nails which they found there, as a base for their repeated assaults on the railway station. Dragan decided to counter-attack and, under cover of mortar fire, his men rushed the nail factory. They managed to seize one of its workshops, but desperate room-to-room fighting with the German troops who controlled the rest of the building produced heavy casualties on both sides.

Not only Dragan's company, but the whole 1st Battalion was being badly mauled by the Germans. The rate of attrition amongst officers was enormous, and on 17 September Lieutenant Fedoseyev took command of the battalion when his predecessor, Lieutenant Chervyakov, suffering from severe wounds, was evacuated to the east bank of the Volga.

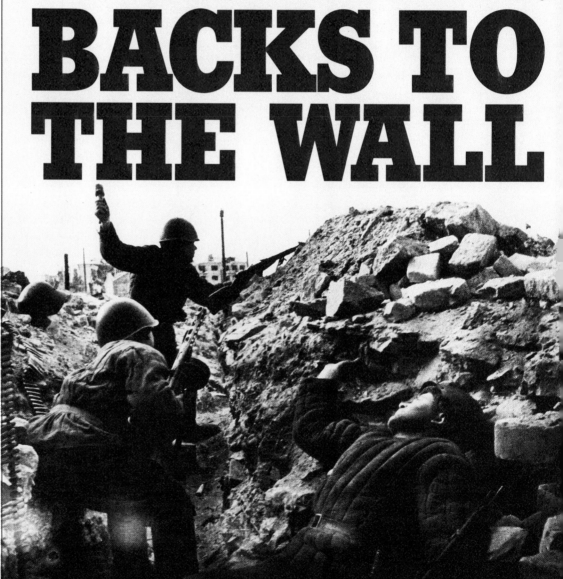

BACKS TO THE WALL

Inside the nail factory, small, intense, brutal battles were fought for the possession of a room or a stairway. Both sides used grenades, knives, rifle butts and the sharpened blades of spades in the battle. Soviet ammunition supplies were desperately low, but one of the Russians' worst problems was lack of water. In an effort to slake their thirsts, the Red Army men fired into drainpipes to see if they contained even the merest drops of water. But there was none to be had, and wounded men lay tormented by thirst as the battle swayed back and forth.

On 21 September a German thrust cut the Soviet battalion in two. Fedoseyev and his entire staff were wiped out in hand-to-hand fighting when the battalion HQ was overrun. Now under Dragan's command, the rest of the battalion began to withdraw yard by yard to the river, disputing each step of the way. However, the remnants of Dragan's company were totally isolated, and German aircraft and tanks pounded the stubbornly-defended ruins of a three-storey building on the corner of Krasnopiteskaya and Komsomolskaya streets to which they had with-

Below left: Soviet troops occupy a trench recently held by Germans (note the German helmet on the left). Right: Red Army forces on the offensive in the ruins of Stalingrad. Right above: Key figures in the defence of the city. From left are Chief of Staff to the 62nd Army, N.I. Krylov; the commander of the 62nd Army, General Chuikov; staff officer K.A. Gurov; and Major-General Rodimtsev, commander of the 13th Guards Division.

STREET FIGHTING

General Vasili Chuikov, the commander of the Soviet 62nd Army at Stalingrad, was an expert on fighting in built-up areas. He had learnt his lessons during the months following the German invasion of Russia. He had very clear ideas on the best method of attacking enemy strongpoints:

'Get close to the enemy's positions: move on all fours, making use of craters and ruins; dig your trenches by night, camouflage them by day; make your build-up for the attack stealthily, without any noise; carry your tommy-gun on your shoulder; take 10 or 12 grenades.

'Two of you get into the house together – you and a grenade; both be lightly dressed – you without a knapsack and the grenade bare; go in grenade first, you after; go through the whole house, again always with grenade first and you after.

'There is one strict rule – give yourself elbow room. At every step danger lurks. No matter – a grenade in every corner of the room and then forward. A burst from your tommy-gun around what's left; a bit further – a grenade, then on again. Another room, a grenade. Rake it with your tommy-gun. And get a move on!

'Inside the object of attack, the enemy may go over to a counter-attack. Don't be afraid. You have already taken the initiative, it is in your hands. Act more ruthlessly with your grenade, your tommy-gun, your dagger and your spade. Fighting inside a building is always frantic. So always be prepared for the unexpected. Look sharp.'

PPSh41 SMG

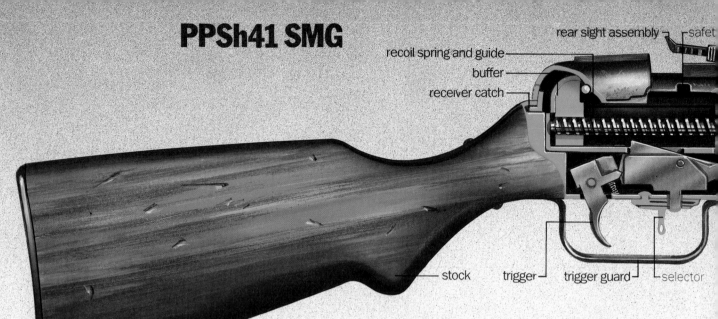

rear sight assembly — safet[y]
recoil spring and guide
buffer
receiver catch

stock — trigger — trigger guard — selector

Above: The Red Army's most important smallarm, the robust and reliable PPSh41 sub-machine gun. Designed by Georgi Shpagin (hence the 'Sh' of the designation) the PPSh41, shown here with its distinctive 71-round drum magazine, was produced in enormous quantities, and whole units were equipped with it, to give them massive firepower at close quarters. Perhaps over five million were manufactured in the Soviet Union during the war, while the communist Chinese produced millions more of their own version, the Type 50, after 1949.

drawn. Dragan held on for four more days but, by the morning of 25 September, only he and 10 other men were left alive. The previous night a lieutenant and a private had fled and, on reaching the other side of the Volga, had reported Dragan and all his men killed. But the survivors fought on.

Dragan fired the last 250-round belt of ammunition for the heavy machine-gun when a platoon of German soldiers was led directly in front of his position by a captured Russian soldier. The prisoner paid for his brave deception an hour later when the Germans shot him in the head in full view of Dragan and his men.

Suddenly, the Russians heard the rumble of approaching German tanks and, certain that they were all about to die, Private Kozhushko, Dragan's orderly, scratched onto the wall with his knife: 'Rodimtsev's guardsmen fought and died for their country here'. With the first German shells, the crumbling building shuddered and collapsed, burying its tiny Soviet garrison beneath the ruins. Dragan lost consciousness, and when he came to he was being dragged from under a pile of rubble by Private Kozhushko. There were six survivors in the shattered basement, and they had to dig their way to the surface with their bare hands.

When they emerged, night had already fallen and they were protected by the darkness. Kozhushko, being the least badly wounded, went off to reconnoitre the area, and when he returned an hour later reported that there were German patrols all around, and that the west bank of the Volga was being mined. The Russians decided to fight their way through if necessary, but as they edged forward under a moonlit sky, they stumbled across a German patrol and were forced to return to their basement refuge. As clouds covered the moon, they moved off again.

Kozhushko crawled forward and knifed a German guard

Once more their way was barred. Kozhushko crawled forward and knifed a German guard, relieved him of his greatcoat, put it on and then approached a second guard. Suspecting nothing, he too was silently disposed of. Dragan and his men moved on across a railway track, through a minefield and down to the Volga. Having gulped down the icy water to satisfy their thirsts, they managed to build a makeshift raft and then floated downstream to an island, where they were picked up by Soviet artil-

barrel

barrel housing

fore sight assembly

barrel assembly hinge

spent round (partially extracted)

gazine
ease catch

magazine

Calibre 7.62mm
Length 84.2cm
Weight (with loaded drum) 5.3kg
Magazine 71-round drum or 35-round box
Rate of fire (practical auto) 90 - 100rpm
Muzzle velocity 500mps
Maximum effective range 200m

Below: Red Army troops
move cautiously forward
through the shattered interior
of one of Stalingrad's
factories. The Russians used
these buildings as
'breakwaters' against the
Germans, and in the fighting
for the 'nail factory' in mid-
September 1942, men of the
13th Guards Division fought to
the last round to stem the tide
of German advance.

lerymen and brought finally to safety.

This episode was only one of many examples of the appalling losses which units of the 13th Guards Division suffered during September 1942 in the central sector of Stalingrad. The 13th Guards (originally the 3rd Airborne Corps) had been attached to the Stalingrad Front from the Soviet Army's central reserve on 9 September, two-and-a-half weeks after the battle had begun.

The 8th German Air Corps had unleashed a devastating air bombardment on the city on 23 August. On the same day, rifles and ammunition had been issued to Stalingrad's factory workers, who had been ordered to prepare to defend their factories. That evening, the 79th Panzer Grenadier Regiment reached the Stalingrad suburb of Spartanovka, and on 24 August the tractor plant in the northern suburbs of the city came under heavy fire.

Stalin refused suggestions of a mass evacuation of civilians from the threatened city, and thus committed the defenders to a fight to the death which was to have a decisive influence upon the whole course of the war. Throughout late August and early September, the situation inside Stalingrad became increasingly critical, and on 12 September both Hitler and Stalin held conferences with their respective commanders. General Friedrich Paulus, the commander of the German Sixth Army, was ordered to launch an all-out offensive to capture the city on 15

September, while, on the Russian side, General Zhukov and Colonel-General Vasilevsky were ordered to work out the basis for the plan which was later to produce the Soviet counter-offensive of November 1942, and the annihilation of the Sixth Army. As an immediate measure, Stalin ordered the 10,000-strong 13th Guards Division, commanded by Major-General Alexander Ilyich Rodimtsev, a veteran of the Spanish Civil War and a Hero of the Soviet Union, to cross the Volga into Stalingrad and hold off the German offensive at all costs.

Rodimtsev's division came under fire when a shell set a barge ablaze near their embarkation point

Forming up in a pine forest on the east bank of the Volga during the night of 14/15 September, Rodimtsev's division came under German fire when a shell set a half-sunken barge ablaze near their embarkation area, illuminating the whole scene for the German gunners, who quickly zeroed in. Rodimtsev ordered an immediate crossing, and the first unit over the Volga was Lieutenant E.P. Chervyakov's battalion.

The guards crossed the Volga through a hail of German fire and, as they neared the west bank, they rolled out of the boats into the water and waded ashore. Once landed, they advanced straight into the battle which was being fought for the narrow strip of the city still held by the Red Army. The Guards relieved the remnants of an NKVD (security troops) unit under Colonel Petrakov, which had been on the verge of launching a counter-attack on a German strongpoint situated in the State Bank building. In desperate hand-to-hand fighting, the 13th Guards established a small bridgehead, but were unable to set up defensive positions, and were forced to fight a fluid battle for control of some of the key buildings which dominated the sector.

With dawn on 15 September, the German dive-bombers were able to prevent the crossing of any further guards units, but nevertheless, the units already in position (the 34th and 39th Regiments and the 1st Battalion, 42nd Regiment) prepared to clear the German 71st Infantry Division from the central railway station, and the 295th Infantry Division from the commanding heights of Mamayev Kurgan – a hill to the north of the city centre. By the morning of 15 September, the lower slopes of Mamayev Kurgan were held by the 13th Guards, but the crest was still in German hands.

At dawn on the following morning, after a 10-minute Soviet artillery barrage, the 42nd Regiment stormed up the slopes of Mamayev Kurgan. Thirty men under Lieutenant Vdovichenko were assigned to clear German machine guns from the crest of the hill. Their mission was accomplished, but only six guardsmen survived, and they faced a vigorous German counter-attack, carried out by infantry with tank and Stuka support. Fighting continued throughout the winter for possession of Mamayev Kurgan,

but from 16 September until the German surrender in February 1943, it remained in Soviet hands, preventing the Germans from dominating the river crossing.

The Soviet tactics were to occupy and defend factories, houses and office buildings as fortresses, which functioned as 'breakwaters', resisting and dividing German assaults. German tanks were channeled towards traps set with men armed with anti-tank rifles and grenades, or else to points covered by Soviet artillery. In these killing grounds, many German tanks were destroyed. After the German tanks had been allowed through to be isolated and knocked out, their supporting infantry would then fall prey to Soviet troops operating from the strongpoints. Snipers were widely employed by both sides. The most famous Soviet sniper was Vasili Zaitsev, credited with killing 242 Germans during the Battle of Stalingrad.

Snipers and German control of the air over Stalingrad reduced movement during daylight to an absolute minimum, and most confrontations took place at night. The sky was lit by the flames of fires burning amongst the shattered ruins, and the sound of battle was always present. Many men must have gone mad.

The 13th Guards had to bear the full weight of the German push towards the Volga from 15 to 26 September, when Paulus shifted the main emphasis of his offensive to the factory suburbs in the north of Stalingrad. As Chuikov later admitted: 'Let me say frankly that had it not been for Rodimtsev's division the city would have fallen completely into enemy

Below: The Red Flag waves triumphantly at the moment of victory in Stalingrad, in February 1943. The battle for Stalingrad was the turning point of the war on the Eastern Front: after it, the Germans were able to do little more than slow temporarily the increasing tempo of Soviet offensives that took the Red Army on its remorseless drive from the banks of the Volga to the Brandenburg Gate in Berlin. And yet when the 13th Guards Division under Rodimtsev had been moved into the city in a desperate attempt to throw back the German offensive in September 1942, it had seemed that nothing could stop the Blitzkrieg. Sheer persistence, however, and the courage of individual soldiers finally ground Hitler's war machine to a halt.

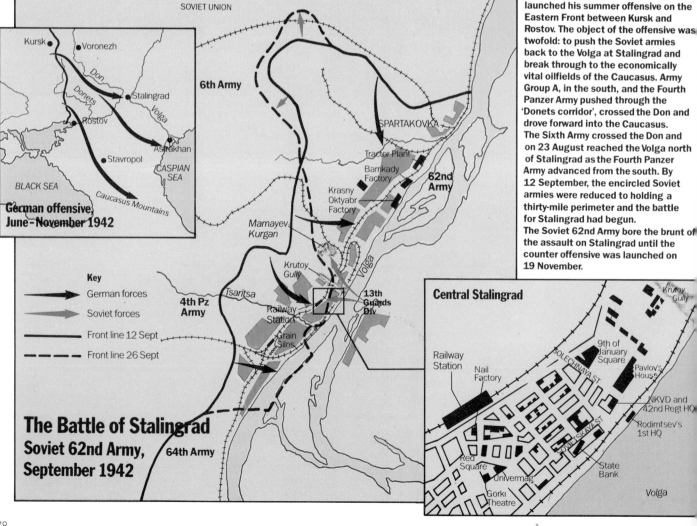

The Battle of Stalingrad
Soviet 62nd Army, September 1942

64th Army

Key
German forces
Soviet forces
Front line 12 Sept
Front line 26 Sept

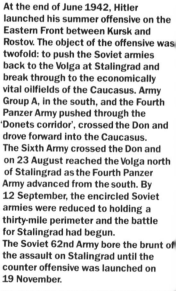

At the end of June 1942, Hitler launched his summer offensive on the Eastern Front between Kursk and Rostov. The object of the offensive was twofold: to push the Soviet armies back to the Volga at Stalingrad and break through to the economically vital oilfields of the Caucasus. Army Group A, in the south, and the Fourth Panzer Army pushed through the 'Donets corridor', crossed the Don and drove forward into the Caucasus. The Sixth Army crossed the Don and on 23 August reached the Volga north of Stalingrad as the Fourth Panzer Army advanced from the south. By 12 September, the encircled Soviet armies were reduced to holding a thirty-mile perimeter and the battle for Stalingrad had begun. The Soviet 62nd Army bore the brunt of the assault on Stalingrad until the counter offensive was launched on 19 November.

hands approximately in the middle of September.'

Even after 26 September, Rodimtsev's division remained under heavy pressure, and on 1 October was hit by a renewed German effort to break through to the Volga and divide the Sixty-second Army in two, this time by cutting through the Soviet lines along the Dolgi and Krutoy gullies. At the same time, some 300 German troops of the 295th Infantry Division infiltrated into the rear of the 34th Guards Regiment through a storm drain. This German force was totally destroyed on the morning of 2 October.

Although the main arena of the battle moved north during late September, the sector occupied by the 13th Guards remained critical to the whole Soviet position, and was still bitterly contested. Seeking to strengthen the division's defences, on 28 September, Colonel Yelin, commander of the 42nd Regiment, sent a squad of men under Second Lieutenant Zabolotnov to capture and fortify two buildings which dominated Lenin Square, near the gutted grain elevator. Zabolotnov occupied the first building, which rapidly became known as 'Zabolotnov's house', and, although Zabolotnov himself was soon killed, the building remained in Soviet hands.

Pavlov's unit held out for 58 days, against everything that the German Army threw at them

The second building, a badly damaged block of flats facing Solechnaya Street, was captured by three men under Sergeant Jacob Pavlov. This small group approached the building by crawling carefully across the rubble-strewn courtyard. Having blasted the ground-floor rooms with grenades, they burst in with sub-machine guns blazing, but the handful of Germans still alive in the building retreated hastily.

German tanks attacked 'Pavlov's house' repeatedly, but were unable to get in close, as the building commanded the whole area, which Pavlov had mined. Pavlov's unit, strengthened to some 60 men,

held out for 58 days against everything that the German Army threw at them, and were eventually linked to the main Red Army lines by a number of tunnels, through which supplies and reinforcements could be moved forward. Pavlov was later awarded the title of Hero of the Soviet Union.

On 19 November 1942, the carefully prepared Soviet counter-offensive smashed into the weak flanks of the German Sixth Army which were manned by Romanian and Italian units. Inside Stalingrad, the grim conflict continued throughout the bitter Russian winter, but on 26 January 1943 tanks of the Soviet Sixty-fifth Army broke through the positions of Paulus' starved and ragged army to link up with the men of Chuikov's Sixty-second Army. On 2 February, all German resistance in the city came to an end, and the defeated German, Romanian and Italian troops were marched off into a captivity which few survived, and which for some German prisoners-of-war was to last until 1955.

The Sixty-second Army was renamed the Eighth Guards Army for its heroic defence of Stalingrad, in which the 13th Guards Division had played an outstanding role. Rodimtsev was named Hero of the Soviet Union for the second time, and Marshal Zhukov later paid fitting tribute to the men of Rodimtsev's division. He was to write, 'September 13, 14 and 15 were difficult days, very difficult days, for Stalingrad. The turning point in those days, and in what seemed to be the last few hours, was the introduction of Rodimtsev's 13th Guards Division into the battle.'

THE AUTHOR J.S. Common is a military historian who has written extensively on issues of national security and international relations for several publications, and is an acknowledged expert on modern armoured fighting vehicles.

GENERAL VASILI CHUIKOV

Born the son of a peasant family in 1900, Vasili Chuikov, the commander of the Red Army at Stalingrad, joined the Communist Party in 1919, and became a leader of a regiment during the Russian Civil War. Six years later, at the age of 25, he graduated from the Frunze Military Academy. After his stint at the academy, Chuikov gained the promotions which enabled him to lead an army in the Russo-Finnish War (1939-1940).

In 1941 he served as an aide to the Chinese leader Chiang Kai-shek, but returned to Russia in May 1942 when he was appointed deputy commander of the Sixty-second Army. In September Chuikov was promoted and asked to take over the defence of the vital sectors of Stalingrad by General Yeremenko and Nikita Khrushchev, Stalin's political deputy in the area. The previous commander of the Sixty-second Army had told Khrushchev that the city could not be defended, Chuikov accepted the mission and swore not to leave the city.

Although the German Army reached the Volga and isolated Stalingrad in the first few days of the offensive, Chuikov retained control of the critical sectors. From September until November 1942, his Sixty-second Army bore the weight of the German attacks and fought a skilful defence of the city, using tactics which Chuikov had developed himself.

After Stalingrad, Chuikov led his men to further victories and in April 1945, commanding the Eighth Guards Army, he took part in the capture of Berlin.

The 8th East Surreys were one of the few British units to capture German ground on the terrible first day of the Somme offensive, 1 July 1916

AS THE LAST seconds ticked away to zero hour, Captain W.P. Nevill clambered over the parapet of the trench. He was followed by the men of B Company, 8th Battalion, The East Surrey Regiment (8th East Surreys). Directly ahead of them, some 400yds away across No Man's Land, they could see shell after shell smash into the German positions, throwing up huge clouds of smoke and dust. The week-long British bombardment appeared to have been highly effective on this sector of the Somme front opposite Carnoy – even the forbidding tangles of barbed wire had been destroyed by 50lb mortar bombs.

Nevill waited until his men had formed themselves into a loose line, and then kicked a football high into the air towards the enemy-held trenches. This was the signal to advance. Each of the four platoons of B Company had been given a football by Nevill, who had hit upon the idea of giving his men a familiar object on which to concentrate during the frightening advance across No Man's Land. Psychologically, this was a brilliant stroke. The men had immediately taken to the idea, painting on one of the balls the words 'The Great European Cup – The Final – East Surreys v. Bavarians', and on another, 'No Referee'. A mere 18 months before, most of the battalion had been civilians, and dribbling the footballs served to distract them from the terror of their baptism of fire.

B Company was holding a re-entrant in the British line, and had to advance several hundred yards before it drew level with C Company's position. There, the men of C Company, led by Captain Pearce, rose from their trenches, shook themselves out into attack formation and joined in the advance. For an all-too-brief moment, the long line pushed forward unscathed, Nevill strolling ahead of B Company, occasionally giving an order to keep the dressing square on the line of advance. Then, at 0730 hours sharp, the screaming of the shells abruptly ceased. There was a brief, eerie silence as the British gunners raised their sights and then the barrage crashed down onto the next objective. Almost immediately, heavy German rifle and machine-gun fire began to rake the British line, coming from their front and their left flank. The East Surreys suffered horrendous casualties in those moments. Captain Pearce was killed outright. Private Willimot, the soldier servant of Second-Lieutenant J.R. Ackerley of B Company, fell to the ground paralysed, a bullet passing through his spine. And then Ackerley himself was hit. His platoon-sergeant, Sergeant Griffin, dragged him into a shell hole and attempted to dress his wound. Fortunately, it was not serious and Ackerley was later sent back to hospital in England.

Many others were not so lucky. Along the 18 miles of the Somme front, from Gommecourt in the north to the junction with the French Army at Maricourt in the south, 143 British battalions attacked on 1 July 1916,

OVER THE TOP

ustaining 57,470 casualties and generally making very few territorial gains. Despite their unpromising start, however, the 8th East Surreys captured all their objectives. They finished the day not, like so many other brave battalions, back in their own trenches and defeated, but looking out into open country, victorious. Tragically, Nevill did not survive the battle. He was hit just outside the German wire and killed instantly.

The road that had led Nevill and his men to the Somme began on 10 September 1914 at Purfleet in Surrey, where three trains had pulled into the government sidings and disgorged 1000 men. As the adjutant, a regular officer named Lieutenant Irwin, led his new charges away, a casual observer would not have been impressed. True, they were keen, but battalion spirit was missing; not surprisingly, for 500 of the recruits were men from Norfolk and Suffolk who had wanted to join their county regiments and were none too pleased to find themselves drafted into the East Surreys. All that was to change over the months to come. Officers of excellent quality began to arrive, and a warm relationship began to develop between officers and men. Some of the new officers were regulars, like Nevill who arrived from the East Yorkshires, and Lieutenant-Colonel Powell from the Royal North Lancashires, but most had been civilians before the war. Many, like the 18-year-old Second-Lieutenant Ackerley (in later life an author) were

little more than boys. Most importantly, the battalion was placed in the 55th Brigade of 18th (Eastern) Division. The divisional commander, Major-General Sir Ivor Maxse, was probably the finest trainer of men in the British Army. On the eve of the Somme offensive, the 8th East Surreys were supremely confident. They were a well trained, cohesive unit which already had served for 11 months in France. No longer mere civilians in uniform, they had become soldiers.

On 1 July they were faced with a formidable task. The Surreys' lines lay at the bottom of a shallow valley, overlooked by trenches held by the 6th Bavarian Reserve Regiment. They had to advance 1450yds and capture four trench systems on a 300yd frontage, and then take the western end of the fortified village of Montauban. On their left was a mass of mine craters. Here, the Germans had abandoned their front-line trench, after filling it with barbed wire and sharpened stakes, and were holding their support line (known to the British as the 'Breslau Support Trench') as the front line. An advance party left in the craters by the Bavarians was to play a crucial role in the fighting of 1 July.

THE EAST SURREY REGIMENT.
Football on the Battlefield at Contalmaison.

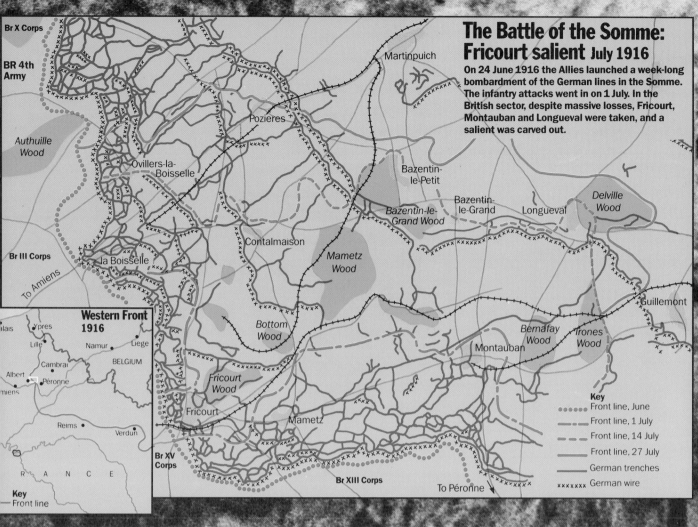

The Battle of the Somme: Fricourt salient July 1916

On 24 June 1916 the Allies launched a week-long bombardment of the German lines in the Somme. The infantry attacks went in on 1 July. In the British sector, despite massive losses, Fricourt, Montauban and Longueval were taken, and a salient was carved out.

Key
- ●●●● Front line, June
- – – Front line, 1 July
- – – – Front line, 14 July
- —— Front line, 27 July
- —— German trenches
- xxxxxx German wire

Western Front 1916

Key
— Front line

The fierce fire that was unleashed at 0730 hours came as a severe shock to the East Surreys. It was all too clear that the preliminary bombardment had not killed all the enemy in their dugouts as had been promised, but the East Surreys' discipline held. A typical example of their spirit was shown by Company Sergeant-Major Hanks of C Company, who was hit as he left the front-line trench. He refused to allow his men to attend to his wounds, instead urging them to continue the advance. He survived the battle, and was awarded the Military Cross. Despite such courage, however, the plan of attack broke down entirely. In place of the long, closely formed 'waves', each 50yds apart, the battalion was reduced to small parties of men who raced for the comparative safety of the Bavarian trenches. They used grenades and bayonets to force their way forward with the greatest gallantry, but with no order or cohesion. Barely 250 men reached Breslau Support Trench unwounded. Many of the casualties were caused by a machine gun situated in the craters, which was able to enfilade both the East Surreys and their left-hand neighbours, the 7th Queens. It was apparent that the force allocated to the task of clearing the craters (two platoons of the 7th Buffs) was simply too weak, and these two units were paying the price of this miscalculation.

The East Surreys' casualties would have been heavier had they not, following a practice that was standard in the 18th Division, moved out into No Man's Land before the barrage lifted. This enabled them to get in among the enemy before the Germans could bring the full weight of their fire to bear. Most of the other battalions attacking on 1 July left their trenches at zero hour, 0730, only to be cut down in No Man's Land. The 18th Division also benefited greatly from the efficiency of their artillery, which successfully cut the German wire. Many other units on that day found the wire uncut.

The battle for Breslau Support was largely one of grenade throwing, or 'bombing' as it was called. By 0750 the 8th Battalion was firmly established in the front enemy trenches and, aided by the arrival of the Bombing Section and two Stokes mortars at about 0815, it had taken all its initial objectives by 0830. These included not only Breslau Support but the trench behind that, Back Trench.

A fresh ordeal was about to begin, however. For the next 30 minutes they were pinned down by heavy enemy fire and were unable to advance. They were being raked with fire from 'The Warren', a heavily defended strongpoint on the extreme right of their front. They were also still under fire from the craters on their left flank, where the Bavarian defenders were still holding off the increasingly desperate attempts of the 7th Buffs to clear their positions. Here, savage fighting was taking place; after the battle several pairs of adversaries were discovered transfixed on each other's bayonets. The craters were finally cleared at about 0930.

For Irwin, by now promoted to major and commanding the battalion in the absence of Lieutenant-Colonel Powell at Corps HQ, mid-morning was an anxious time. From the odd scraps of information being brought by runner (the only effective form of communication) it became clear that the battalion

Above: Major-General Sir Ivor Maxse, commander of the British 18th (Eastern) Division on the Somme. Due largely to his guidance, his troops did not suffer as much as other battalions in the initial assault on the Somme, and they achieved lasting gains. Left: One man who survived the carnage – a wounded Tommy is manoeuvred to safety by stretcher bearers on the second day of the Somme offensive.

Below: The exploits of the East Surreys captured the national headlines back in Britain and a military legend was born. Bottom: With bayonets fixed, soldiers traverse the wire on the killing grounds of the Somme. Bottom right: Two years later, members of the 8th East Surreys rest with RAMC stretcher bearers near Albert during the successful offensive of August 1918.

was virtually leaderless and so depleted that he was forced to appeal to the 7th Buffs for reinforcements. Worse, at 0900 a wounded officer arrived with the grim news that the Germans were threatening the right flank with a counter-attack down Valley Trench. The crisis of the battle was at hand.

The high morale of the East Surreys enabled them to weather the crisis. At about 0900 the hostile fire from The Warren began to slacken as the defenders, alarmed by the rapid advance of the 30th Division towards the centre of Montauban, began to retire before their line of retreat was severed. Immediately, ignoring the enfilading fire from the craters, the East Surreys began to push forward parties of bom-

bers, and by 0915 they had fought their way into Train Alley, which was part of the Pommiers Line. Ten minutes earlier, a platoon of the 7th Buffs – all that could be spared from the 55th Brigade's dwindling reserve – had been despatched to block the counter-attack down Valley Trench.

Irwin learned from a runner of the renewed advance of his men at 0921. Although they were on the German fourth line, having advanced 550yds, it was obvious that the attack was losing its impetus as the leaderless men of the 8th consolidated their gains. Handing over command of Battalion HQ to the adjutant, Captain Clare, Irwin set out at 0944 for the enemy trenches. On his way he met the medical officer, Captain Gimson, who had a grim tale to tell of the battalion's casualties (for his courageous and selfless work in tending the wounded on 1 July, Gimson was recommended for the VC, eventually being awarded the DSO). Successfully completing the hazardous journey across No Man's Land, Irwin eventually reached the remnants of the battalion in Train Alley. On the way he had collected scattered groups of men. Second-Lieutenant Janion, the only unwounded officer of C Company (now reduced to about 20 effectives) was discovered leading a party of three men; Sergeant Griffin was found in command of another 10. Irwin's dynamic leadership transformed his bone-weary soldiers. He energetically reorganised Pommiers Line – for the threat of a German counter-attack could never be discounted – and scraped together 70 men to renew the advance. At 1100 he sent these men, drawn from both the East Surreys and the 7th Buffs, along Breslau Alley (a lateral communication trench well to the rear of the German positions). Organised into two waves under the command of Sergeant Willis, the attack was a far cry from the carefully ordered advances envisaged before the battle, but it met with no opposition and Willis succeeded in occupying the whole trench.

From Train Alley, Irwin had a panoramic view of the battlefield. When he saw the Surreys line the parapet of Breslau Alley, just a few yards short of the main perimeter trench defending Montauban, he

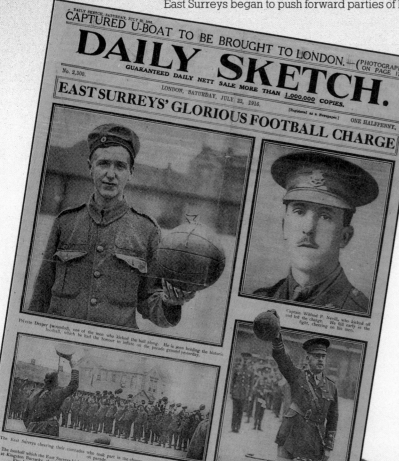

DAILY SKETCH, SATURDAY, JULY 22, 1916.

CAPTURED U-BOAT TO BE BROUGHT TO LONDON. (PHOTOGRAPHS ON PAGE 12)

DAILY SKETCH.

No. 2,300. GUARANTEED DAILY NETT SALE MORE THAN 1,000,000 COPIES.

LONDON, SATURDAY, JULY 22, 1916. [Registered as a Newspaper.] ONE HALFPENNY.

EAST SURREYS' GLORIOUS FOOTBALL CHARGE

Private Draper (wounded), one of the men who kicked the ball along. He is seen holding the historic football, which he had the honour to inflate on the parade ground yesterday.

Captain Wilfred P. Nevill, who kicked off and led the charge. He fell early in the fight, cheering on his men.

The East Surreys cheering their comrades who took part in the charge, on parade.

The football which the East Surreys kicked off from the parapet and dribbled to the German lines at Kingston Barracks, the Headquarters of the Regiment, yesterday. Five hundred of their comrades were killed and wounded in the charge.

Colonel Treeby holding up the ball, which was sent over from the front, to be kept as a regimental trophy of the glorious day. Colonel Treeby, addressing officers and men, said the East Surreys had nobly played the great game on July 1 was blown up on the Square. The East Surreys had nobly played the great game, but they had not died in vain—they had helped to bring us nearer to the goal of victory.

lised that German resistance had virtually col-
...sed in this sector and the time for the final push
...arrived: the drive to occupy Montauban Ridge
...lf. At 1145 he sent orders to Captain Bowen of D
...mpany, who was still encountering stiff resistance
...the extreme left flank, to disengage and push
...ward into the gap. Irwin then proudly watched the
...ance to the battalion's final objective. Now led by
...otain Clare, the remnants of the battalion pushed
...wn Mine Alley. Then, for the second time that day,
...British gunners ceased to send their shells
...eaming onto the enemy trenches. Previously, the
...uing silence had heralded the assault; this time, it
...s saluting its triumph. As the barrage lifted, the
...t Surreys surged forward and reached their goal:
...ntauban Ridge. The time was 1220. It had taken
...m nearly five hours to advance 1450yds.

Lance-Corporal Bilson staggered ack the following day, cross-eyed and with his uniform in tatters

...e price they paid for their success was dreadfully
...h. Seven officers and 140 men had been killed; 272
...n and seven officers had been wounded, one
...cer mortally. Most of the casualties had been
...tained in the first 20 minutes. At first the 'butcher's
...' was thought to be even higher, but some of the
...sing drifted back – men such as Lance-Corporal
...son, who staggered back the following day, cross-
...d and with his uniform in tatters, having been
...wn up by a shell and left unconscious for 24 hours.
...wever, as the 8th East Surreys rested on Mon-
...ban Ridge on the afternoon of 1 July, the officers
...sing around a bottle of champagne previously set
...de to be drunk in Montauban 'on der tag' (on the
...), they were jubilant. Their division, and the
...ghbouring 30th Division, had punched a hole
...an through the German lines on a day when there
...been almost unrelieved failure everywhere else
...ng the front.
...he failure of General Sir Henry Rawlinson, the
...mmander of the Fourth Army, to exploit this
...cess is one of the most controversial aspects of the

opening day of the Battle of the Somme. He passed up
the opportunity to send his reserves – perhaps even
including cavalry – through the gap to occupy the
woods beyond. The penalty for this failure was paid
by the British Army in the form of ghastly battles of
attrition that lasted for the next five months, when the
woods – Delville, Trones, and Mametz – had to be
wrested yard by yard from the Germans.

Rawlinson's inaction cannot detract from the
magnificent achievements of the 8th East Surreys. To
put them into context, it should be mentioned that 13
villages were supposed to fall to the Fourth Army on 1
July; in fact, only three were captured, one of them, of
course, being Montauban. The 8th East Surreys, a
mere Kitchener battalion of an unfashionable regiment, had triumphed when so many of the smarter
Regular units had failed. Their dogged determination in carrying out the assault on Montauban Ridge,
regardless of loss and in the face of the most formidable difficulties, was fully recognised by the award of
15 decorations. They included DSOs for Major Irwin
and Second-Lieutenant Janion, an MC for Company
Sergeant-Major Hanks, and an MM for Sergeant
Griffin.

Paradoxically, in the long run their success was to
cost many lives. Overnight, the 18th Division
achieved a reputation as an elite formation, and for
the rest of the war it was used as a 'stormer' division,
frequently thrown into the attack against the tough-
est German positions: only a fortnight later, they led
the assault on Trones Wood, and in 1917 they were to
fight at Passchendaele.

Today, Montauban Ridge is a quiet backwater of
eastern France, with little to remind the visitor of the
desperate fighting of July 1916. However, in the
nearby village of Carnoy is a British military cemet-
ary. There, among the beautifully tended graves is
that of Captain Nevill. He was the originator of one of
the most famous incidents of World War I, for the
footballs of B Company rapidly passed into legend as
newspapers in England took up the story. Maxse
spoke only the truth when he said that on 1 July the 8th
Battalion, the East Surrey Regiment, 'had made for
itself an immortal name', for the battalion's reputation
has long survived the unit's disbandment in 1919.

THE AUTHOR W.B. Brabiner is a freelance writer who
specialises in 20th century warfare. His numerous
articles have described many aspects of military
affairs from World War I to the present day.

THE SOMME

By October 1914, the fluid
battles of August and
September had given way to
entrenched warfare on an
unchanging front which
stretched from the North
Sea to the Vosges
mountains. The original
British Expeditionary Force
(BEF) suffered severe
casualties in the battles, and
Field Marshal Lord
Kitchener raised large 'New
Armies' of idealistic,
patriotic Commonwealth
volunteers to defend the
Western Front and prepare
for a mass offensive which,
it was hoped, would bring
the war to an end.

It was the intention of
General Sir Douglas Haig,
commander-in-chief of the
BEF, to mount the offensive
in Flanders. He was
persuaded, however, by
General Joseph Joffre, the
French chief of staff, to fight
in Picardy, in the rolling
uplands overlooking the
Somme river. The Somme
sector marked the junction
of the British and French
armies on the Western
Front, and Joffre was
anxious to commit Haig to
greater involvement in the
war with a joint offensive.
On 21 February 1916 the
Germans began a
concentrated attack on the
Verdun sector of the
Western Front, knowing that
France would sacrifice
unlimited manpower to
defend it. The battles for
Verdun were protracted
and costly, and Joffre
insisted that Haig should
begin the offensive to
relieve pressure on Verdun.

In the early years of the American combat involvement in Vietnam, infantry commanders were frustrated by a lack of solid tactical intelligence. To solve this problem, they set up their own 'home-grown' reconnaissance forces

'NECESSITY IS THE mother of invention' is a well-worn cliché, but in the annals of warfare it will always have a place. Battles, campaigns and even wars can be planned to the finest detail, but on the ground things rarely turn out as expected, and nowhere more so than on the ground in Vietnam.

On 5 May 1965 the 'Sky Soldiers' of the US 173rd Airborne Brigade flew in to Bien Hoa air base in South Vietnam – the first US Army ground combat unit to be committed to the war. They were soon followed by the 1st Brigade of the 101st Airborne, and through 1965 and 1966 complete divisions poured in to fight the jungle war. The tables of organisation and equipment for the US Army fighting units reflected the planners' expectations of the most likely scenario of war at that time – conventional, main-force actions, probably in Europe or Asia. But the nature of the escalating battle for Vietnam soon proved their expectations to be very wide of the mark.

On the ground, the main problem for American infantry commanders was getting hold of sufficient intelligence to get to grips with the enemy. Consider the types of force and the nature of the terrain they were up against. Hostile forces were grouped generally into three categories – local-force Viet Cong (VC), main-force VC and regular units of the North Vietnamese Army (NVA). Local-force VC stayed in or near their home villages, watching US Army and South Vietnamese (ARVN) units, collecting information and planting mines and booby-traps. They blended into the local scene, were lightly

Below: A seven-man Lurp poses for a picture for *Life* magazine before setting out on a mission in the Mekong Delta in 1968. Lurps travelled relatively light since their mission required considerable stealth and mobility, but were well armed. From left to right this particular patrol fields a 'blooper' (M79 grenade launcher), a Colt Commando and three M16 assault rifles. A good supply of ammunition is carried, along with grenades, combat knives and radio equipment with which to relay their observations back to the main force.

armed and only fought when ordered to by higher command. Main-force VC units were more heavily armed and their ranks included well-trained sapper teams whose mission was heavy demolition during attacks on US and allied installations. These main-force units hid out in base areas in the hills or jungles, sallying forth to attack and then melting back into the fastness when their mission was completed. Regular NVA units also remained in base areas until committed to battle, which was fought according to a well-rehearsed plan and in concert with VC units.

To inflict damage on US and ARVN installations, the main-force VC and NVA units had to come out of their base areas and they also had to be resupplied with weapons, ammunition, food and other necessities. It soon became clear that one of the most essential tasks for the US military was to find these base areas and interdict enemy movement in and out of them. Once a base area had been pinpointed, it could be attacked. Also, any VC and NVA units moving in or out could be engaged and destroyed,

RECONDO

thus thwarting plans for assaults on US installations.

In identifying enemy base areas, aerial reconnaissance was, of course, helpful, but analysing the photo imagery took time. By the time the interpreters had finished with the pictures and transmitted their findings to a fighting unit, the enemy had moved on. What was needed was immediate and reliable tactical intelligence. The problem was, where to get it. The formal US Army organisation made no provision for extensive and really effective long-range, close reconnaissance and so, faced with the frustration of trying to bring to battle an elusive and often invisible enemy, the infantry commanders took matters into their own hands. Their solution to the problem was the creation of informal units known as Long-Range Reconnaissance Patrols (LRRPs – pronounced 'Lurps'). These patrols were to provide skilled 'eyes and ears' for their parent formation out in the remote parts of an operational area, collecting tactical intelligence and giving early warning of enemy movements.

The next challenge was to create the units. Infantry battalions at that time had a reconnaissance platoon of about 40 men, led by a lieutenant, and, although trained in the skills of long-range reconnaissance, one platoon was insufficient for the level of effort needed. This shortage was exacerbated by the fact that most line units were chronically under strength. Each battalion, however, had an anti-tank (AT) platoon. Since the enemy had no armoured vehicles during the early years of the war, the AT platoon was somewhat redundant, so its strength was converted into an additional reconnaissance resource. The change of role gave most battalions a force of between 50 and 80 men to be employed as Lurps.

The experience of the 1st Battalion, 327th Infantry, in forming Lurps was typical of more than 80 infantry battalions in Vietnam. In mid-1965, the battalion commander, Lieutenant-Colonel Joseph B. Rogers, initiated long-range patrols in his area of operations and their work immediately paid off in reliable tactical intelligence. To expand the Lurp force, he converted his AT platoon to reconnaissance duties and called for volunteers from the rifle companies. He got them. The 1st Battalion was an airborne unit so all his men were already volunteers, but even in the non-parachute infantry units the call for volunteers

for Lurp work met with success. The idea of operating independently, far out in the enemy area, appealed to many young soldiers.

Colonel Rogers broke down his Lurp force into seven-man teams, each led by an experienced NCO as team leader. Other units used five or six-man teams. Teams had to be kept small because the UH-1 'Huey' helicopter, used to transport the Lurps to their area of operations, could only carry seven men and their equipment – and even then it was a tight fit and a heavy load.

The composition of Lurp teams was a local option but was usually like this: team leader, radio operator, medical aidman and scouts. All except the medic were armed with M16 assault rifles, fragmentation and smoke grenades, and knives. Many men also carried a .45in pistol, and the team took along a supply of Claymore anti-personnel mines for protecting patrol bases and laying ambushes on trails used by the enemy. On patrol, the Lurps wore floppy hats or bandanas to save weight and increase their field of vision. Heavy steel helmets and armoured vests were left back at base camp.

Two Lurp teams were landed at night by helicopter in the vincinity of likely enemy base areas

Colonel Rogers trained his Lurps as realistically as possible. The men infiltrated suspected VC-controlled areas at night and on foot where they set up a patrol base and conducted team reconnaissance of the area. Stringent control over light, noise and smoking was observed. Continuous stress was placed on the individual patrol skills of navigation, stealthy movement, marksmanship, communication and adjustment of supporting fire.

After the initial training period, Colonel Rogers' Lurps were issued with Vietnamese camouflage fatigues, known as 'tiger suits', which were striped in random patterns for maximum concealment in the jungle. The tiger suits and unconventional head gear set the Lurps apart from the other troops in the battalion, giving them a certain distinction that added elan.

The pattern of training and equipping the Lurps was similar in US battalions throughout Vietnam, and General Westmoreland's HQ soon came up with an

Above: A reconnaissance patrol radioes its findings back to base. For their clandestine mission, the Lurps soon discarded their steel helmets and armoured vests in favour of less formal military attire and the liberal application of camouflage paint. This practice persisted

when the Lurps were formalised into Ranger Companies and was taught to their fellow Rangers in the South Vietnamese armed forces (below left).

unofficial definition of Lurps: 'A specially trained military unit, organised and equipped for the specific purpose of functioning as an information gathering agency responsive to the intelligence requirements of the tactical commander.'

As the Lurps were formed in the various units and began fanning out through operational areas, the quality of intelligence improved immensely. Lurps were placed in position to maintain surveillance over routes, areas or specific locations for extended periods, reporting all sightings of enemy activity within their area of observation. Checking out previously reported enemy locations and detecting the movement of enemy forces allowed the brigade or battalion commander to decide whether to commit his infantry units to attack, or to look elsewhere.

A typical example of the value of Lurp intelligence can be seen in the operational record of the 1st Battalion, 327th Infantry. In February 1966, several agents reported a large number of NVA troops in an area north of Tuy Hoa. As the battalion noted: 'In typical agent fashion, the location of the enemy force was given as "somewhere" in a 16-kilometer square.' Instead of committing the battalion for the usual 'walk in the sun', on the off-chance of making contact with the enemy, two Lurp teams were landed at night by helicopter in the vicinity of two likely enemy base areas.

After five days of extensive patrolling throughout the area, the teams reported only occasional sight-ings of local guerrillas. This did not warrant the commitment of the whole battalion and its strength was saved to fight another day.

That day was not long in coming. Another agent reported an enemy force near the Special Forces camp at Dong Tre, estimated as 'several companies', and seven Lurp teams were sent into the area with a radio relay established to receive their incoming reports. After a day of patrolling, one of the teams located a main-force VC company. While they shadowed the VC, another Lurp team selected and secured a suitable helicopter landing zone (LZ). The battalion then launched a surprise heliborne night assault into the LZ and was led by the Lurps into contact with the VC. The infantry mauled the enemy company, killing 50 men in the firefight.

More often than not, however, Lurp missions did not result in contact with the enemy. There were two reasons for this. First, because the area of operations was huge, and small, dispersed forces could be concealed easily. Second, because if the enemy detected the Lurp team, they could avoid them if they so wished. To increase their chances of avoiding enemy detection, Lurps were inserted into a patrol area by helicopter, some distance away from where they would be operating. They then infil-

Below: A Lurp deploys. The patrols were taken into the area of operations in choppers, but once on the ground (right) the men disappeared into the jungle and proceeded towards the reconnaissance target area on foot (right below).

FROM LURPS TO RANGERS

When US forces were first committed to the war in Vietnam, normal intelligence channels were more concerned with the so-called 'big picture', and information they were able to supply was not particularly helpful to commanders on the ground. The first ad hoc units formed to fill this gap and provide tactical intelligence quickly proved their worth and very soon most infantry units had formed their own Lurp forces.

This piece of improvisation on the part of local commanders soon became more formalised and by late 1967 each division had a Long Range Patrol company assigned to it. In January 1969 the Lurp concept was expanded even further and the LRPs were organised as Ranger infantry companies. Their parent unit was the reactivated 75th Infantry, which traced its lineage back to Merrill's Marauders of World War II fame. The strength of each company was standardised at 118 men (three officers and 115 enlisted men), organised into a company HQ and two platoons. Following the Lurp concept, the platoons were broken down into six-man patrols.

With the expansion in organisation came an extended role and Ranger companies often provided the manpower for specialist missions and brigade or divisional reaction forces.

Into the jungle. With his M16 at the ready (far left), a member of a Lurp snakes slowly through the undergrowth. He is travelling light, which indicates that he is on a short security recce out from a Lurp base. Left centre: Lurp leader Sergeant Michael D. Frazier keeps watch for enemy movement as he brings up the rear of a patrol. Left below: Complete silence and a watchful eye were basic to the tradecraft of the Lurps. Left: A US Ranger oversees the training of the Biet Dong Quan (Vietnamese Rangers) in hand-to-hand combat.

trated on foot to the designated patrol base and began their reconnaissance from there. A typical mission lasted four or five days and, on completion, the Lurp would move stealthily to an agreed pick-up point for extraction by helicopter.

Although the Lurps were primarily a reconnaissance force, when required they could, and did, fight. Their usual recon mission could be expanded into a combat ambush, or the taking of prisoners to be brought back to base for interrogation. There were many possibilities.

The Lurps worked hard and their record is impressive. Between February and March 1968, for example, the Lurp force supporting the 199th Light Infantry Brigade was operating about 50km northeast of Saigon. Extending the reach of the 199th by conducting reconnaissance and combat-reconnaissance, the idea was to watch trails and river-crossings, find the enemy, and enable the brigade to commit heavy forces against him. Over the two month period, Lurp teams were sent out 117 times and suffered no losses. Forty emergency extractions by helicopter were recorded, while NVA and mainforce VC troops were sighted on 91 occasions. Contact was made in one third of these cases. Reaction forces were committed 10 times, either to hit the enemy or extract the Lurp. In all, 48 enemy troops were killed, and 18 prisoners were taken.

High-level recognition for the Lurps' accomplishments came in many forms. One was the establishment of the Recondo (a combination of 'recon' and 'commando') School by General Westmoreland's headquarters, to which units could send prospective Lurp leaders to receive specialist training that was difficult to provide within the unit's own resources. Back in Washington, the Army decided to set up actual tables of organisation and equipment for the long-range patrol detachments.

'Every major battle the 4th Infantry Division got itself into was initiated by the action of an LRP'

Individual commanders also made official comments on the value of the Lurp contribution. Major-General William R. Peers, who commanded the 4th Infantry Division during the epic battles it fought with the 173rd Airborne against regular NVA regiments in the Central Highlands in late 1967 and early 1968, stated:

'Every major battle that the 4th Infantry Division got itself into was initiated by the action of a Long-Range Patrol – every single one of them. That included the battle of Dak To, for the Long-Range Patrols completely uncovered the enemy movement. We knew exactly where he was coming from through our Long-Range Patrol action.'

By late 1967 the LRRPs had become known as Long-Range Patrols and eventually, as the war continued, the Army expanded the Lurp detachments

LURP RATIONS

As the number of LRRP actions increased and experience was gained, the requirements for specialised equipment were clarified. One acute need was for lightweight, portable combat rations.

The normal US Army combat ration of the day was the C-Ration – a collection of canned foods, providing close to 3000 calories. The tins contained such 'delicacies' as sausage patties (in congealed white fat), beans and frankfurters, spaghetti and meatballs and several others. The diet was monotonous.

A Lurp team member, assigned to a jungle mission, expected to be out for five days and had to carry five bulky boxes, each weighing nearly two pounds. This reduced his capacity for carrying weapons, ammunition, grenades and other essential gear. Disposing of the cans on their undercover missions was a problem, and because they could not light fires, the rations had to be eaten cold. However, the Army's food-research laboratory at Natick, Massachusetts, was experimenting with methods to reduce the size and weight of individual combat rations and, the troops hoped, to make them more appetising. The research effort was accelerated and the Natick wizards concentrated their efforts on the 'freeze-dry' process. The results of their work produced a meal that was two thirds lighter than the C-ration. The chili meal was especially zesty and the production of banana flakes and other more interesting culinary delights made the whole package far more acceptable to the troops.

The freeze-dried meals came in sealed pouches that could be squeezed or bent and tucked away anywhere a man had space. To eat his meal, he had only to add the specified amount of water, stir or knead the contents, and let it sit for a few minutes. The meals were tasty either hot or cold. They were quickly dubbed 'Lurp rations'. Freeze-dried meals are now sold widely for use by campers and trekkers everywhere.

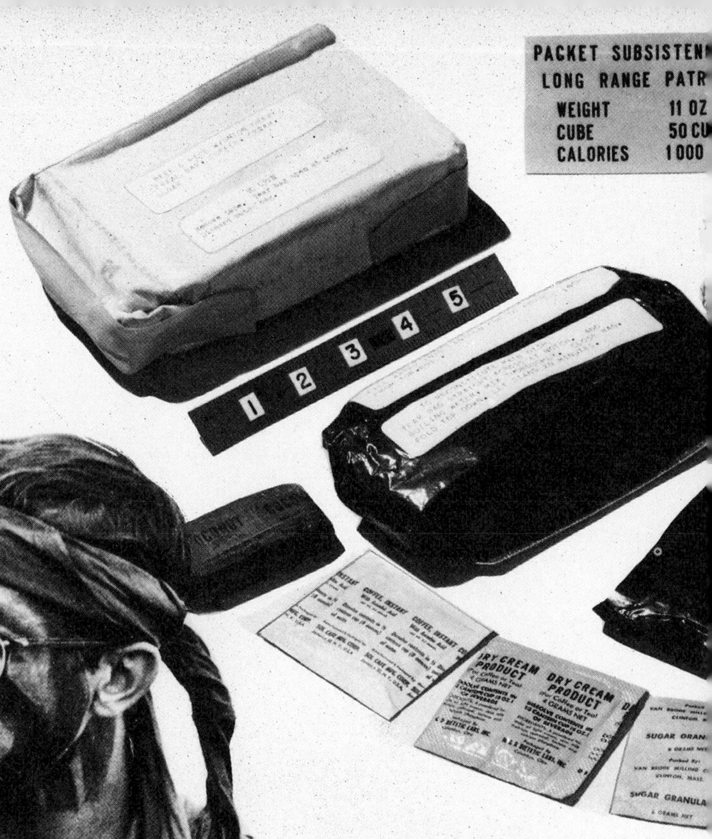

PACKET SUBSISTEN
LONG RANGE PATR
WEIGHT   11 OZ
CUBE   50 CU
CALORIES   1000

Left: Thanksgiving Day – C-Ration style. A Lurp gazes with some amazement at a morsel of what the label on the box described as 'Turkey Loaf'. Later in the war, however, the Lurps were issued with freeze-dried rations that were less bulky, much lighter and easier on the taste buds. Below: A Lurp tucks in to a bag of re-hydrated chili.

MACV RECONDO SCHOOL

On 15 September 1966, by direction of General Westmoreland, the Military Assistance Command, Vietnam, Recondo School was established by the US Army 5th Special Forces Group at Nha Trang on the eastern seaboard of South Vietnam. The purpose of the new training facility was to prepare selected troops from both US and Allied units in long-range reconnaissance techniques – techniques that had already proved their worth both in the clandestine operations conducted by the Special Forces and in the work of the 'home-grown' Lurps of the regular divisions.

The school opened with 60 students doing a three-week course but by January 1967 the number of students in training had doubled. Included in the Recondo curriculum were all those skills essential to small-unit, undercover patrol work in hostile territory. The Lurps sent to the school went through a rigorous programme of instruction in survival, escape and evasion, insertion and extraction by helicopter, land navigation, silent movement, field medicine, communications and photography. The training was realistic and practice operations were carried out on Hon Tri in the Bay of Na Trang where the students often came into contact with the enemy.

Above: The Lurp ration. The opened pack contains one complete meal – spaghetti with meat sauce, a coconut bar, cocoa beverage, coffee, cream and sugar. Below: Training Lurps at the MACV Recondo School.

into fully fledged Ranger companies, assigning one to each division and brigade. From 1 January 1969, the 75th Infantry was reactivated as the parent unit of all LRP Ranger companies. By the time US combat units pulled out of Vietnam, 13 Ranger companies had been authorised.

The Rangers expanded the forces available to perform the roles originally assigned to the 'home-grown' Lurps and also worked in an advisory capacity to the South Vietnamese Rangers.

But, even with the additional strength of the Ranger companies, most units kept operating their own Lurps. Most Ranger teams were deployed far back into the jungles and mountains to detect regular NVA units, but the need for local tactical intelligence was still acute. The 173rd Airborne, for example, had expanded its Lurp force into a Ranger company but also set up 'Hawk' teams in all of its rifle companies, which performed close-in reconnaissance along the same lines as their Lurp predecessors.

In a war with no boundaries, and where the enemy was elusive and the terrain formidable, the Long-Range Reconnaissance Patrols proved invaluable. In the past they have not received the same level of recognition as units such as the Green Berets, but as an example of the ingenuity of local infantry commanders in meeting local needs, the Lurps were one of the most successful units of their kind.

THE AUTHOR F. Clifton Berry, Jr is a Washington-based writer on aerospace and military subjects. He fought in Vietnam as operations officer of a light infantry brigade.

DARBY'S RANGERS

The 1st Ranger Battalion was formed in June 1942 in Northern Ireland as an American version of the British Commandos. It was originally intended that the battalion should take part in commando operations against Nazi-occupied Europe, and a small contingent participated in the Dieppe raid of August 1942. But the Rangers first saw action as a battalion, under the leadership of Lieutenant-Colonel William Orlando Darby, in Operation Torch, the US invasion of North Africa in November 1942.

They played a distinguished role in subsequent operations in Tunisia, and in April 1943 Darby was authorised to expand the Rangers. Spreading his experienced officers and men among new volunteers, by June he had formed three Ranger battalions – the 1st, 3rd and 4th. Although they lacked any centralised command, the three battalions were known as Darby's Rangers and frequently fought together, notably in the landings at Gela, Sicily (1st and 4th Battalions, 10 July 1943), the Chiunzi Pass near Salerno in September 1943, and the Winter Line north of Naples during the following October and November.

In December 1943 the three battalions were at last officially put under Darby's unified command as Ranger Force, under which title they spearheaded the January 1944 Anzio landings. The landings were initially a success, but on 30 January, advancing inland to Cisterna, 1st and 3rd Ranger Battalions were encircled by a superior German force and 4th Battalion could not break through to relieve them. Only six out of 767 men escaped the encirclement.

Above: The shoulder patch worn by US Rangers.

DARBY'S RANGERS

In February 1943, Lieutenant-Colonel William Darby led the hand-picked men of the 1st Ranger Battalion in an audacious night attack on the Sened Pass, Tunisia

BY THE BEGINNING of February 1943, the 1st Ranger Battalion was a restless, thoroughly discontented body of men. All of them had volunteered for the Rangers as the quickest possible route to the sharp end of war, where danger and fear would be compensated for by the exhilaration of action and daring exploits. But after almost eight months of continuous training, broken by only one brief explosion of combat, they were stuck in the dull North African port of Arzew with no outlet for their energies but bar-room brawls and seemingly endless training routines for operations that never happened. The battalion commander, Lieutenant-Colonel William Orlando Darby, knew he must find an opportunity for his men to put their commando training into practice or they would begin to drift back to the units from which they had been taken the previous summer. Fortunately, that opportunity came at Sened Pass.

The Ranger battalion had seen its only combat so far in Operation Torch, the US invasion of North Africa, seizing the port of Arzew in an amphibious night attack on 7/8 November 1942. After the invasion, Allied forces pushing eastwards had run into stiff Axis resistance in Tunisia. The Sened Pass was a

key position in the south of the Axis line, for through it ran the mountain road from central Tunisia to the coastal town of Sfax. The pass was held by Italian troops with German armour in support, and some 20 miles of no-man's land separated it from forward Allied positions. Darby was ordered to lead his men in a lightning raid against this strongpoint, with the aim of inflicting maximum damage on men and material, thus undermining enemy morale. From Darby's point of view, the most important effect would be on the morale of his own troops and on the future of the Ranger concept in the US Army.

When the 1st Ranger Battalion was formed at Carrickfergus, Northern Ireland, in June 1942, its designated function was to give combat experience to a wide range of US troops by participation in commando operations, then the only form of action available in Europe. These men were then to return to their original units, where they would provide a backbone of battle-hardened soldiers to stiffen the ranks of their inexperienced colleagues. With this end in view, volunteers were requested from every branch of the US Army formations in Northern Ireland – 34th Infantry Division and 1st Armored Division – artillerymen, infantrymen, tankers, signallers

Operation Torch gets under way. Bottom left: Rangers are carried across the Mediterranean in high spirits for the first operational task of the US Army in the European theatre in World War II. Below: Against little opposition from the Vichy French, elements of the Anglo-American force wade ashore at Arzew in Algeria. Bottom: Crouched low behind his machine gun, one of Darby's Rangers guards a captured enemy emplacement overlooking Arzew. In a skilful night assault, the Rangers silenced a brace of enemy fortresses that threatened the Allied fleet.

and even rear echelon personnel such as cooks and storesmen. But all were rigorously selected for their elite qualities: they had to be 'fully trained soldiers of the highest possible type', with 'natural athletic ability, physical stamina…, initiative, judgement and common sense'. Even men with dentures were rejected as unfit. Any inferior men who may have slipped through the initial selection procedure were soon weeded out during training at the hands of the British Commandos and the Royal Navy: courage, physical endurance and fighting skills of a high level were needed to stay the course.

There was no question that, by November 1942, the Rangers did constitute a Commando-style unit of excellent quality. The US Army commanders, however, having abandoned the original idea of using the Rangers simply to blood untried soldiers, were hard pressed to find a serious use for this new creation. The landings at Arzew gave Darby's men a chance to show their paces, but subsequent ideas for commando operations in North Africa failed to in-

spire the high command with sufficient enthusiasm. It was clear that on the whole Darby's superiors were either hostile to the Ranger concept or could find no place for its style of action in their tactical plans. 'Top Brass' had shown plenty of interest in Ranger training techniques – their rehearsals of opposed landings, carried out with live ammunition on the North African beaches, made an exciting spectacle – but less imagination for using their skills in actual combat.

The Rangers were fortunate in their battalion commander, Darby, who saw them through this difficult period. The fierce training routines he imposed were not necessarily popular with the rank and file – one wit remarked: 'We may not have many battle honours, but when the war is over the Rangers will have the top training honours in the whole Army'. But the training kept men at a peak of fitness – and exhaustion. Discipline was unrelenting. Darby imposed punishments for quite minor misdemeanours that were themselves a schooling in endurance – brutal route marches across hot, rough terrain, or painful penalties such as remaining for hours in the North African sun, stripped to the waist, until the skin burnt to blisters. But Darby took so much punishment himself in training that his tough approach won him respect and admiration, as well as fear (several Rangers admitted to being more scared of Darby than they were of the enemy).

The news of the planned raid on Sened Pass was received in the ranks with relief and enthusiasm, coupled with the hard-nosed cynicism that was many men's stock in trade, and the usual nervous tension associated with the approach of battle. On 7 February the Rangers were flown to II Corps headquarters at Tebessa, Tunisia, and then moved by truck to Gafsa, the southernmost point in the loose-knit Allied line. The day after their arrival in this oasis town, the Rangers were briefed on their mission. Three of the battalion's seven companies – Companies A, E and F – were to carry out the raid. First, they would be driven to a French outpost some 24 miles from Gafsa. The following night, they would advance through the barren desert and mountain terrain to a position within a few miles of the Sened Pass. There they would lie up during the daylight hours, ready to launch their assault when darkness fell. Having hit the strongpoints held by Italian Bersaglieri, the Rangers would have to get well clear by daybreak or their chances of survival would be slim. The return journey to their own lines was potentially the most hazardous part of the whole enterprise.

It was a mission tailor-made for the Rangers. For weeks prior to the operation, they had repeatedly rehearsed night attacks, living a virtually nocturnal existence. Darby had developed his own method of manoeuvring in pitch darkness, using a system of hooded lights to co-ordinate the movement of companies engaged in an assault. Now had come the chance to see how it worked in practice, and for the Rangers to put everything, from their speed-marching to their weapons skills, to the test.

Darby and his executive officer, Major Herman W. Dammer, had already reconnoitred the target and were now awaiting the three assault companies at the French outpost. At 2130 hours on 10 February 1943, the companies boarded the trucks at Gafsa and set out to join their commanders. The Rangers were meticulously prepared for swift silent movement. Apart from their weapons, each man carried one ration pack, one water canteen and a groundsheet (known to the Americans as a shelter-half). They left behind such items as their standard-issue cups, that might have clinked a warning to the enemy, and every potentially creaky piece of leather was carefully softened. Faces blacked up under their skull caps – tin helmets were not worn – the Rangers huddled together for warmth in the cold desert night as the trucks rolled towards their destination.

The enemy remained oblivious to the Ranger presence on the high ground above them

Within minutes of dismounting from the trucks at the French outpost, the companies were formed up and set off, a column of 180 men following Darby through the pitch darkness into the djebel. Darby set a ferocious pace and no-one could afford to lose touch for more than an instant with the man in front or they would risk becoming hopelessly lost in the night. As the going got rougher, through mountain ravines and up small cliff faces, Rangers delayed by a difficult ascent found themselves running to keep up with the column, their lungs pumping hard in the thin mountain air. The column covered 14 miles by daylight.

As dawn broke, the Rangers reached their first objective, a large depression between two mountain peaks. Here they were to spend the dangerous daylight hours, about six miles from the Sened Pass. German reconnaissance aircraft were known to patrol the area, so the Rangers had at all costs to camouflage their bivouac from aerial observation. Each man installed himself under his shelter-half, stretched from boulder to boulder or between outcrops of rock, concealing him equally from enemy spotters and from the heat of the sun. No movement was permitted. Exhausted by the previous night's

Below: Carbines at the ready a pair of Darby's Rangers scan the rooftops of Arzew for signs of enemy snipers. Note the familiar motif of 'The Sain on the back of the helmet of the right-hand ranger.

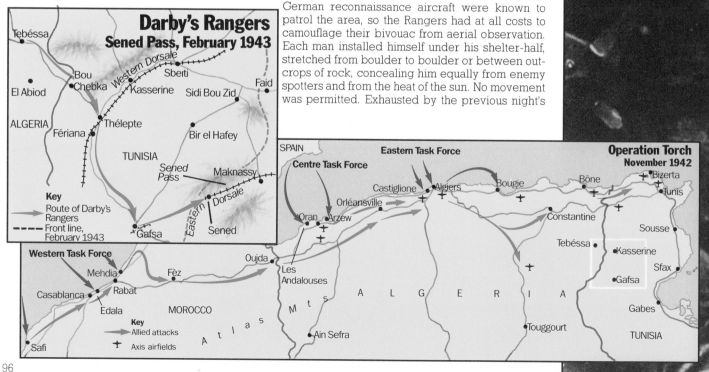

Darby's Rangers
Sened Pass, February 1943

Tebéssa
Bou Chebka
El Abiod
ALGERIA
Fériana
Thélepte
Western Dorsale
Sbeïtla
Kasserine
Sidi Bou Zid
Faïd
Bir el Hafey
TUNISIA
Sened Pass
Maknassy
Eastern Dorsale
Gafsa
Sened

Key
→ Route of Darby's Rangers
--- Front line, February 1943

Western Task Force
Mehdia
Fèz
Casablanca
Rabat
Edala
MOROCCO
Safi
Atlas
Key
→ Allied attacks
+ Axis airfields

SPAIN
Centre Task Force
Eastern Task Force
Oran
Arzew
Les Andalouses
Orléansville
Castiglione
Algiers
Bougie
Bône
Bizerta
Tunis
Constantine
Sousse
Tebéssa
Kasserine
Sfax
Gafsa
Gabes
TUNISIA
ALGERIA
Oujda
Touggourt
Ain Sefra
Mts

Operation Torch
November 1942

efforts, the Rangers slumbered through the day as best they could, while Darby and the other senior officers kept watch over the six mile-wide plain that separated them from the Italian positions defending the pass. Four times in the course of the day, Darby spotted German armoured patrols trundling across the plain, raising a thick dust cloud behind them. But the enemy remained oblivious to the Ranger presence on the high ground above them.

Towards evening, the Ranger section leaders assembled for their final briefing, given by Captain Roy A. Murray, a veteran of the ill-fated Dieppe raid of the previous summer. He pointed out the three hills in front of the Sened Pass where the Italian strongpoints were located. Under cover of darkness, the Rangers were to cross the plain in a column and approach to within half a mile of the enemy. The three companies would then spread out, Company A on the left flank, Company E in the centre and Company F on the right. They would advance in complete silence until they were on top of the enemy

before opening fire. A maximum of 10 prisoners could be taken. The Italians were believed to be experienced troops and they were dug into well prepared positions, with machine guns and cannon in support. Only the element of surprise, and the Rangers' high level of training in night fighting, would give the Americans a decisive advantage.

As night fell, the Rangers blacked up, rubbing a mess of dirt and spittle into their faces and hands, and moved down onto the plain. There they halted, waiting for the moon to set before advancing further. It was 0100 hours before darkness was complete. Then, following a compass bearing, the column moved silently forward across the pebble-strewn ground. After half an hour a whispered warning – 'enemy patrol' – passed swiftly back along the column. The Rangers halted, peering into the pitch darkness, until word came that the unseen enemy had been quietly neutralised by the knife of a scout.

At 0200 hours the order came for the column to

RANGER TRAINING

The Rangers were formed as a conscious imitation of the British Commandos, and it was the Commandos who were entrusted with their initial training. In July 1942, at Achnacarry in Scotland, the Commandos introduced the Rangers to the full gamut of special force exercises and skills – speed marches, cliff climbing, obstacle courses, landings in inflatable dinghies, the use of Bren gun, grenade, knife and bayonet, and assault tactics. Live ammunition was used in many of the exercises, and the going was extremely tough even for such carefully selected volunteers. By the end of the Commando course, one Ranger had died by drowning, three had been wounded –two by bullets and one by grenade fragments – and about 40 had suffered sprains. The Rangers were then passed on to the Royal Navy for a month's amphibious assault training near Argyle, and this was followed by a month at Dundee chiefly spent rehearsing attacks on pillboxes and other strongpoints. Once the nature of the Rangers' first combat mission was known – a night assault on the port of Arzew – they were sent to practise opposed night landings at Loch Linnhe. By the time they went into action, the Rangers had undergone the most thorough training possible, and the tradition of maintaining a level of training that was little less demanding than actual combat was upheld throughout the Rangers' period in North Africa. By the Italian campaign, however, continuous fighting and heavy losses had made it necessary to recruit many individuals who had received little or no Commando instruction, and the decline in military standards within the unit may well have been instrumental in the destruction of Darby's Rangers at Cisterna in January 1944.

William Orlando Darby was born on 8 February 1911 at Fort Smith, Arkansas. After graduating from West Point Military Academy in 1933, he joined the field artillery as a second lieutenant and remained an artillery officer until the United States entered World War II. In January 1942, Darby transferred to the 34th Infantry Division as aide-de-camp to the divisional commander, in which post he was sent to Northern Ireland as part of the first wave of US forces in Britain. In June 1942 he was selected to set up the new Ranger battalion.

On the face of it, Darby was a surprising choice – an artillery officer proud of his traditional West Point training. But he was aggressive, self-confident and fearless, a born leader who inspired by personal example.

Throughout the North African, Sicilian and Italian campaigns of 1942-43, Darby remained officially commander only of 1st Ranger Battalion, with the rank of lieutenant-colonel, despite having set up 3rd and 4th Ranger Battalions and having frequently commanded much larger forces. In December 1943 he was finally promoted colonel in command of Ranger Force, comprising the 1st, 3rd and 4th Ranger Battalions, for the Anzio operation.

The disaster at Cisterna on 30 January 1944 virtually destroyed Darby's Rangers. After briefly commanding the 179th Infantry Regiment, in April 1944 Darby was sent back to Washington to join Operations Division, War Department General Staff. He fretted at being left out of the action, however, and in April 1945 he manoeuvred his way into the post of Assistant Divisional Commander, 10th Mountain Division, on the Italian front. On 30 April, with the war almost over, he was killed by a stray artillery shell. Darby was posthumously raised to the rank of brigadier-general the following month.

spread out into their assault formation. This was a manoeuvre that the battalion had practised relentlessly in training. The system the Rangers had evolved to avoid confusion and maintain well organised command in the darkness involved the use of red and green flashlights, partially taped over to reduce them to pinpoints. Each platoon leader carried a green light which he shone backwards towards his men, guiding them through the dark. The company commander, stationed in the rear, could follow the movement of his platoons by observing these lights, and he himself carried a red light with which to indicate his own position back to Darby's headquarters. Darby could then radio through instructions correcting the companies' line of advance if they were pulling too wide or drawing too close together. The much-rehearsed manoeuvre worked to perfection on the night, and the Rangers were soon advancing on the enemy in perfect formation, spread out along a half-mile front.

They had got to within 200yds of the enemy positions when at last they were spotted. An instant later the first machine gun cut a searing trail of tracer fire through the darkness, a dozen others joined in along the front from left to right, and the Italians' 47mm cannon were also soon in action, their shells throwing up showers of pebbles and rock over the Rangers who had flung themselves flat on the sloping ground. Sticking to their orders to hold fire, the Rangers crawled forward under the enemy onslaught. Squad leader James Altieri described those desperate moments:

'I felt naked. There were no rocks to hide behind. There were no helmets to give us the illusion of protection. There was nothing between the enemy's field of fire and our crablike forms ... I cradled my rifle in my arms and slithered forward into the hell of fire crackling over our heads like a hot blow-torch. I could hear the rest of the squad behind me, grunting, gasping. I could hear the babble of Italian voices ahead, bewildered, shouting commands. And I could hear an occasional cry of pain as some of our men were hit.'

There was a momentary respite for the Rangers when they reached the last rise up to the enemy's outer line of defences, for here they were beneath the field of fire. Hurriedly they prepared for the assault and, at a shouted command, hurled grenades upwards into the enemy positions. Immediately, the Rangers were on their feet and charging forward, firing their Tommy guns from the hip into the Italian machine-gun nests. The first defensive line was quickly overrun, the defenders given no chance by the speed of the attack. Meanwhile, the Rangers' mortars opened up, concentrating their fire on the enemy vehicle park, well away from their own side's area of attack.

Inside the Italian defences, the Rangers identified centres of resistance by muzzle flashes in the darkness and homed in for the kill. Most dangerous were still the 47mm cannon, their shells whooshing through the night with a noise like express trains. One Ranger, Pfc Elmer W. Garrison, had his head knocked clean off his shoulders by the cannon in the Company F sector before it was put out of action.

Most of the action was now at close quarters, as the Rangers took on the enemy with bayonet and knife inside their dug-outs. Altieri, dazed by a grenade explosion, unwittingly stumbled into an enemy trench, finding himself face to face with an Italian soldier in a space so narrow he could not bring his rifle up to his hip to fire. After a second of bewilderment and panic, he remembered the commando knife worn on his right leg:

'Almost mechanically I released my grip on my rifle, reached down, gripped the handle of my knife, then with a lightning thrust brought it up with all my strength into his stomach ... I felt the hot blood spurt all over my right arm as I pulled the knife out, then rammed it home again and again. As the body sagged and slid to the ground, I reeled and vomited.'

The Rangers pushed themselves to the limit to cross the plain before they could be discovered

All over the battlefield, in similar moments of brutality, Rangers were discovering the distance that separated the harsh realities of war from training, however thorough. Carried forward by the fierce impetus of their own attack, they killed mercilessly until effective enemy resistance had ceased. Only then did men regain the composure and control to take prisoners and tend to their own wounded. Charges were placed against the Italian cannon and exploded to complete their destruction, while at improvised medical posts the wounded were patched up as best possible.

There were two and a half hours left until dawn, and Darby rapidly organised the withdrawal. Most of the fit Rangers would head back to the French outpost at top speed, led by Major Dammer; from there, trucks would carry them back to Gafsa. Darby would lead a second column composed of the wounded, Italian prisoners and volunteers to aid and guard them. The second column would, of necessity, make slower progress and might not reach the outpost by daybreak. It ran an awful risk of interception.

Some of the 18 wounded could walk, but others, such as Corporal Garland S. Ladd, whose left foot had been shot off at the ankle, had to be carried on stretchers improvised from groundsheets and rifles. It took from four to six men to carry one stretcher, and even then it was far from easy. All water rations remaining were given to the wounded, so the rest had to struggle not only with the harsh mountain country and their extra burdens, but also with a burning thirst. They had 20 hard miles to cover.

Darby moved up and down the column, urging men on and taking his turn at carrying the stretchers. At one point, the stretcher bearing Corporal Ladd began to slip, threatening to tip the badly wounded man onto the ground. The sergeant holding the back of the stretcher thumped the back of the man in front and told him in no uncertain terms to slow down. When the man turned round, the sergeant saw it was

Below left: Partially hidden by a protective smokescreen, Rangers armed with rifles and a Browning Automatic Rifle (BAR) practise their assault drill. Below left: Lieutenant-Colonel William Darby talks tactics with a fellow officer from the seat of his motor cycle. After North Africa, Darby saw service in Sicily and Italy before meeting his death in action. Below right: A Ranger sergeant prepares for combat by sharpening his bayonet.

Darby. 'I'm sorry,' Darby said, 'but we have to keep going.' And they did. By daybreak the second column had marched 14 miles through the mountains; six more miles of pebbled desert plain separated them from their goal. Their blackened faces running with sweat in the hot morning sun, the Rangers pushed themselves to the limit to cross the plain before they could be discovered. At last they encountered a unit of British armoured cars coming out to cover the last stage of their withdrawal. Two hours after daybreak, the exhausted Rangers were eating broth and bread at the French outpost. That night the trucks arrived to take them to Gafsa, where they were greeted by an enemy bombing raid that came close to killing the men who had survived the whole operation unscathed.

The following afternoon, cleaned up and rested, the battalion saw nine enlisted men and four officers, including Darby, decorated for their part in the raid. Perhaps more flattering than the congratulations of their own commanders, however, was the news that the German radio had nicknamed them 'the Black Death'. For the loss of one man killed and 18 wounded, the Rangers had killed about 100 Italians, destroyed six cannon and 12 machine guns, and taken 11 prisoners who had provided valuable intelligence.

THE AUTHOR R. G. Grant graduated in Modern History from Trinity College, Oxford. He has written extensively on the military campaigns of the 20th century.

COLONIAL FIREFIGHT

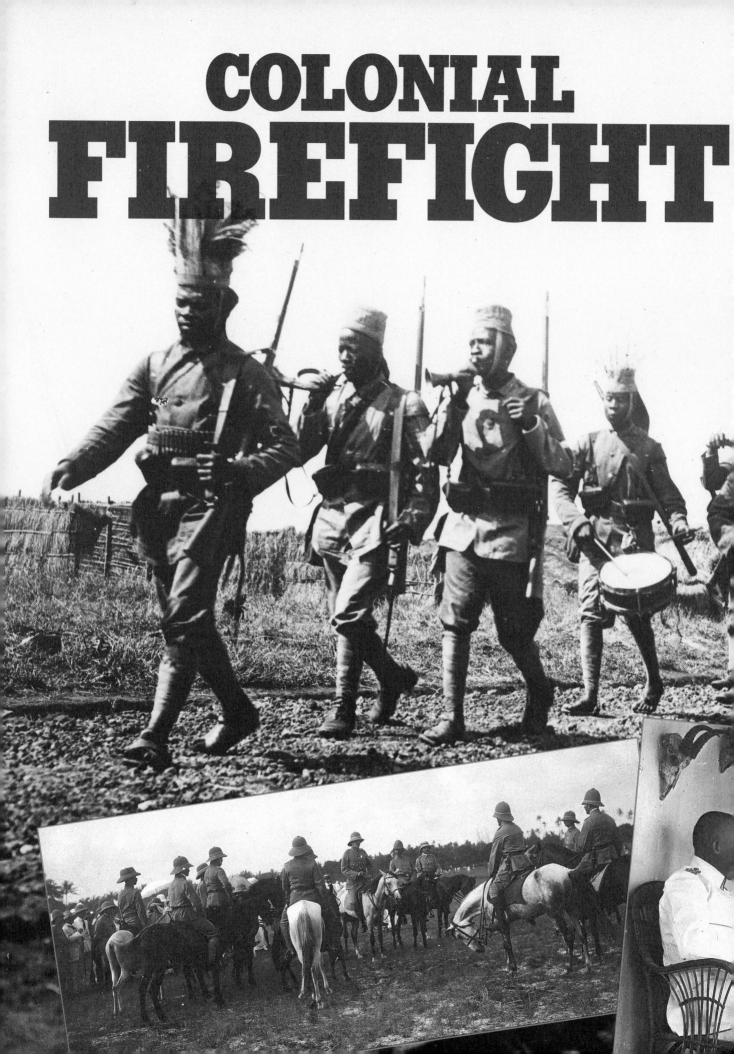

In November 1914, the Schutztruppe in German East Africa successfully beat back a British invasion force

ON THE EVENING of 3 November 1914, Oberstleutnant (Lieutenant-Colonel) Paul von Lettow-Vorbeck, the commander of the Schutztruppe (defence force) in German East Africa, arrived on the western outskirts of the port of Tanga. During the day, units of the Schutztruppe had been in action against a considerable force of British Imperial troops landed from the sea. After hours of fierce fighting the local German commander had decided, in the face of overwhelming odds and the prospect of further landings, to withdraw his troops to the west of Tanga. Lettow-Vorbeck was determined to assess the situation for himself and, accompanied by two officers, he rode into Tanga on a bicycle. He found the town deserted, and when he reached the harbour he saw the British transports a quarter of a mile away, ablaze with lights and making a lot of noise. As they rode back, an Indian sentry challenged them, but he made no attempt to halt the bicycles. After this reconnaiss-

Below left: Askaris on the war-path. Paced by drums and horns, East African recruits of Germany's colonial defence force march in to confront the British. Bottom left: Horse-mounted German officers of the Schutztruppe (defence force), photographed on the declaration of war. Bottom right: Paul von Lettow-Vorbeck (on left), master tactician and leader of the highly successful German East African campaign.

NCO, Schutztruppe, German East Africa 1914

This NCO's uniform is in yellow-khaki with white piping, and white epaulettes with a black and red twist. His grey slouch hat has the white top and cockade of German East Africa. His rifle is the 7.92mm Model M1891.

THE SCHUTZTRUPPE – GERMAN EAST AFRICA

When Germany went to war in August 1914, the fate of the distant colony of German East Africa seemed sealed. Cut off from supplies and surrounded by hostile territories, it was expected that the briefest of Allied campaigns would ensure a surrender. But that calculation took no account of one remarkable soldier and his small but resolute fighting force.

Prior to the war, order was maintained in the territory by a defence unit known as the Schutztruppe. Commanded by Oberstleutnant (Lieutenant-Colonel) Paul von Lettow-Vorbeck, it consisted of 260 Germans and 2472 askaris (native East African soldiers), and these men had, through constant bush operations, developed into a well-disciplined unit of great skill and endurance. The Schutztruppe was organised into 14 independent field companies, each comprising up to 20 German officers and NCOs and 200 askaris. They operated as self-contained, mobile tactical units and had their own supply and transport elements. The askaris were trained according to the standard German infantry drill regulations, with direct orders given in German and lengthier orders in Swahili. Discipline was enforced by flogging, but the Germans made sure that pay and status were sufficiently high to ensure loyalty.

Armament was not plentiful for, although each company had up to four machine guns, the Schutztruppe had few artillery pieces and eight of the field companies still used the antiquated Mauser Model 1871 single-shot rifle. In addition to the Schutztruppe, Lettow-Vorbeck could draw on 2200 police and a number of Schutzenkompagnie (sharpshooter companies) recruited from the German farming community.

Above: Some of the opening shots of the war in German East Africa were fired by the Royal Navy. Here, HMS *Severn* shells Tanga in August 1914, in order to force a local truce. Above right: The hurriedly recruited Indian infantry battalions within the British-led Expeditionary Force 'B' were no match for the well-trained askaris of the Schutztruppe and heavy casualties were sustained in the fighting at Tanga. Background: By contrast, the British contingents of the force benefitted from sound military discipline. That Lettow-Vorbeck could take on such a numerically superior force and win says much for the quality of his leadership.

ance, Lettow-Vorbeck was determined to defend Tanga against the next British attack, and he began to deploy his forces at dawn on 4 November. The coming battle was to determine the course of the war in East Africa for the next four years.

In August 1914 Lettow-Vorbeck had been presented with the almost impossible task of defending German East Africa. The territory covered 650,000 square miles of forests, swamps, bushland and highlands which stretched from the Congo Basin to the Indian Ocean and from Lake Victoria to Portuguese East Africa. To the west, it was bordered by the Belgian Congo, to the north it was threatened by British East Africa, and to the east by the Royal Navy. To the south there was a measure of security in the shape of the still neutral Portuguese East Africa. The population consisted of 7,650,000 Africans of 53 different tribes, 15,000 Indians, Arabs and Goanese and only 5336 Germans. Lettow-Vorbeck had no intention of remaining on the defensive, however, and was determined to attack the allies where they were most vulnerable, along the border of British East Africa. Over the next two months he concentrated the bulk of the Schutztruppe in the north around Kilimanjaro and ordered raids into British East Africa. Then, in October 1914, captured British newspapers and intercepted mail convinced Lettow-Vorbeck that the British were concentrating an amphibious force to land at Tanga. At the end of that month Lettow-Vorbeck motored or rode over most of the area between Moshi and the port. Although Tanga itself was held only by one field company, reinforcements could be concentrated fairly quickly by using the rail link with Moshi in the north.

British action on the outbreak of war in August 1914 had been to shell Dar es Salaam from the sea and establish local truces there and at Tanga. The few battalions of King's African Rifles in British East Africa were dispersed inland on punitive expeditions. The British government decided to reinforce East Africa with the aim of landing an expeditionary force to seize the German coastal areas. It called upon the Indian government to provide such a force, but as the best Indian troops had already been sent to France and the Persian Gulf, those organised into Expeditionary Force 'B' and sent to East Africa could best be described as a 'scratch force'.

It consisted of 8000 troops, organised into two brigades and commanded by Major-General A.E.

Aitken. The 27th Brigade consisted of the 2nd Loyal North Lancashire Regiment and three Indian infantry battalions. The Imperial Service Brigade consisted of two and a half battalions of very mediocre Indian infantry. None of the senior officers had ever seen their men before, and the Indian troops were described by one officer as 'the worst in India'. Poorly trained, badly armed, and lacking experienced officers and NCOs, they had also been subjected to a month's sea passage, which had reduced the majority of them to a state of collapse due to sea sickness.

At a conference held at Mombasa on 31 October between the senior officers of the Expeditionary Force, local commanders and the senior naval officer, it was decided to land at Tanga while a land force attacked south across the border. It was assumed that Tanga was lightly held and that Lettow-Vorbeck would be distracted to the north. Aitken rejected the offer of troops from the King's African Rifles as he expected the landing to be effected without serious opposition. Then, to the amazement of some of the military officers present, the captain of HMS *Fox*, the escorting cruiser, announced that he would have to inform the Germans at Tanga that the local truce was finished before hostilities began. Thus, on 2 November when the Expeditionary Force anchored off Tanga, the whole day was wasted and the opportunity for surprise lost while negotiations were conducted between the local German authorities and the captain of *Fox*.

Nearly 1000 troops assembled around Tanga, arriving either by forced march or packed into lorries

As soon as the local German district officer had seen the Expeditionary Force sail into view off Tanga he had telegraphed the news to Lettow-Vorbeck at Moshi, who immediately sent orders to his field companies scattered along the frontier to concentrate on Tanga. Over the next 48 hours nearly 1000 troops assembled around Tanga, arriving either by forced march, or packed into lorries or the carriages of the single-track railway which ran from Moshi to Tanga. The day's delay on 2 November not only lost the British the element of surprise, it also gave the Germans just sufficient time to organise a defence.

The British finally decided to land on the beaches on the headland at Rase-Kasone, about a mile to the east of Tanga. This indirect approach was adopted because the captain of *Fox* was worried about

Right: Paul Lettow-Vorbeck, pictured during his triumphal ride through Berlin on 2 March 1919. Although his return to Germany was delayed by the formalities of repatriation, he received a hero's welcome from Germans who had avidly followed his campaign in the newspapers.

PAUL VON LETTOW-VORBECK

The commander of Germany's Schutztruppe in East Africa, Paul von Lettow-Vorbeck, was unquestionably one of the most outstanding German officers in World War I. That his force successfully resisted the British without supplies or reinforcements is largely attributable to his strength of character, determination and professional ability. Every inch a Prussian officer of the old school, Lettow-Vorbeck had followed an unusual military career for his generation. Following his graduation from the Kriegschule, he had served almost continually abroad, gaining valuable experience in colonial and guerrilla warfare. He had fought in the Chinese Boxer Revolt of 1900-01, and during the German campaign of 1904-06 against the Herero tribe in South West Africa, he served both as a staff officer with General von Trotha, and as commander of an independent company detachment. He was wounded in 1906 and, while returning to Germany to recuperate, he had the opportunity to see East Africa for the first time. Lettow-Vorbeck believed in leading from the front, inspiring the men and sharing their privations. He also had a flair for languages, and could speak the Swahili of his African troops. Appointed as commander of the Schutztruppe in January 1914, he immediately carried out a whirlwind of inspections and then began the process of converting his men into disciplined, confident soldiers. An intensive training programme was put into effect, based on a system of tactics originated by Lettow-Vorbeck himself. That his methods succeeded is demonstrated by the fact that, despite the efforts of the 100,000 Allied troops that were brought against him, only the fall of Germany itself could force his surrender.

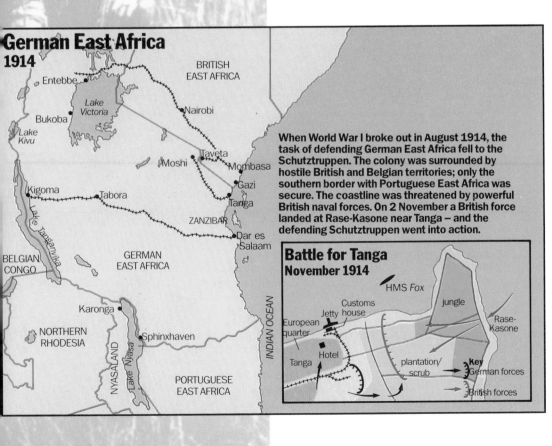

German East Africa 1914

BRITISH EAST AFRICA

Entebbe
Lake Victoria
Bukoba
Nairobi
Lake Kivu
Moshi
Taveta
Mombasa
Kigoma
Tabora
Gazi
Tanga
ZANZIBAR
Dar es Salaam
BELGIAN CONGO
GERMAN EAST AFRICA
Karonga
NORTHERN RHODESIA
Sphinxhaven
Lake Nyasa
NYASALAND
PORTUGUESE EAST AFRICA
INDIAN OCEAN

When World War I broke out in August 1914, the task of defending German East Africa fell to the Schutztruppen. The colony was surrounded by hostile British and Belgian territories; only the southern border with Portuguese East Africa was secure. The coastline was threatened by powerful British naval forces. On 2 November a British force landed at Rase-Kasone near Tanga – and the defending Schutztruppen went into action.

Battle for Tanga
November 1914

HMS *Fox*

Customs house
Jetty
jungle
European quarter
Rase-Kasone
Tanga
Hotel
plantation/ scrub

Key
German forces
British forces

risking his ship in the waters of a harbour which might have been mined, and because Aitken believed that the Germans might defend the approach to the jetty. As a result of this decision the troops were obliged to undertake a difficult route march through inhospitable terrain against an enemy of unknown strength. Tanga was only five degrees south of the Equator and its climate was hot, damp and conducive to fever. The countryside was carpeted with thick trees and spiky undergrowth which made movement difficult.

At dusk on 2 November, the 13th Rajputs and the 61st Pioneers were landed at Rase-Kasone. They were disorganised, frightened and exhausted and almost immediately came under rifle and machine-gun fire, so it was decided to let them rest before commencing the advance in daylight. The Germans who had fired on them were patrols sent out from the 17th Field Company, which had taken up a defensive position in a railway cutting on the outskirts of the town. It was at this position that the 13th Rajputs and the 61st Pioneers met the enemy on the morning of 3 November. The Germans waited until half the battalion of Rajputs were within 200yds and then opened fire with machine guns. The effect of this fire was not only to stop the advance, but also to precipitate the accompanying porters into hasty flight. At this point the Germans counter-attacked, with the askaris (native East African recruits) cheering, blowing horns and bugles, and firing their rifles. The Rajputs and the Pioneers broke and fled in terror back towards the beach, sweeping aside their surviving British officers. At the end of the day order had been restored, but casualties had risen to over 300 and the Expeditionary Force was back at its start line. Ironically, the local German commander decided that he had insufficient troops to defend Tanga against the expected British attack and he withdrew to the west of the town. At that point Lettow-Vorbeck arrived and began to prepare a new defensive position.

In the boiling heat, many Indian soldiers dropped out with heat exhaustion and thirst

Lettow-Vorbeck's plan was determined by the nature of the terrain:

'In the north, the houses of the European town at the harbour provided cover from view, and therefore also from the fire of the cruisers close by. The town was surrounded by continuous cocoanut and rubber plantations, which extended almost to Rase-Kasone, and in which, besides the native town, a few native patches of cultivation were scattered about. Undergrowth occurred along a few points and the ground was absolutely flat. It was probable that the enemy, whether he landed at Rase-Kasone only, or simultaneously at several points, such as Mwambani, for instance, would press upon our south, or right wing. Here to the south of Tanga, the ground afforded us also the prospect of greater power of manoeuvre. I decided to meet the attack, which I expected with certainty, on the eastern edge of Tanga, and to echelon strong reserves behind our right wing for a counter-attack against the enemy's flank.'

Lettow-Vorbeck put his best-trained field company to the east of Tanga and echeloned another to the rear. He positioned himself further back where he could control his reserves and where he was close to the telegraph line. He realised he was taking a risk with his troops outnumbered eight to one, but he

calculated that they were better trained and led than the British force.

Aitken began to land his full force of 8000 troops on the beaches at Rase-Kasone with the simple objective of marching westwards on Tanga. For his spearhead he used the 2nd Loyal North Lancs and the 101st Grenadiers, with the unreliable 63rd Light Infantry sandwiched between. Behind them were the 13th Rajputs, the 98th Infantry Regiment and the 61st Pioneers. In the boiling heat it took two hours before the force reached the outskirts of Tanga, and many Indian soldiers dropped out with heat exhaustion and thirst. At 1500 hours an askari reported to

The high standard of the Schutztruppe's training amply compensated for its limited supplies of weapons and ammunition. Well-sited machine guns (top) and light artillery in improvised emplacements (right) brought a heavy toll, while askari troops (above) attained a high level of marksmanship with their antiquated rifles.

Lettow-Vorbeck, 'The enemy is ready'. The Germans began to fire on the advancing Loyal North Lancs and the 101st Grenadiers who, in the words of one German officer, 'fought magnificently'. The German 16th Field Company, which Lettow-Vorbeck estimated was outnumbered 20 to one, was driven back and had to be reinforced.

But behind the Loyal North Lancs the 63rd Light Infantry broke and fled, carrying with them the 13th Rajputs and the 61st Pioneers. Captain R. Meinertzhagen, a British intelligence officer who witnessed the rout, wrote in his diary:

'It was most demoralising. We collected most of them, made them lie down and keep quiet, but they were all gibbering like terrified monkeys and were clearly not fit for it at any price. Individuals were letting off their rifles in any direction and many men were deliberately firing at our advancing troops.'

But panic was not an Indian prerogative, and German askaris to the south of Tanga began to withdraw. Lettow-Vorbeck and some of his staff rushed up to stop them. The German commander wrote:

'To this day I can see the fiery and determined Captain von Hammerstein, full of fury, throwing an empty bottle at the head of a retreating askari. After all, they were for the most part young companies, only just formed, who were fighting at this point, and they had been staggered by the intensity of the enemy's fire.'

Lettow-Vorbeck then realised that the British left flank was unprotected and did not reach further south than the German right wing. He organised concentrated machine-gun fire to be poured into the unprotected British left flank. This, combined with a swarm of extremely angry and ferocious African bees disturbed by the firing, completed the British rout. At this point *Fox*, on Aitken's urgent request, began to provide covering fire, but many of the shells fell amongst the British and Indian troops. To their disgust, the Loyal North Lancs were ordered to withdraw from the town because they were unsupported. At dusk, there was confusion on both the German and British sides, as Lettow-Vorbeck observed:

'At this time, in the dense forest, all units, and in

many instances friend and foe, were mixed up together, everybody was shouting at once in all sorts of languages, darkness was rapidly setting in; it is only necessary to conjure up this scene in the imagination in order to understand how it was that the pursuit which I set in motion failed completely.'

Lettow-Vorbeck, on the right flank, had ordered the troops there to pursue the enemy, but when he moved to the left flank he found hardly anybody there because the bulk of his force had withdrawn to the west of Tanga, mistakenly believing that this was his order. So, on the night of 4 November, neither the British nor the Germans were organised to continue the fight, and yet a little effort and determination on either side could have secured victory.

Unbeknown to Lettow-Vorbeck, Aitken had already given up the fight and decided on re-embarkation. To cover this, on 5 November Aitken issued false orders over his ship's radio and ordered the Loyal North Lancs to make a feint attack from Rase-Kasone. Throughout 5 November Lettow-Vorbeck did little except re-occupy his positions in Tanga and harass the ships with machine-gun fire. Believing that the British were planning a further attack, Lettow-Vorbeck reluctantly decided at 1700 hours to withdraw inland from Tanga where his defence would be easier. It was at this point that Aitken sent a British officer under a flag of truce to negotiate an honourable withdrawal. So Lettow-Vorbeck suddenly realised that he had won.

The immediate cost of the battle at Tanga was that the Germans suffered 147 casualties while the British suffered 817. Of greater importance for Lettow-Vorbeck and the ability of the Germans to continue the war, however, was the capture of a large amount of British equipment due to the hasty nature of their evacuation. The haul included eight machine guns

and 600,000 rounds of ammunition, and it was to take the combined efforts of over 100,000 allied troops before German East Africa was finally occupied in 1916. But even then, Lettow-Vorbeck kept his Schutztruppe intact: he withdrew into Portuguese East Africa and fought on for another two years before eventually surrendering in Rhodesia, several days after the Armistice in Europe of November 1918.

The Germans were lucky at Tanga – lucky that the British gave up the element of surprise; lucky that the Indian troops were largely inexperienced and poorly led; lucky that the British failed to exploit moments of German panic or precipitate withdrawal. But the Germans were also lucky in the positive sense that they had a professional commander in Lettow-Vorbeck. He had strategically concentrated the bulk of the Schutztruppe in the north and was a resourceful tactical leader. Although not experienced in military operations beyond internal security, the majority of the German field companies were well trained and commanded. Apart from some of the newly recruited young soldiers, the majority of the askaris were brave and loyal, and this important fact was to form the basis of Lettow-Vorbeck's continuing success in drawing large numbers of allied troops away from more important theatres of war to the backwater of East Africa.

THE AUTHOR Keith Simpson is senior lecturer in War Studies and International Affairs at Sandhurst. He is a member of the Royal United Services Institute and the International Institute for Strategic Studies.

During 1914 and early 1915, the German cruiser SMS *Königsberg* roamed the Indian Ocean and sank several important British warships. Eventually in need of a re-fit, she was concealed in the jungle-covered delta of the Rufiji river, where she was attacked and wrecked by the monitors HMS *Severn* and *Mersey*. Her 10 4.1in guns were salvaged, however, and mounted on improvised carriages (below) for use on land. Bigger than any artillery pieces fielded by the British, they gave the Schutztruppe a powerful punch, and they participated in several key moments of Lettow-Vorbeck's campaign.

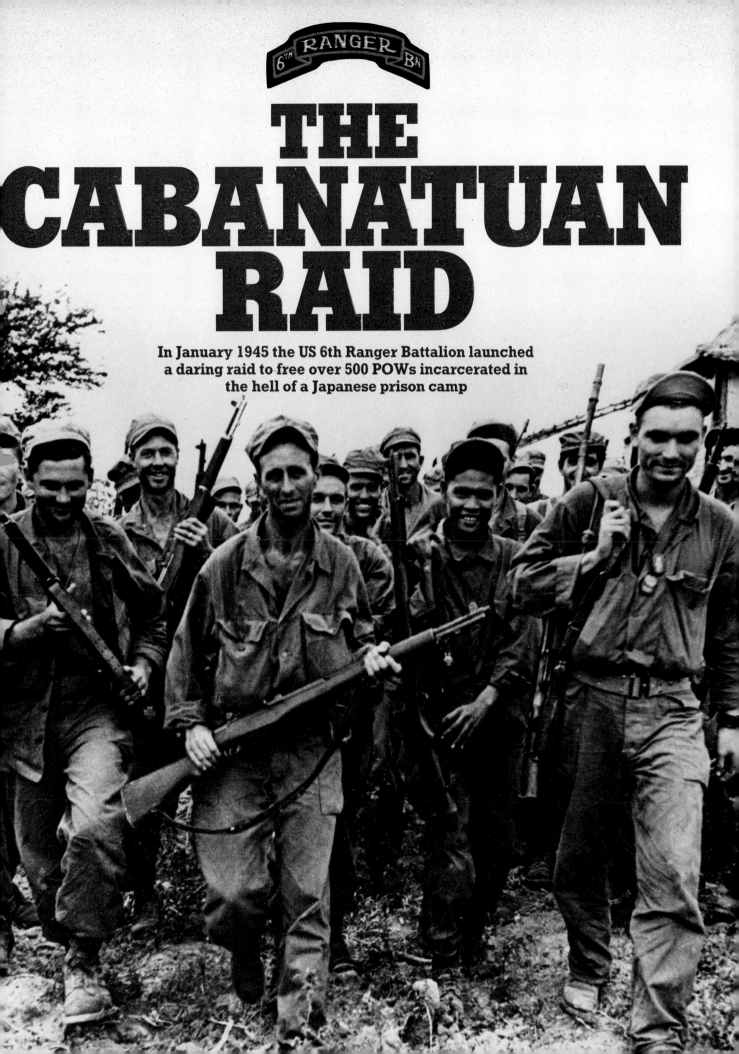

THE CABANATUAN RAID

In January 1945 the US 6th Ranger Battalion launched
a daring raid to free over 500 POWs incarcerated in
the hell of a Japanese prison camp

IN MOST DISCUSSIONS concerning American special forces' capabilities, the Son Tay raid into North Vietnam in November 1970 and the abortive Iranian hostage mission of April 1980 are cited again and again, but the Cabanatuan rescue operation during World War II – one of the most successful POW rescue missions – is virtually forgotten. Yet the raid had enormous symbolic importance, and it demonstrated to the men who had spent so many years in captivity that their country had not forgotten them.

When General Douglas MacArthur's forces, spearheaded by the US Sixth Army under Lieutenant-General Walter Krueger, landed on Luzon in the Philippines on 9 January 1945, rumours began to filter through of American prisoners held captive by the retreating Japanese forces. Three years earlier, when MacArthur had withdrawn from the Philippines in the face of the Japanese invasion, troops remaining on the Bataan peninsula of Luzon had been captured and forced to endure the 60-mile 'Bataan Death March' to a prison camp at Cabanatuan. Fears now grew that the surviving POWs would be executed once the Japanese began to lose their grip on the Philippines. Major Bob Lapham, an American guerrilla leader on Luzon, reported that the prison had been located, and plans were drawn up for a lightning rescue mission.

The raid would be extremely hazardous, since the men chosen for the operation would have to make their strike more than 25 miles behind enemy lines. Lieutenant-General Krueger therefore picked the best men available.

Chosen to carry out the mission were the 6th Ranger Battalion and the Alamo Scouts, a specialist unit similar to the Long Range Reconnaissance Patrols that the Americans were later to use in the Vietnam War. One of the Scouts, Sergeant Galen Kittleson, had the distinction of participating in both the Cabanatuan mission and the Soy Tay raid.

The raid behind Japanese lines would require

Below right: General Krueger, commander of the US Sixth Army, in conference with Generals Murray and Patrick of the 6th Division on Luzon. Below left: POWs on the 'Bataan Death March'.

Right: Men of the 6th Ranger Battalion on their way to the POW camp at Cabanatuan, 25 miles behind Japanese lines.

great stealth, and this prohibited the use of the entire Ranger Battalion. Accordingly, Lieutenant-Colonel Henry Mucci, the battalion CO, detailed Company C, commanded by Captain Robert W. Prince, to execute the raid. The company was reinforced by the 2nd Platoon of Company F, making a total of 121 Rangers.

Additional firepower would be provided by Philippine guerrilla units led by Captain Pajota. These would join up with the Alamo Scouts and carry out a recce of the target, in addition to setting up roadblocks and ambushes to delay any Japanese attempts to reinforce the camp. The Alamo Scouts would have only 36 hours to march the required 27 miles to their objective, but the men were honed to the peak of physical fitness and well versed in the arts of jungle warfare. The Rangers would also have a tough march ahead of them, though one of their main worries was the two Japanese tanks that were reported to be guarding the POW camp. To deal with this threat, and any other they might encounter, the Rangers were well equipped with bazookas and anti-tank grenades procured from the US 6th Infantry Division. Apart from this, however, the Rangers travelled light. They carried only Browning automatic rifles, M1 rifles, M1 carbines and .45in automatics, in addition to their fighting knives, medical supplies, rations for two days and water. Each Ranger also carried his own ammunition.

Travelling throughout the night, the Rangers had moved to within five miles of the camp by dawn

The raid was originally scheduled for 29 January, and by 2000 hours on the 27th the Alamo Scouts were already deep within Japanese territory. The following day the Scouts were joined by Philippine guerrillas led by Captain Pajota, and both groups made their way towards the camp to carry out a preliminary reconnaissance. The Rangers left their camp at Guimba, 25 miles northwest of Cabanatuan, that same afternoon, making their way towards the guerrilla headquarters of Captain Joson at Lobong. The reinforced company then moved into enemy territory, fording the Talavera river at midnight. The assault force had now covered 15 miles, but the men kept pushing on towards their target. Joson's guerrillas provided the flank guard, and sent out patrols to watch for the Japanese and the 'Huks' – left wing guerrillas. Great care had to be taken when crossing major highways for fear of enemy traffic, but the crossings were made without incident. Travelling throughout the night, the Rangers had moved to within five miles of the camp by dawn. Pajota's guerrillas had already moved into blocking positions, their task being to prevent Japanese troops on the opposite side of the Cabu river from reinforcing the camp during the Ranger assault.

At 0600, Mucci and the Rangers arrived at the village of Balangkare, where they were met by Alamo Scouts who had attempted a recce of the POW camp. However, the Scouts reported that the open terrain had prevented them from getting close to the target, and that there were large numbers of Japanese troops entrenched in positions across the Cabu river and at Cabanatuan City. As Mucci began to formulate his strategy in the light of this new information, the guerrillas brought some better news into the camp. Captain Pajota reported that he had requisitioned local *carabao* carts to carry the POWs, who were expected to be extremely weak

THE ALAMO SCOUTS

The Alamo Scouts were established as part of the US Sixth Army on 28 November 1943; their mission was to act as a special reconnaissance unit. Candidates were chosen for courage, intelligence, stamina and adaptability, all of which were put to the test in a five-to-six week training and selection course. This incorporated quick reaction shooting, hand-to-hand combat, radio techniques, small boat handling and land navigation. Up to two teams, each comprising six men, were chosen from each class to join the Alamo Scouts. The remaining graduates (from an original class of five officers and 25 to 50 enlisted men) were returned to their units, where they could exploit their newly acquired scouting skills. During the life of the Alamo Scouts, 10 such courses were run.

The missions were specifically selected by Lieutenant-General Walter Krueger (above), and included the gathering of intelligence on beaches, possible landing sites and the deployment of enemy forces. The Scouts were therefore infiltrated in advance of landing forces in New Guinea, the Solomon Islands and the Philippines. Two Alamo Scout teams,, drawn from the 11th Airborne Division, were parachute-qualified, but this skill was never used operationally.

During the two years of their existence, the Alamo Scouts carried out 70 operations, during which time not one of their number was killed in action. Although the unit was highly classified, most of the 120 men who served with the Scouts were awarded the Silver or Bronze Star.

Cabanatuan
January 1945

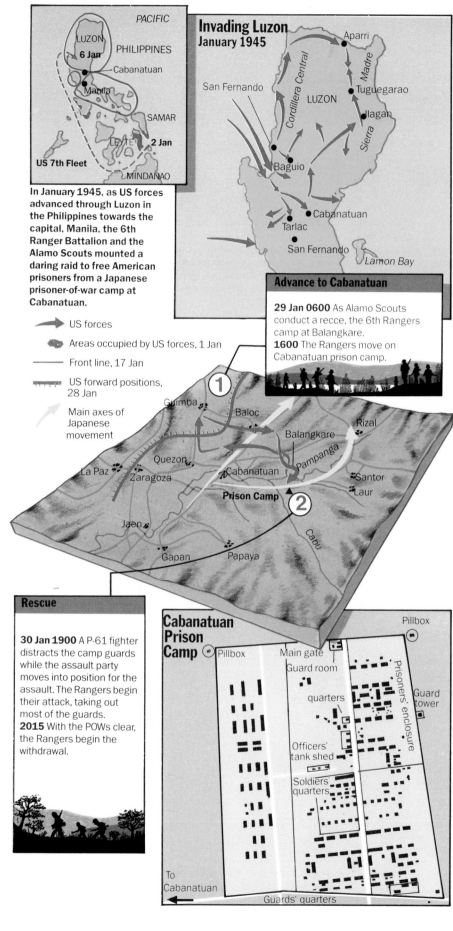

PACIFIC

LUZON
6 Jan
PHILIPPINES
Cabanatuan
Manila
SAMAR
LEYTE
2 Jan
MINDANAO
US 7th Fleet

In January 1945, as US forces advanced through Luzon in the Philippines towards the capital, Manila, the 6th Ranger Battalion and the Alamo Scouts mounted a daring raid to free American prisoners from a Japanese prisoner-of-war camp at Cabanatuan.

➤ US forces

Areas occupied by US forces, 1 Jan

—— Front line, 17 Jan

US forward positions, 28 Jan

Main axes of Japanese movement

Invading Luzon
January 1945

Aparri
San Fernando
Cordillera Central
Madre
LUZON
Tuguegarao
Sierra
Ilagan
Baguio
Cabanatuan
Tarlac
San Fernando
Lamon Bay

Advance to Cabanatuan

29 Jan 0600 As Alamo Scouts conduct a recce, the 6th Rangers camp at Balangkare.
1600 The Rangers move on Cabanatuan prison camp.

Guimba
Baloc
Quezon
Balangkare
Rizal
Pampanga
La Paz
Zaragoza
Cabanatuan
Santor
Prison Camp
Laur
Jaen
Cabu
Gapan
Papaya

Rescue

30 Jan 1900 A P-61 fighter distracts the camp guards while the assault party moves into position for the assault. The Rangers begin their attack, taking out most of the guards.
2015 With the POWs clear, the Rangers begin the withdrawal.

Cabanatuan Prison Camp

Pillbox
Pillbox
Main gate
Guard room
quarters
Prisoners' enclosure
Guard tower
Officers' tank shed
Soldiers' quarters
To Cabanatuan
Guards' quarters

---

after their long ordeal. In addition, residents near the camp had been told to evacuate their homes quickly so that they would not be caught up in the attack, and peasants along the approach route had been ordered to keep their dogs inside – if their barking alerted the enemy to the Rangers' approach, the element of suprise would be lost.

Mucci's plan was actually quite simple; hit the camp hard and fast, killing the Japanese guards before they had an opportunity to exact vengeance on the POWs. The Rangers were lean, mean and ready for action as they moved out from Balangkare towards the camp at 1600 hours on 29 January. Before travelling very far, however, they received reports from the Alamo Scouts of a Japanese division moving up the road through Cabu. As a result of this fresh intelligence Mucci was forced to delay the attack for 24 hours. Falling back to the village of Plateros to wait until the coast was clear, the Rangers were surprised by a feast in their honour. While the Rangers ate their fill, however, the Alamo Scouts maintained their vigil near the camp.

Less than a minute after the first shot had been fired the Rangers were pouring into the camp

By 1430 on 30 January, the Alamo Scouts had carried out successful recces of the camp, and were able to provide Mucci with detailed information regarding the target. The location of the POWs, guard towers, main gate, barracks and pillboxes were collated into a sketch map, and the Scouts estimated enemy strength at some 200 to 300 soldiers. To gain this intelligence, the Scouts had infiltrated into a shack just outside the perimeter fence, while Lieutenant Tombo of the guerrillas donned peasant clothing and walked right up to the main gate, located at the northern end of the compound. On the afternoon of the 30th, guerrillas managed to slip notes to some of the POWs warning them to be ready, though the notes were so cryptic it is doubtful whether the prisoners realised their significance.

As the Rangers moved out from Plateros, a six-man bazooka team under Sergeant White, together with Captain Joson's guerrillas, was tasked to set up a road block 800yds southwest of the camp. The Rangers would be responsible for stopping any enemy tanks approaching once the attack was under way. Captain Pajota's guerrilla unit was to engage the Japanese on the northeast bank of the Cabu river and hold them off until the Rangers had completed their mission at the prison camp. The guerrillas would then withdraw from the Ranger retreat route in order to draw the Japanese away. In addition, the guerrillas would be in charge of cutting all phone lines on either side of the camp, thereby reducing the risk of enemy reinforcements bearing down on the Rangers.

Mucci's plan of attack called for Company C's 1st Platoon, led by Lieutenant William O'Connell, to hit the main gate and drive into the compound killing as many guards as possible. Company C's 2nd Platoon under Lieutenant Melville Schmidt, would follow and release the prisoners. Only when the POWs were clear would the Rangers pull back. At 1700 on 30 January, the Rangers, Alamo Scouts, and a party of guerrillas moved into position for the attack. When Pajota's guerrillas moved towards the Cabu river, they discovered that the Japanese commander had failed to post sentries on the bridge. They thus planted explosive charges and, as a backup, mined

THE 6TH RANGER BATTALION

The 6th Ranger Battalion began life as the 98th Field Artillery Battalion, a unit that lost its pack artillery to Merrill's Marauders. Lieutenant-General Krueger, impressed with the success of the Alamo Scouts, decided that he needed a Ranger unit for his Sixth Army.

The 98th Field Artillery was chosen to be converted, and Lieutenant-Colonel Henry Mucci was assigned to train the men for their new role as Rangers. The 6th Rangers therefore came into being on 20 August 1944, comprising six rifle companies, an HQ company and a medical detachment. Mucci trained the men hard, and, in the tradition of special force officers, he led by example. At full strength, the battalion comprised 600 rangers. On 17 October 1944, the six companies of the 6th Rangers spearheaded the re-conquest of the Philippines, sweeping through Leyte Gulf and landing at Dinagat. For the remainder of October, the battalion was responsible for patrolling the area around the port of Loreto.

In the Lingayen Gulf landings on Luzon, on 9 January 1945, the battalion came ashore at White Beach.

After VJ Day on 15 August 1945, the Rangers were gradually demobilised – the first 139 men leaving the 6th Rangers on 20 August. For the remainder of the battalion, there was a five-month spell in Japan as part of the army of occupation. At the end of November, the 6th Rangers held their final parade – before Lieutenant-General Krueger – and the unit was disbanded on 30 December 1945.

Left: Three of the men who led the daring raid on Cabanatuan POW camp. Lieutenant-Colonel Henry Mucci (top) commanded the 6th Rangers whose Company C, under Captain Robert Prince (far left), was detailed for the mission. Sergeant Theodore Richardson (left) opened the camp gate and had his pistol shot from his hand in the process.

the road on the Cabanatuan side of the river – in case the charges failed to blow the bridge and the Japanese tanks made it across.

Shortly before 1900, as the Rangers neared their target, a P-61 Black Widow nightfighter buzzed the camp, drawing the guards' attention and enabling the Rangers to infiltrate across the open ground. According to the plan, all units were to be ready for the assault by 1930, though the attack was delayed by 15 minutes to ensure that everyone was in position. As the Rangers began their attack, withering fire from Company F's 2nd Platoon, under Lieutenant John Murphy, killed most of the guards in the towers and pillboxes. Simultaneously, guerrillas cut the telephone wires. Within 30 seconds, all guard positions had been neutralised. The Rangers then immediately turned their fire on the Japanese barracks to stifle any possible counter-attack before it could begin. Under the cover of this deadly fire, the assault platoons had breached the compound's fences with wire cutters, and less than a minute after the first shot had been fired the Rangers were pouring into the camp. With deadly accurate bazooka fire, other Rangers knocked out four tanks and two trucks – loaded with Japanese soldiers. Everything was going to plan, each man performing the task expected of him down to the finest detail. At the same time as the Ranger assault, the guerrillas had attacked the Japanese at the Cabu and blown the bridge.

Bursting into the POW compound shouting 'It's OK…we're Yanks! Get the hell out of here!' the Rangers began herding prisoners towards the gates. When the assault platoons revealed their identity, the POWs seemed confused – the Rangers had not been formed until after they had gone into captivity – but they had little doubt that their rescuers were Americans when they heard the cursing in fluent English ringing through the camp as the Rangers dealt with the enemy.

Remarkably, throughout the raid, American casualties were very low, the greatest threat coming when a Japanese mortar team managed to loose off three rounds that seriously injured several men and mortally wounded Captain Fisher, the Ranger surgeon. Rangers quickly silenced the mortar before it could inflict any more damage. During the assault, the P-61 circled overhead in case additional air support was required. At 2005 it attacked a Japanese column on the road, thereby preventing enemy reinforcements reaching the camp just as the Rangers were clearing the last prisoners from the compound.

Hurrying to clear the camp, the Rangers found that many POWs were so weak that they needed to be carried to the carts. Nevertheless, by 2015 they began to pull out after checking that all the POWs were safely clear. One POW was in fact left behind because he had fallen asleep in the latrine, though

Aftermath of liberation. Many of the POWs were too ill to walk from the camp (far left and left) and had to be carried out to safety on carts. Left centre: Private Lloyd Hitchens of the Rangers chats to two of the POWs after the daring rescue. Below left: The survivors of the camp pose for the camera during their recuperation at a base hospital.

fortunately he was rescued by guerrillas later that evening. Another POW died of a heart attack at the camp gate. During the pull back, one other Ranger was killed, but casualties were incredibly light, and by 2030 the Rangers and POWs were heading for the Pampanga river. By 2045 all Rangers and POWs were across the river and Captain Prince set off a flare to let Pajota's guerrillas – engaging a 1000-strong Japanese force – know that they could now break off the attack and withdraw. The Alamo Scouts and Joson's men acted as rearguard for the retreating Rangers, setting up an ambush near the Pampanga river bank.

Throughout the Ranger assault, the guerrillas' efforts to keep a heavily armed Japanese force from crossing the Cabu river were extremely successful. In fact, rather than break off when they saw Prince's flare, they kept firing until 2200 hours, in a bold attempt to prevent the Japanese from following the retreating Americans. So effective had the guerrilla attack been, however, that there was really little chance of enemy pursuit. The guerrillas had killed over 1000 Japanese soldiers without suffering a single serious injury themselves!

If his force was hindered in the slightest he would call in an artillery strike and destroy the village

Throughout the night, the column of Rangers and POW-laden carts advanced towards American lines that had moved closer to Cabanatuan during the two days since the Rangers had left. At one Huk village, Mucci quickly solved a potential problem by informing the Huk leader that if his force was hindered in the slightest he would call in an artillery strike and destroy the village. Finally, a little after 1100 on 31 January, the column reached the front lines of the US Sixth Army. The POWs were finally safe. That evening the Alamo Scouts of the rearguard made it back to American lines.

For the loss of two Rangers killed, 516 POWs had been rescued and 1275 Japanese killed. More than that, the Rangers and the Alamo Scouts had helped repay a small part of the debt owed to the survivors of the Bataan Death March, as well as to those who had not survived. America had returned to the Philippines with a vengeance.

THE AUTHOR Leroy Thompson served in Vietnam as a member of the USAF Combat Security Police. He has published several books including *Uniforms of the Elite Forces* and *Uniforms of the Indochina and Vietnam Wars*.

Britain declared war on Germany on 4 August 1914, and the nations and territories that constituted the far-flung British Empire were quick to provide aid to the mother country. Within weeks of the outbreak of war, thousands of Australians had answered the call of the recruiting posters, and the 1st Infantry Division of the Australian Imperial Force (AIF) had been formed by the end of August. The division had three brigades, comprising a total of 12 battalions. The first Australian troops arrived in Egypt at the end of November 1914, and were deployed to protect the Suez Canal from the Turkish Army in Palestine. At Gallipoli, the Australian and New Zealand Army Corps (ANZAC) was provided with a test of courage and military ability that it was to pass with flying colours. Following the evacuation of the Allied expeditionary force from the Gallipoli Peninsula, the Australians were transported to France and saw action in the Battle of the Somme in 1916, fighting with distinction during the capture of Pozières on 20 July. Their aggressiveness and high spirits were unsurpassed.

The army continued to expand, and by 1917 the order of battle of the Australian Imperial Force comprised five infantry divisions, five light horse brigades and support units, including heavy artillery and mechanical transport formations. Each division had its own field artillery, trench mortar battery, machine-gun battalion, engineer battalions and ordnance units.

With the addition of four divisions from Canada and one from New Zealand, the Dominion units became increasingly important as the vanguard of the British Army on the Western Front.

During the Gallipoli campaign of 1915, the ANZACs demonstrated their tenacious fighting spirit with a fearless attack on the Turkish defences at Lone Pine

IN JULY 1915, despite the intense heat of the Mediterranean summer, Dominion engineers of ANZAC (the Australia and New Zealand Army Corps) worked furiously, digging tunnels and saps out from the Australian trenches towards the Turkish defences on Lone Pine. Making inroads into the hard rock of the Gallipoli peninsula was a slow and difficult business, but it could be done. The Allied expeditionary force had landed on the Gallipoli beaches in April, with the ANZACs coming ashore at 'Anzac Cove' on the western coast. During the next three months, both sides had constructed an extensive tunnel system beneath No-Man's Land.

Above ground, the sharp ridges and steep-sided gulleys of Gallipoli favoured the Turkish defenders and hampered Allied mobility. Entrenched in the high ground overlooking Allied positions that were clustered along the shoreline, the Turks undoubtedly possessed the upper hand. Anzac Cove was particularly vulnerable in this respect; almost the entire area was open to long-range machine-gun fire and the attentions of enemy snipers.

The decision to attack the Turkish positions on Lone Pine was based on two considerations. The first was the belief that its capture would relieve pressure on a number of Australian strongpoints. Second, it was hoped that the battle would divert Turkish reserves south from Suvla Bay, where a large British landing was planned for the night of 6/7 August. In effect, the Australian attack on Lone Pine was only a feint – but the Allied command argued that an easy landing at Suvla could mean the difference between victory and defeat for the whole campaign.

The Turks had devoted much time and effort to strengthening Lone Pine; facing it was a bulge in the Australian line known as the 'Pimple', itself strongly defended. At their nearest, the two forward trench lines were only 70yds apart, extending to a maximum distance of 130yds. Behind the Turkish front line were the usual support lines linked to one another by a maze of communication trenches. In constructing the Lone Pine position, the Turks had set up numerous machine-gun emplacements, able to sweep all of No-Man's Land.

The Australian defences consisted of a main firing line, with its parapet and parados clearly visible to the Turks. Some 20yds forward of this, however, was a parallel line of sunken gallery trenches, connected to the main firing line by a number of tunnels. In addition, three tunnels ran out from the gallery trenches towards the Turkish line – in each was a large charge of ammonal, primed to explode at the onset of the attack.

The assault was set for the afternoon of 6 August, to be carried out by the four battalions of the Australian 1st Brigade, 1st Australian Division, under the command of Brigadier-General Nevill Smyth. The 1st Battalion would be held back as the brigade reserve, ready either to support the main attack, or, if Lone Pine fell to Australian infantry, to take the brunt of the inevitable Turkish counter-attack. Of the three assault battalions, the 2nd was deployed on the right, the 3rd in the centre and the 4th on the left. Each

ANZACs

battalion sent 50 men forward into the gallery trenches, their task being to race ahead of the main advance, leap over the Turkish front line and attack the enemy in the second and third-line trenches. The bulk of the main force was instructed to deal with the Turkish front-line defences, before advancing forward to join up with the survivors of the advance guard. Once reunited with the advance guard, the battalions were to set up a defensive position before nightfall. The troops of the 1st Australian Brigade were well-trained volunteers with plenty of fighting experience behind them. Above all, their morale was at its peak – 'they were ripe for a fight' one observer noted.

At 1630 hours the preliminary bombardment opened up: the brigade's meagre allotment of field guns and howitzers being reinforced by some long-range gunnery from naval vessels out at sea. The hour-long bombardment was a limited one, a consequence of chronic shortages of ammunition.

Above left: Embarked on the *Lutzow*, an ex-German cruiser, ANZAC troops sail towards the Gallipoli peninsula in April 1915. Although the campaign soon stagnated into trench warfare (above right), the inimitable ANZACs were unyielding in their attempts to storm the Turkish lines. Below: The 'bull-dog rush' of the Dominion troops.

However, it helped flatten and cut the barbed wire in front of the enemy trenches, as well as forcing the Turkish front-line troops to keep their heads down.

At 1730 the guns ceased, whistles blew and the 1st Australian Brigade clambered over the parapet into No-Man's Land. Simultaneously, the three mines went up, causing confusion among the Turkish ranks. However, within seconds they had leapt up to their fire-steps and unleashed a hail of bullets onto the advancing Australians. The ordeal of Private C.R. Duke of the 4th Battalion, out on the left of the

The Battle for Lone Pine
ANZACs at Gallipoli, August 1915

In early 1915, the Allies sought to break the deadlock on the Western Front by opening a new front in the east. On 25 April, 70,000 British, French and Australian and New Zealand troops landed on the Gallipoli Peninsula as part of the Allied Expeditionary Force. The British 29th Division landed on the south of the peninsula, on five beaches at Cape Helles. The ANZACs landed further north, above Gaba Tepe, and the French made a temporary landing at Kum Kale, on the Asiatic side of the Dardanelles. However, the Turkish defenders were well entrenched and the campaign soon degenerated into trench warfare. Heavy Allied casualties resulted in a new strategy by the summer of 1915. ANZAC forces were tasked with a diversionary attack on Turkish frontline trenches at Lone Pine, allowing a further Allied landing to take place at Suvla Bay to the north.

The Gallipoli Peninsula

GREECE

Gallipoli Peninsula

SEA OF MARMARA

TURKEY

AEGEAN SEA

Gallipoli Peninsula

Suvla Bay

Anzac Cove

Lone Pine

● Boghali

Gaba Tepe

Kilid Bahr

Maidos

Chanak Kale

Kepnez

Krithia

Sedd el Bahr

Cape Helles

Dardanelles

Kum Kale

TURKEY

Key
----- Allied positions,
10 August 1915

The Assault on Lone Pine

6 June 1630 Preliminary bombardment opens up.
1730 Three assaulting battalions of the 1st Australian Brigade clamber over the parapet and surge into No-Man's Land. Enemy machine-gun fire takes a heavy toll.
1745 The ANZACs reach the Turkish trenches and engage in close-quarters fighting.
1805 Several posts are established in the Turkish positions.

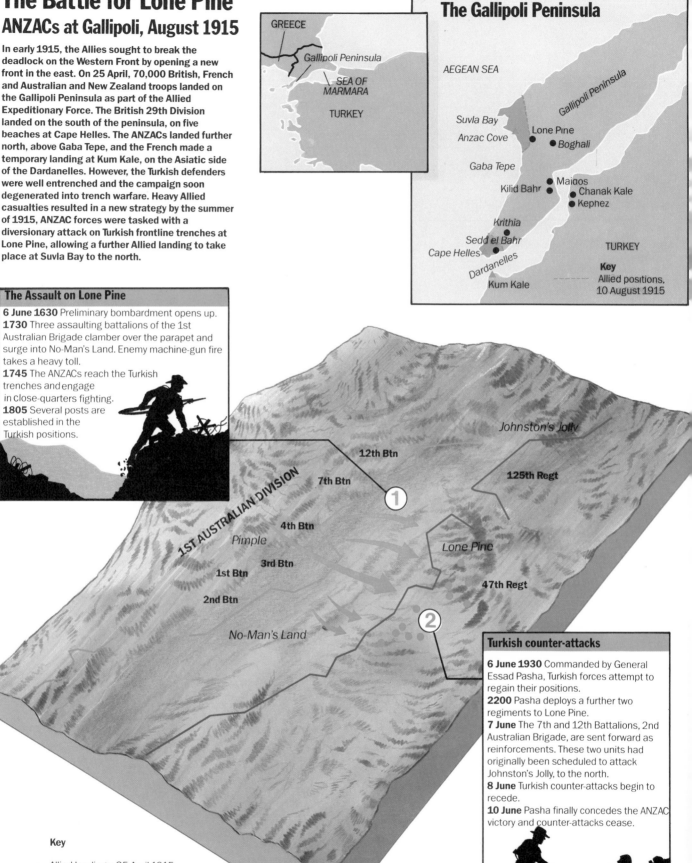

Johnston's Jolly

12th Btn

125th Regt

1ST AUSTRALIAN DIVISION

7th Btn

①

4th Btn

Pimple

Lone Pine

3rd Btn

47th Regt

1st Btn

2nd Btn

②

No-Man's Land

Turkish counter-attacks

6 June 1930 Commanded by General Essad Pasha, Turkish forces attempt to regain their positions.
2200 Pasha deploys a further two regiments to Lone Pine.
7 June The 7th and 12th Battalions, 2nd Australian Brigade, are sent forward as reinforcements. These two units had originally been scheduled to attack Johnston's Jolly, to the north.
8 June Turkish counter-attacks begin to recede.
10 June Pasha finally concedes the ANZAC victory and counter-attacks cease.

Key

▲ Allied landings, 25 April 1915
ANZAC front line, 5 August 1915
Turkish front Line, 5 August, 1915
→ Direction of ANZAC advance
● Posts established in Turkish trenches, 6 August 1915

Towards the end of 1914, the main theatre of war on the Western Front had ground down to a costly stalemate with little prospect of either side securing a decisive victory. However, with the entry of Turkey into the war as a German ally in early November 1914, Britain was provided with an opportunity to exert her maritime power in a new theatre of operations. Forcing the Dardanelles was seen by the Allies as the first step to an assault on Constantinople. Initially, the First Lord of the Admiralty, Winston Churchill, believed that this objective could be achieved by the Royal Navy. The naval attack began on 19 February 1915, but the results were disappointing in the face of strong Turkish resistance from coastline howitzers. When heavy losses were suffered at the hands of Turkish mines, the call went up for combined land and sea operations. A combined British, French and ANZAC expeditionary force, under the command of General Sir Ian Hamilton, was thus assembled in the spring of 1915. Its aim was to secure the Gallipoli Peninsula.

An amphibious assault was launched on 25 April, but logistical difficulties and well-organised Turkish defences meant that the Allied footholds at Cape Helles and Anzac Cove were very tenuous. It proved impossible to push inland, and a tactical stalemate developed. In early August, while ANZAC forces made diversionary thrusts towards the Sari Bair mountains, fresh landings were made at Suvla Bay. However, initial successes were thrown away by command failures and overall inexperience, and the beachhead was not fully exploited. This inability to make any headway on the peninsula led to growing demands for an Allied withdrawal.

During December 1915 and January 1916, well-planned evacuations enabled the troops to withdraw without loss of life – one of the few redeeming features of an otherwise disastrous campaign.

advance, was typical of many:

'The tension as we waited for the whistle was unbearable. We had some 70 or 80yds to go and as the fire grew hotter we might have been doubling over crisp straw as this was the impression the noise of the firing made on me. We had to go straight to the third-line trench over the top of the others. I got to this trench absolutely exhausted and was regaining my breath when a big Turk came charging along, being pursued by two Australians; as he passed me I shot him in the back. Immediately we met more Turks and I made an attempt to bayonet one but my bayonet stuck in his leather equipment and, as he was about to shoot me, he himself was shot by a rifle fired over my shoulder. I fired at a dark head peering from around the traverse and two bombs [grenades] came back in reply. I was paralysed with fear waiting for them to explode but none of us was seriously hurt. We got on to the fire-step to face Turks apparently about to attack when enfilade fire hit us all, killing six and leaving two of us wounded.'

Those troops attacking the main enemy front-line trench found the overhead cover of logs and sleepers that protected it largely intact, making it impossible for most of the men to get into the trench itself. Throughout this ordeal, the Australians were shot at from loopholes in the Turkish defences as they tried to hack a way in. One observer from the Australian side of No-Man's Land looked on helplessly:

'Men could be seen feverishly seeking a way into the trenches. One man rendered the most valuable service by working along the front of the Turkish trenches beneath the parapet, tearing down the loopholes that were made of clay and straw with his bayonet.'

A second wave of Australians struggled over No-Man's Land and launched themselves into the attack: some men joined in the task of dismantling the main Turkish fire trench, while others advanced towards the enemy communication trenches. Reaching their objective, these men jumped down and proceeded to work their way back to the covered trench.

The Turkish artillery reacted quickly to provide support for its defending infantry. Within five mintues of the Australian attack beginning, the enemy was tearing up No-Man's Land and had located the

Below: Australian troops man a crowded forward trench. The soldier on the left is using a periscope to monitor Turkish positions. To his right, a 'sniperscope' is being set up. Above: A wounded ANZAC makes his way to the field hospital.

Australian forward and second-line trenches. This caused casualties amongst the reserves and slowed down their movement up to the front line. The Australians fighting it out with the Turks for the Lone Pine position sent desperate arm signals for reinforcements and another wave was sent across. The once-packed Australian front-line trenches were emptying rapidly, leaving only a simple holding line. For Brigadier Smyth and his battalion commanders, the battle raged on in a state of almost total confusion; the five separate attempts by signallers to lay telephone wires across No-Man's Land had proved futile. The combination of high explosive shells and shrapnel had repeatedly severed the signal wires. After nearly half an hour of fighting, the walking wounded began to fall back to the Australian lines. With them came the news that although the three lines of Turkish trenches has been taken, they were far from secure. The fighting continued.

'From the north and south the enemy dashed forward with fixed bayonets'

The struggle to gain control of the trenches was exceptional in its ferocity – the Australians pressed on regardless of casualties while the Turks refused to give way. As small bands of Australians fought their way along the firing bays and traverses of Lone Pine's labyrinthine defences, the dead and dying choked the trenches, four and five men deep. One young soldier vividly remembered the sight of two men who had bayonetted each other simultaneously and remained impaled together. Both sides threw grenades around the traverses, especially the Turks who had large stocks at hand. To counter this, there were many instances of Australians fearlessly catching live grenades and throwing them back at the enemy.

The Australians kept up the pressure, and gradually the Turks began to give way. A notable coup that helped to knock the heart out of the Turkish defence was gained by Major Stevens of the 2nd Battalion, who had led a charge down a main trench, bombing and shooting as he advanced. The journalist Philip Schuler, who was at Lone Pine, recounts Stevens' exploit:

'Major Stevens came face to face with a German officer at the mouth of the tunnel. In this tunnel were some 70 Turks. The Australian was fired on at point blank by the German, but the shot missed its mark and the officer was shot dead by a man following Stevens. The Turks in the tunnel surrendered. They had gone there at the commencement of the bombardment, as was their custom, and had not had time to man the trenches before the Australians were on them.'

At 1830 hours the 1st Battalion was sent forward to strengthen the line and allow the remaining three, now very battered, battalions a temporary rest. Schuler was now in the Lone Pine system and there he recorded the next round of events:

'At 7pm, when the first clash of arms had passed, the enemy made their first violent and concerted effort to regain their lost trenches. It was a furious onslaught, carried on up the communication trenches by a veritable hail of bombs [grenades]. In some places we gave way, in others we drove the enemy further along his trenches. From the north and south the enemy dashed forward with fixed bayonets. They melted away before our machine guns and our steady salvoes of bombs. The Au-

stralians stuck to their posts in the face of superior numbers – four to one; they fought right through the night, and as they fought, strove to build up cover with whatever material came nearest to hand. Thousands of sandbags were used in making good the position.'

During the night, two of the tunnels that had been used for blowing the mines in front of the Turkish positions were tidied up and extended to form improvised trenches. One was used for sending up ammunition, food and drink, digging equipment and reinforcements, and the other served as a conduit for the steady stream of wounded coming back from Lone Pine.

Under cover of darkness, as the Australians built trench stops and swapped over the parapets and parados, the Turks launched attack after attack – their battle cries of 'Allah! Allah!' drowned out by the noise of Australian machine guns and rifles whose withering fire beat them back time after time.

For the next few days the Turks continued their relentless counter-attacks, throwing men forward regardless of the mounting casualties. Exchanging their fighting role from attackers to that of defenders, the Australians found the second phase of the battle as hard as the first. Although the 7th and 12th battalions of the 2nd Brigade moved up to reinforce the position, the Turks got into the Australian trenches on numerous occasions, and were either killed or ejected only at the point of a bayonet. Acts of the greatest courage were commonplace during this

Having reached Lone Pine, the assaulting battalions were subjected to a succession of frenzied Turkish counter-attacks. The Australians continued to surge forward, however, and at one point, pickets had to be posted in the ANZAC communication trenches leading up to Lone Pine to prevent men entering the fray without proper authority. Two days after the initial assault, the 7th Battalion (badge shown above) was moved forward to reinforce the captured positions. In the ferocious struggle that followed, four of the battalion's men earned the Victoria Cross: Corporal W. Dunstan (far right, above); Corporal A. Burton (far right, centre); and Lieutenants W. Symons and F. Tubb (right, from left).

Two hours after the initial assault by the 2nd, 3rd and 4th Battalions, the 1st Battalion rushed forward to consolidate the forward positions at Lone Pine (left). These reserve troops had waited in queues for the chance to push their way forward, and Captain A.J. Shout (bottom right) and Lieutenant L. Keyor (below) were later awarded the Victoria Cross for gallantry. Above: Private J. Hamilton (right of picture) of the 3rd Battalion, was also awarded the VC at Lone Pine.

Below: The grim reality of trench warfare. The attack on Lone Pine, so-called because of a solitary tree that stood behind the Turkish lines, claimed enormous casualties from the ANZACs – over 1700 all ranks. Turkish losses were even greater – estimated at 5000. Throughout the battle for Lone Pine, the men of the Australian 1st and 2nd Brigades had faced the enemy with a fighting spirit that astonished Allied commanders. General Sir Ian Hamilton, commander of the Allied expeditionary force, later commended their performance as 'a glory to Australia.'

Corporal, Australian Infantry, Gallipoli 1915

This soldier wears an Australian service dress tunic, corduroy breeches, woollen puttees and brown leather boots. On his head he wears an Australian bush hat. He is equipped with a leather bandolier, worn round the waist, which is part of the equipment used before the issue of 1908 webbing. Armament consists of a .303in SMLE Mk III Rifle, fitted with a 1907 Pattern sword bayonet with curved quillon.

epic defence, and the award of seven Victoria Crosses confirmed the Australians' sacrifice. Lieutenant F.H. Tubb of the 7th Battalion conducted one such defensive action with a party of 10 of his compatriots. Eight men were detailed to defend the parapet around an endangered and barricaded post. Two men, Corporals Webb and Wright, remained on the floor of the trench to catch and return grenades thrown in by the Turks. Meanwhile, Tubb stood on the parapet and gunned down the attacking Turks with his revolver. Inevitably, the corporals paid the ultimate price for their gallantry: Wright had a grenade blow up in his face, killing him, and Webb had both his hands blown off – he later died through loss of blood. Another attack caused the Australian outpost a further five casualties, including Tubb who was badly wounded in the arm and head. Refusing to give up, however, Tubb fought on supported by Corporals Dunstan and Burton. The Australian barricade was blown down a number of times but on each occasion the three soldiers rushed forward to rebuild the barricade. A grenade killed Burton and wounded Dunstan, but reinforcements arrived before the Turks could get into the trench. The attackers were permanently repelled. Tubb, Burton and Dunstan were all awarded the Victoria Cross.

By 10 August the Turks had finally accepted that the Australians had won Lone Pine, leaving hundreds of their dead piled up in front of the Australian trenches. The 1st Brigade suffered heavily too, losing over 50 per cent of its strength as a result of battlefield casualties. However, the 'Diggers' could look out triumphantly from their smashed up trenches secure in the knowledge that they had outfought 'Johnny Turk'.

The Australians had achieved their twin aims of capturing Lone Pine and drawing in the Turkish reserves. The British landings at Suvla Bay thus met with little opposition, and, although they failed to alter the final outcome of the campaign, it was through no fault of the indomitable Australians. At Lone Pine they forced the world to recognise the arrival of a new military nation. As battlefield soldiers, Australia's infantry had no betters.

THE AUTHOR Adrian Gilbert has edited and contributed to a number of military and naval publications. His book *World War I in Photographs* covers all aspects of the Great War.

HAND TO HAND COMBAT

The Scots Guards' attack on Mount Tumbledown during the Falklands War was a grim struggle against a tenacious foe

IF GOOSE GREEN was the best known of the battles for the Falklands, then perhaps the most hard-fought was the struggle for Mount Tumbledown, which took place on 13/14 June 1982 when the 2nd Battalion of the Scots Guards assaulted a well-defended position held by the best Argentinian unit in the Falklands, and, in a bitterly-contested night action, completely outfought the enemy, sending them back to Stanley and surrender.

The significance of the battle was duly recognised after the end of hostilities when the Scots Guards were awarded the battle honour 'Tumbledown Mountain'. Only the two battalions of The Parachute Regiment shared the distinction of battle honours in the Falklands campaign, for Goose Green, Mount Longdon and Wireless Ridge. Tumbledown was a soldiers' battle – its hand-to-hand fighting with fixed bayonets would have been recognisable to the veterans of World War I – and it was one that demonstrated the age-old military virtues of disci-

pline under fire, resolute leadership and simple, straightforward courage.

The two brigades that formed the land element of the British forces – 3 Commando Brigade and 5 Infantry Brigade – had undergone considerable

THE SCOTS GUARDS

In 1642 a Scottish regiment was raised to guard Charles I while he led his army in Ireland. Its motto: *Nemo me impune lacessit* (No-one molests me with impunity). Scattered by Cromwell at Worcester in 1651, it was re-formed as the Scottish Regiment of Foot Guards 15 years later in 1666, and was renamed the 3rd Regiment of Foot Guards in 1712. The regiment distinguished itself in the heroic defence of Hougoumont farmhouse at Waterloo in 1815. Redesignated the Scots Fusilier Guards in 1831, it fought in the Crimea, where it won five VCs, and was finally named the Scots Guards in 1877. It went on to fight campaigns in Egypt, Sudan and South Africa.

In World War I the two battalions of Scots Guards suffered appalling losses in the first battle of Ypres. In a famous attack at Loos they encountered 'a tornado of shrapnel fire'. Five VCs were won on the Western Front.

In World War II the regiment recruited the short-lived 5th Battalion ('the Snowballers') for the abortive Finnish campaign, and a 3rd Battalion in 1941. Scots Guards held Rommel's armoured advance at Rigel Ridge in the Western Desert. In 1944 the 3rd Battalion served in the 6th Guards Tank Brigade in northwest Europe. One VC was won in Tunisia. The Scots Guards today comprise two of a total of eight battalions in the Brigade of Guards.

Right: Heavily laden and ready for action, guardsmen wait for a helicopter to move them forward. The man on the left is in charge of the stand of an 81mm mortar. **Below:** The Scots Guards come ashore at San Carlos, preparing for the fight ahead.

Queen Elizabeth 2

Above: On board the *Queen Elizabeth 2* on the way south to the Falklands, men of the Scots Guards pose for a group photograph. Right: A Sea King helicopter lifts stores onto the *Canberra*, to which the battalion transferred at South Georgia, in order to keep the *Queen Elizabeth 2* out of the war zone. Above right: Testing weapons (here, a GPMG) during the final stages of the voyage to the Falklands. Right, main picture: Guardsmen dig in while supplies are heli-lifted forward, in preparation for the attack on the mountains around Stanley. Below: Brigadier Tony Wilson, commander of 5 Infantry Brigade.

reorganisation in the early stages of the campaign. The Scots and Welsh Guards and the 1st Battalion, 7th Gurkha Rifles, were assigned to reinforce an under-strength 5 Infantry Brigade that had 'lost' its two para battalions to 3 Commando Brigade when it had steamed south in early April.

While preparations were under way for 5 Brigade's departure for the Falklands in early May the Scots Guards conducted an intensive training programme at Sennybridge in Wales. The Welsh terrain was broadly similar to that of the Falklands and every attempt was made to simulate likely battlefield conditions. One notable exception was the weather; a Welsh summer – no matter how wet – was little preparation for the bitter cold encountered by the battalion in a Falklands deep in winter.

On 12 May the Scots Guards set sail for the South Atlantic aboard the liner *Queen Elizabeth 2*, and in conditions of comparative luxury the men went through weapons drill, physical exercise workouts and other forms of basic training that were possible within the ship's confines.

After transferring to the *Canberra* in order to ensure the safety of the *QE2* from Argentinian air attacks, the Scots Guards landed at San Carlos on 2 June. While San Carlos remained the logistic centre of British operations in the Falklands, by early June the fighting had moved elsewhere. Brigadier Tony Wilson, 5 Brigade's energetic commander, was determined that his men would get their share of the action and while 3 Commando Brigade advanced on Stanley from the west, his troops were to push forward from the south via Fitzroy and Bluff Cove.

The problem was the transport of his two battalions of guards from San Carlos over to the other side

Left: A section of Argentinian marines awaiting the British advance. Note their US M1 helmets with camouflage covers and tinted goggles.
Below: Scots Guardsmen at San Carlos manning a 0.5in Browning machine gun. The gun is tripod-mounted and fitted with an anti-aircraft sight.

5TH MARINE INFANTRY BATTALION

The fortified sangars on Mount Tumbledown were defended by men of Argentina's crack 5th Marine Battalion. Distributed among the fortified positions were their mortars and 10 sustained-fire machine guns.
The Argentinian Marine Corps is 10,000 strong and is divided into two Fleet Marine Forces, each of which includes an amphibious infantry brigade and two independent battalions, one for riverine and one for Antarctic operations.
The 5th Marine Battalion consists of 600 men, and alongside the marine infantry in the Falklands were combat support units from the 2nd Fleet Marine Force: the Amphibious Reconnaissance Group was landed with 12 Panhard AML Model 245 light armoured cars and 15 Mowag Roland armoured personnel carriers; while the 1st Marine Anti-Aircraft Regiment had a battery of Tigercat surface-to-air missiles and a single Roland SAM unit. However, the armoured vehicles were never used as they proved far less suitable for the rugged Falklands terrain than the tracked Scorpion and Scimitar light tanks of the British.

of the island. A straightforward cross-country march was ruled out and it was decided that a sea passage was the best solution. On the night of 5 June the assault ship HMS *Intrepid* slipped out of San Carlos Sound with 600 Scots Guardsmen aboard (the Welsh would follow the next night on HMS *Fearless*) and steamed south around East Falkland to Lively Island at the mouth of Choiseul Sound. There, because of the risk of land-based Exocet missiles sited on the coastline south of Stanley, *Intrepid* would launch her four LCUs (Landing Craft Utilities) which would then head northwards to Bluff Cove to disembark their guardsmen.

The voyage to Lively Island and the transfer to the LCUs went without a hitch but from then on events took a marked turn for the worse. By the early hours of 6 June weather conditions had deteriorated and within the exposed landing craft – intended for simple ship-to-shore operations – the guardsmen were soaked by flying spray, whipped up by 70-knot gusts of wind. Unwelcome drama was added to the battalion's discomfort when two warships were spotted bearing down on the LCUs, much to the consternation of the convoy's commander who, having been told that there would be no British ships in the area, had to assume that they were Argentinian.

Starshell burst over the LCUs – seemingly a prelude to a deadly barrage of high explosive which would send the defenceless craft to the bottom – but just in time a frantic exchange of Aldis messages flashed across the heaving seas, identifying all parties – the destroyer HMS *Cardiff* and the frigate HMS *Arrow* and the landing craft – as 'friendly'. Shortly before dawn, after a gruelling seven-hour voyage, the LCUs rounded Bluff Cove and the soaked guardsmen came ashore, meeting elements of 2 Para who had secured the Fitzroy-Bluff Cove area some days earlier.

The Scots Guards relieved 2 Para at Bluff Cove, establishing a defensive position in anticipation of new orders to move on to Stanley. The sheep-sheds around Bluff Cove were used on a rotational basis to dry the men out, an important factor in ensuring that cases of exposure and trench foot were kept to a minimum.

On the night of 7 June the battalion's reconnaissance platoon was sent forward along the coast to discover the whereabouts of two 105mm guns and a radar system thought to be around Port Harriet House, due south of Stanley. Although this information proved to be faulty, the patrol established a covert base forward of Port Harriet House to gather intelligence of Argentinian positions and the terrain around Stanley. This useful exercise was the battalion's first operation of the campaign. In marked contrast, the Welsh Guards suffered a baptism of fire over the adjoining bay at Fitzroy; they were surprised by a low-level attack by Argentinian aircraft that destroyed *Sir Galahad*, badly damaged *Sir Tristram* and caused heavy casualties. Responding to this attack as best they could, the Scots Guards claimed two Argentinian aircraft in a hail of small-arms fire, which did something to avenge the losses of their fellow guardsmen.

The battle for Stanley was planned as a two-phase assault. The first phase was to be conducted on the night of 11/12 June by 3 Commando Brigade who would secure Mount Longdon, Two Sisters and Mount Harriet, while the second phase would follow a day later and rely on 5 Infantry Brigade to take the 'inner circle' of hills overlooking Stanley. The key position in 5 Brigade's assault was Tumbledown itself, the Scots Guards' objective.

The exposed slopes of Tumbledown made a perfect killing ground for the Argentinian machine guns

The commander of the battalion, Lieutenant-Colonel Mike Scott, was far from happy with the plan of attack for Tumbledown. This called for an assault at first light against the mountain's southern slopes. Tumbledown dominated the surrounding terrain and its craggy rocks provided excellent defensive positions for the Argentinians, while the exposed slopes spreading out from Tumbledown made a perfect killing ground for their machine guns sited on the high ground. After detailed consultation with his officers and supporting battery commander, Colonel Scott concluded that a daylight assault would be suicidal folly and instead proposed a flanking attack at night, to be launched from the west of the summit.

The assault would be well supported and the battalion was provided with a fire plan that included five batteries of 105mm Light Guns, naval gun-fire from HMS *Active* and *Yarmouth*, plus the use of mortars from 42 Commando and the Gurkhas. Also promised was a strike by Harriers in a ground-attack role. Scott's plan called for a spirited diversionary assault from the southeast, spearheaded by the reconnaissance platoon, while the main advance, approaching from the west, would be conducted in three phases, each involving a company attack against a different section of Tumbledown.

The assault had originally been scheduled for the night of 12 June but a shortage of helicopters to fly the battalion to its assembly areas west of Goat Ridge ensured a postponement to the following night. One advantage of the delay was that it gave Colonel Scott a chance to show his company officers the objective in daylight and to discuss details of the forthcoming attack. On the morning of the 13th the

Guardsman, Scots Guards, Falklands 1982

This soldier wears a variety of winter clothes in standard British Army DPM. He is kitted out in cold weather overtrousers and over his parka is a nylon waterproof jacket (distinguishable by its bright colour). 'Northern Ireland' gloves and a pile-lined cap complete his cold-weather clothing. Fixed to his 7.62mm SLR is the Individual Weapon Sight Type SS20, an image-intensifying night-sight which can be used for target sighting up to a range of 700m. The SS20 works by electronically boosting weak natural light sources – such as starlight – to produce an effective image.

battalion was airlifted to its assembly area and the men dug in – a wise precaution as the Argentinians shelled the battalion for much of the day. The only casualty was one guardsman wounded.

Final battalion orders were issued at 1400 hours and company commanders went back to their units to run through the details of the assault with their junior officers. The recognition signal for the advance was the well-known Scottish phrase 'Hey Jimmy!', the reasoning behind it being that the Spanish-speaking Argentinians would be unable to pronounce the English letter 'J'. The three companies of the battalion were to advance down Goat Ridge, with G Company in the lead, followed by Left Flank and then Right Flank Companies. (The 2nd Battalion's company names derive from the positions they hold in ceremonial parades: G Company stands in the centre, with Left Flank and Right Flank Companies on either side.) Phase One of the plan entailed G Company capturing the westmost section of Tumbledown; in the next

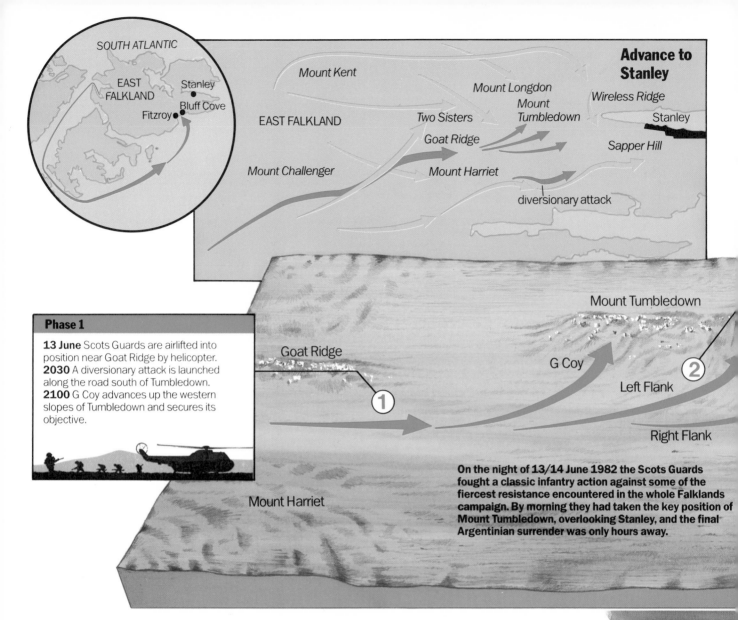

Advance to Stanley

SOUTH ATLANTIC

EAST FALKLAND

Stanley
Bluff Cove
Fitzroy

Mount Kent

EAST FALKLAND

Mount Longdon

Mount Tumbledown

Two Sisters

Wireless Ridge

Stanley

Goat Ridge

Sapper Hill

Mount Challenger

Mount Harriet

diversionary attack

Mount Tumbledown

Goat Ridge

G Coy

Left Flank

Right Flank

①

②

Phase 1

13 June Scots Guards are airlifted into position near Goat Ridge by helicopter.
2030 A diversionary attack is launched along the road south of Tumbledown.
2100 G Coy advances up the western slopes of Tumbledown and secures its objective.

Mount Harriet

On the night of 13/14 June 1982 the Scots Guards fought a classic infantry action against some of the fiercest resistance encountered in the whole Falklands campaign. By morning they had taken the key position of Mount Tumbledown, overlooking Stanley, and the final Argentinian surrender was only hours away.

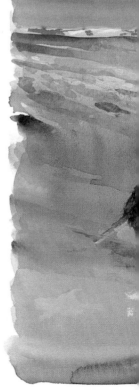

phase Left Flank would move through G Company and launch its assault on the main part of the mountain. Major John Kiszely was Officer Commanding Left Flank and a soldier respected by officers and men alike; his inspiring leadership was to be an important factor in the gaining of the summit. Phase Three involved Right Flank (commanded by Major Simon Price) moving round Left Flank and securing the eastern part of the mountain.

H-Hour for the main attack was set at 2100 hours, but 30 minutes before G Company crossed its start line the diversionary attack was launched. Commanded by Major Nicholas Bethell (back from a tour with the SAS) it consisted of three four-man assault groups drawn from the reconnaissance platoon and a fire-support group from battalion headquarters, together with a troop of Scorpion light tanks from the Blues and Royals.

The weather was bitterly cold and in the clear starlit night the diversionary force could make out Tumbledown and Mount William on their left as they advanced towards the Argentinian positions. The Scorpions had been assigned the task of drawing the enemy's fire and they moved down the main Stanley road. Argentinian tracer fire and various flares lit up the area, enabling Bethell's guardsmen to locate the enemy's forward positions.

The assault groups advanced towards the enemy

sangars, covered by the three GPMGs of the fire support group led by Company Sergeant-Major Braby. A general fire-fight ensued as the guardsmen pushed onwards while the Argentinians poured fire down upon them. Braby's men then dashed forward with tracer winging over their heads and alongside the assault groups they rushed the end sangar in the Argentinian defensive line; once there a GPMG was set up which enfiladed the other sangars. The Argentinians continued to resist but the guardsmen opened up a tremendous barrage of fire, which included the lobbing of innumerable phosphorus and high explosive grenades. The enemy fell silent; the attack had succeeded.

This attack had taken two hours and by now the main assault was well under way on Tumbledown, so with two guardsmen killed and four more wounded it was time to withdraw. The Argentinians now began to shell the retreating guardsmen but thanks to the boggy ground the fire had little effect. Covering the withdrawal Major Bethell and another guardsman were wounded by grenade shrapnel but worse followed when Lance-Sergeant Miller trod on an anti-personnel mine that severely wounded him, and three others were injured when another mine exploded.

The two dead guardsmen had to be abandoned. The survivors, carefully picking their way through

Mount Tumbledown
2nd Battalion, Scots Guards, 13/14 June 1982

Key
→ Scots Guards
→ Other British forces

Phase 2

13 June 2230 Left Flank passes through G Coy positions and is pinned down by heavy Argentinian fire.
14 June 0230 British artillery pounds Argentinian positions and Left Flank attacks up the slope towards the summit of Tumbledown. The guardsmen advance with fixed bayonets, urged on by Left Flank's commanding officer, Major John Kiszely. Overcoming stiff Argentinian resistance, Kiszely and 15 Platoon reach the summit.

Stanley

③

Mount William

Phase 3

As Left Flank continues to advance under fire, Right Flank launches an attack on the eastern edge of the mountain, taking bunker after bunker.
0815 Right Flank seizes its objective and the Argentinian forces fall back on Stanley. Some five hours later, as 2 Para march on Stanley, the cease-fire is announced.

the minefield with torches, arrived back at the start line just after midnight; by then Tumbledown was lit up by the artillery explosions and tracer fire of the main assault. Despite the casualties suffered, the attack had the desired effect of diverting enemy attention to the southeast, a fact confirmed by the captured Argentinian battalion commander after the battle.

At 2100, G Company advanced towards its objective on the western flank of Tumbledown. There was some sporadic artillery and mortar fire but the company's advance was not spotted by the Argentinians and, in the event, the leading platoon found their objective abandoned. The men of G Company quietly prepared their positions – undetected by the Argentinians – ready to support Left Flank which passed through them at 2230. Left Flank soon came under heavy fire from the Argentinians and G Company provided covering fire where it could for the guardsmen now beginning their difficult ascent of the higher slopes of Tumbledown.

Major Kiszely's tactical plan was to advance with two platoons forward and the third in reserve. Both forward platoons were to attack in parallel formation, moving eastwards; the left-hand platoon under 2nd Lieutenant Stuart clambered over the crags on the northern section of the ridge while Lieutenant Mitchell's platoon moved towards enemy positions on the lower slopes to the right.

'They have to skirmish through the position and get stuck in with their rifles and bayonets'

As Left Flank began to come under increasingly heavy and accurate fire it was realised that the enemy positions had been very well sited, and consisted of an intricate system of interlocking bunkers and sangars, some cut deep into the rock. The Argentinian battalion holding the mountain was the 5th Marines, a well-armed and well-trained unit which had no intention of quitting its excellent position. The main Argentinian firepower was provided by numerous 0.5in Browning machine guns, used to cover the main approaches of attack, and 7.62mm FN automatic rifles, some fitted with high-grade nightsights, which in the hands of Argentinian snipers began to exact a rising toll, killing two guardsmen and mortally wounding a sergeant.

Kiszely had advanced with Mitchell's platoon and he explained the opening stages of the attack:

'We were opened up on from about 300 metres by a couple of machine guns. The platoon led by Lieutenant Mitchell put in a section attack but it was beaten back. The section has two groups, one with a GPMG while the rest make a flanking attack. They have to skirmish through the position and get stuck in with their rifles and bayonets. They had bayonets fixed from the start. They throw grenades into the trenches and then mop up. There is no messing around; it is a question of getting on and keeping going.'

In the days leading up to the assault on Tumbledown many of the battalion's officers had buttonholed their fellow officers in 2 Para and the Royal Marines to find out what it was like fighting the Argentinians and the best ways of dealing with them. Their replies were invariably the same as that reported by Lieutenant Robert Lawrence (who suffered an appalling head wound and was awarded the Military Cross for his role in Right Flank's attack):

'I had spoken to some paras a couple of days beforehand and they had said, "Get within two hundred metres and they'll give up, and if they are in bunkers, hit them with 84mm rocket launchers and that bunker will drop out."'

The Scots Guards followed these basic tactics, blasting the Argentinian strongpoints with 66mm and 84mm rocket launchers as well as M79 grenade launchers but the Argentinians held firm.

The Scots Guards were now pinned down on the lower slopes of Tumbledown and remained there for two to three hours, unable to break the enemy defences. At the same time the planned fire support was proving difficult to bring to bear and in their exposed positions at the foot of Tumbledown the guardsmen of Left Flank were effectively contained.

They charged forward to the next ridge overpowering the Argentinians with rifles, grenades and bayonets

Kiszely had explained to his men how the Argentinians were expected to collapse after a concerted attack and a good blasting from the anti-tank weapons. As the attack ground to a halt in the first couple of hours of the 14th, Kiszely noted: 'There was a bit of a crisis of confidence. The boys were thinking: is the boss spinning us a line or what?" We were getting quite close hits with these anti-tank weapons, but they were staying there and fighting back.'

Kiszely realised that he would have to wait for the artillery to get on target to keep the enemy's heads down, otherwise an unsupported advance up the fire-swept slopes of Tumbledown would be suicidal. The pressure was on Left Flank to get the assault going but both Kiszely and Scott knew they had to wait for the artillery to do their work.

By 0230 British artillery rounds had begun to pound down in front of Mitchell's men and Kiszely ordered him to put in a platoon attack on the first ridge. With bayonets fixed they charged up the slope followed by Kiszely and company headquar-

Below left: Scots Guards, near Goat Ridge, moving up to a Westland Scout helicopter. Goat Ridge was the main piece of high ground before Tumbledown on the Scots Guards' axis of advance to Stanley. Note the SAS man in the right foreground, carrying an M16 – the standard US Army assault rifle. The M16 was lighter than the British Army's SLR, and had the capacity for fully automatic fire. As such, it was preferred by many British soldiers, and the SAS, able to choose their own weapons, used the M16 on occasion. Below right: Moving out, with packs on backs and SLRs at the ready.

ters. They made it to the ridge and then began a confused series of small fights from crag to crag.

As long as they could keep up the momentum, Kiszely felt that Left Flank could make the summit. The guardsmen were scattered around in the rocks and Kiszely ran forward calling out, 'Come on, come on', but found himself alone. '15 Platoon, are you with me?' he shouted out but again there was no reply. Fearing the worst he called back into the darkness. 'Come on, 15 Platoon, are you with me?' To his relief a voice replied, 'Aye sir, I'm with you,' followed by another, 'Aye sir, I'm fuckin' with you as well.'

They charged forward to the next ridge, overpowering the Argentinians with rifles, grenades and bayonets. Kiszely himself killed three enemy soldiers, shooting two and bayoneting the third. As the assault continued, the need to clear enemy bunkers and guard the increasing numbers of Argentinian prisoners depleted Left Flank's strength so that when Kiszely finally reached the top of Tumbledown he had only six men with him. Kiszely looked down. As he said later: 'It was amazing. I never imagined seeing Stanley lit up. We were so close we could see the grid plan of the streets, with vehicles moving. I could not believe my eyes.' Suddenly an Argentinian machine gun opened up and badly wounded three guardsmen. The rest only just managed to keep the ridge in British hands until reinforcements arrived in the form of Right Flank under Major Price.

Although the battle was turning in the Scots Guards' favour the Argentinians were far from broken and hung onto their positions on the eastern side of Tumbledown. Price decided to hold one platoon back in reserve to provide covering fire for the other two platoons which were sent forward around Left Flank. M79 grenade launchers and 66mm LAWs (Light Anti-tank Weapons) were the

BRITISH ARTILLERY SUPPORT

The British Artillery support in the Falklands was supplied by 18 105mm Light Guns of 3 Commando Brigade and a further 18 of 5 Infantry Brigade. Usually deployed in batteries of six guns apiece, each gun has a crew of six men.

Most transport of the guns was done via helicopter airlift. A Sea King or Puma would take out the gun, slung under the craft with cables, with four of the crew aboard. A lighter helicopter such as the Wessex would bring up about 24 shells and the other crewmen. Finally a complement of 100 shells would follow, slung below in a net. Wastage of nets was unexpectedly high and helicopters were forced to wait while the net was unloaded in order to claim it for further use.

Of the 100 shells, about 80 would be 16.1kg high explosive. The thin hardened steel of their manufacture allows 20 percent of their weight to be explosive and gives maximum lethal fragmentation effectiveness. The other shells would comprise white phosphorus, smoke and illumination shells, the ratio depending on the requirements of the battery commander.

Illumination shells (which eject a magnesium flare at a selected height, from where it floats down on a parachute) were used to give overhead battlefield illumination: they were also pitched behind enemy lines to silhouette their positions and expose them to fire. Though normally equipped with laser target designators and night vision instruments, the spotters dumped this extra weight and used hand-held laser rangefinders and detached rifle nightsights, combining their observations with traditional map and compass work. Their tasks complete, the Light Gun, extremely accurate with a range of 17km, could be brought to bear.

COURAGE CAUGHT ON

'I think everybody learnt something about themselves on Tumbledown; some with shame, some with pride, some with surprise. Fear is infectious; but what I never realised until Tumbledown is the fact that in exactly the same way courage is also infectious. In those first few moments when the bullets are flying around and everybody is lying down, looking around to see what the bloke next door is doing or what the platoon commander is doing, you realise that probably nobody has done this before. They are questioning themselves; how do you behave, what are you meant to do? If the first thing they see is people being scared, people running away, people not there with a rifle looking out for the enemy but lying hiding, cowering under a rock, they will do that as well. If, however, they see people doing courageous things, they will think this is obviously what one is meant to do in battle, and so will do it. Now that's something that surprised me, and I was very lucky because in my company – and absolutely nothing to do with me – that's what caught on, because people were seen doing very brave things early in the battle. People who under other circumstances might have lain behind the rock were doing very brave things right the way through the battle. Courage caught on – it was absolutely contagious.'

Major John Kiszely, commander of Left Flank

favoured weapons of the guardsmen of Right Flank but, as Left Flank had found, the Argentinians often had to be forced from their sangars at the point of a bayonet. Inevitably the advance became fragmented and the platoon commanders experienced considerable difficulty in directing their men towards their objectives in the darkness.

Lieutenant Lawrence's platoon became pinned down alongside Left Flank, under fire from an Argentinian machine-gun nest. Lawrence began to crawl towards the Argentinians armed with a phosphorus grenade while his platoon covered him with an intense barrage of rifle fire. Bullets ricocheted off the rocks around him, and at one point he found himself under fire from three directions, from the Argentinians in front of him, from his own platoon behind him and from men of nearby Left Flank. Finally Lawrence edged himself to a position just below the rock covering the Argentinian position:

Left: Triumphant Scots Guards on the summit of Mount Tumbledown. Below: Under an escort of Scots Guards, a file of Argentinian prisoners is marched to Stanley after the battle.

'I threw the grenade,' he explained afterwards, 'and I screamed to my platoon to come on. It was probably the most fantastic thing in my life because they all did just that; every single man leapt up and charged forward. We went in so mad without thinking and just ran over the machine-gun post. And having been told that there was just one machine gun in it, we found out there were three!'

The determination of Right Flank to close with the enemy proved to be the key to victory, and bit by bit the Argentinians were pushed back off the mountain. By 0815 hours Right Flank had secured its objective and the Scots Guards were finally in possession of Mount Tumbledown. The battalion had suffered 50 casualties – nine dead and 41 wounded – but the exhausted guardsmen could look down and see their opponents, the Argentinian 5th Marine Infantry Battalion, streaming back towards Stanley.

THE AUTHOR Adrian Gilbert has edited and contributed to a number of military and naval publications and is a co-author of *Vietnam: The History and the Tactics*.

DEATH WALKERS

Portuguese paratroopers in Angola were operating in hostile terrain, where ambushes were common, the roads were strewn with mines, and death lurked around every corner

CORPORAL VINCENTE Mocosso Mavungo, a Cabindan-born black African serving in the Portuguese Army, sat in the back of a Unimog truck, a heavy machine gun in a turret above him and his standard-issue G3 German assault rifle within easy reach. Although it was broad daylight, visibility was so poor in the sweltering, putrid jungle of the Cabinda Enclave that one of Mavungo's colleagues remarked that they should switch on the truck's headlights.

As the Unimog skirted a swamp, a burst of fire from the right – known and feared by the Portuguese as the *flagelação* or whipping burst – killed both Mavungo's companions. Simultaneously, an explosion underneath the front wheels brought the truck to a lurching halt, the two men in the cab were severely wounded by the upward blast that tore off the roof. Instinctively, Mavungo seized his rifle, flipped the safety catch off and began replying to the fire from the surrounding jungle.

A grenade exploded at the rear of the truck, a fragment searing his back, while his face was creased by another fragment from one of the bullets spraying into the truck. Mavungo hurled his own grenades – the long, tubular Portuguese grenades with four-second fuses – and jumped down to retrieve those of his dead comrades. He threw these, too, into the undergrowth, but by now his ammunition was expended and the pain of his wounds was becoming intense. He suddenly remembered the machine gun and dragged himself up to the bullet-proofed turret and began to swing the gun on its mounting. He had fired off the first belt when he finally collapsed from his wounds. Four hours later another Portuguese patrol found Mavungo and the two badly wounded Portuguese still in the cab. The other two lay dead on the ground while, in the jungle fringe, eight guerrillas also lay dead. Almost a year later, in June 1968, Mavungo was awarded the Cross of War, Third Class, for his courage in the ambush.

Corporal Mavungo's home, the Cabinda Enclave, is a small part of Angola separated from the main body by a strip of Congo territory. His patrol had come into contact with guerrillas of the MPLA who, based in sanctuaries in the Congo Republic, had begun infiltration operations into Cabinda in 1963. The practice of operating from friendly territory across the borders of the Portuguese colonies was being repeated elsewhere. The FNLA, for example, was launching its attacks into the heavily wooded mountains of north Angola from bases in neighbour-

Left: Armed with a G3 assault rifle, a Portuguese soldier inches forward through the hostile Angolan bush on the trail of guerrillas. Bush patrols were carried out in absolute silence – the only form of communication being sign language – and were so successful in this respect that the Portuguese were called the 'death walkers'. When the Portuguese colonial revolts first broke out in the early 1960s, the initiative lay with the nationalist guerrilla groups who were faced with a relatively weak Portuguese military presence. By 1968, however, Portugal had greatly strengthened its forces in Africa and was engaged in all-out warfare against guerrillas in Angola, Mozambique and Guinea. Right: A Portuguese bush patrol launches a surprise raid into a village in Mozambique in search of guerrillas and weapons caches. Above, inset: The third series cap badge of the Portuguese paratroopers.

PORTUGUESE AFRICA

By the early 1960s, Portugal had become the only European colonial power still holding on to its African possessions. Nationalist movements emerged in Angola, Portuguese Guinea and Mozambique.

The first of these appeared in 1956, the Angolan Movimento Popular de Libertação de Angola (MPLA) and the Guinean Partido Africano da Independência da Guiné e Cabo Verde (PAIGC). Two years later another group was founded in Angola, the Frente Nacional de Libertação de Angola (FNLA), from which a significant offshoot movement was formed, the União Nacional para a Independência Total de Angola (UNITA). Meanwhile, men in Mozambique formed the Frente de Libertação de Moçambique (FRELIMO).

The first outbreak of guerrilla activity occurred in March 1961 in Angola, and was followed by armed conflict in Portuguese Guinea in 1963 and Mozambique in 1964. Portuguese response was to build up their troops to engage and defeat the guerrillas.

By 1974 it was clear that although the Portuguese had succeeded in imposing a stalemate in the warfare, there was little possibility of decisive victory over the nationalists. The army itself came to believe that a fundamental change in government policy was necessary. In April 1974 the right-wing government of Marcello Caetano was overthrown in a coup and by November 1975 all the colonies were independent.

'FORCES OF INTERVENTION'

ng Zaire. One of the first tasks of the growing Portuguese army was thus to seal off border routes.

The Portuguese 'forces of intervention' usually divided a colony into a number of territorial or theatre commands – there were five in Angola and three in Mozambique. Units were made available at theatre level for the interventionary role. Below theatre level, tactical responsibility was shared by sector commands, and further sub-divided into battalion and company commands. Intervention forces could also be made available at local level for specific tasks such as immediate reinforcement and convoy escort, or similar mobile roles.

Precise tactics were determined by the nature of the terrain in each colony, which varied from the flooded interior of Guinea to the open savannah of eastern Angola. Much also depended on the season, since all the colonies were subject to the tropical or semi-tropical climatic cycle of a cool dry season (April to September in Angola and Mozambique, and October to March in Guinea) followed by a hot rainy season (in the remaining months). For instance, large-scale operations by the Portuguese were only possible in the dry season, while their guerrilla foes preferred to operate in the rainy months when thicker vegetation and low cloud cover reduced the threat from the air. The Portuguese had air superiority until the guerrillas introduced surface-to-air missiles in the early 1970s.

Each Alouette carried five men and mounted either a machine gun or a 20mm grenade launcher

Air power offered the opportunity of attacking guerrilla infiltration routes and also provided a quick-reaction force. Ultimately, however, the Portuguese needed to get to grips with the guerrillas on the ground, and the introduction of the Alouette helicopter in 1966 transformed Portuguese strategy. The elite units now had far greater mobility. In Angola, for example, the arrival of the helicopters coincided with the opening of the MPLA's 'eastern front' in the Moxico and Bié regions. By 1971 some 60 Alouettes were available, each carrying five men and able to mount either a machine gun or a 20mm grenade launcher. Parties could now be dropped either to reinforce ground patrols or to block guerrilla escape routes. In 1966, 1968 and 1972, large-scale operations in eastern Angola compelled the MPLA to stop their infiltration from Zambia, thus limiting them to their original operations from the Congo Republic.

Heliborne operations were only a part of the Portuguese response to guerrilla activity. In other respects, technology was not of paramount importance to Portuguese counter-insurgency. Thus, cavalry was used effectively, with three squadrons deployed in Angola from 1966, and more under training in Mozambique by 1974. Cavalry was used to protect the flanks of advancing troops in difficult terrain and, when supplied by helicopter, could mount extended patrols. It might be added that the horses sometimes acted as effective shock absorbers when troops strayed into a minefield.

The mine was by far the most effective weapon of the guerrillas. In 1970, over 50 per cent of Portuguese casualties in Angola were caused by them. The newer and more sophisticated mines could not be located by mine detectors (few of which were in any case available) and so the Portuguese resorted to the *pica* or sharpened stick. Depending on the width of the track to be cleared, one or two men ahead of a

'FORCES OF INTERVENTION'

The uprisings in Portugal's major African territories provoked the immediate deployment of large numbers of troops. The majority of these troops were conscripts who were not involved in anti-guerrilla warfare. Instead, they performed garrison duties in strategic villages and carried out 'social promotion' programmes, such as building amenities, to turn the local populations against the guerrillas.

It was the 'forces of intervention', professional soldiers of the Portuguese Army, heavily supported by black recruits, who met the guerrillas in combat. These elite fighting units included paratroops, marines, commandos and naval fusiliers, and up to 35 per cent were black Africans.

Also fighting in the territories were highly organised local formations such as the Commandos Africanos, the Grupos Especiais (GE) and the airborne Grupos Especiais de Paraquedistas (GEP), of which over 90 per cent were black Africans.

In addition to units fielded by the army, the Portuguese secret police organised a force known as the *Flechas* (arrows) which acted as a long-range reconnaissance group in Mozambique. The majority of the *Flechas* were guerrillas who had been captured and 'turned' by the Portuguese. They were highly valued and enjoyed many privileges.

G3A3

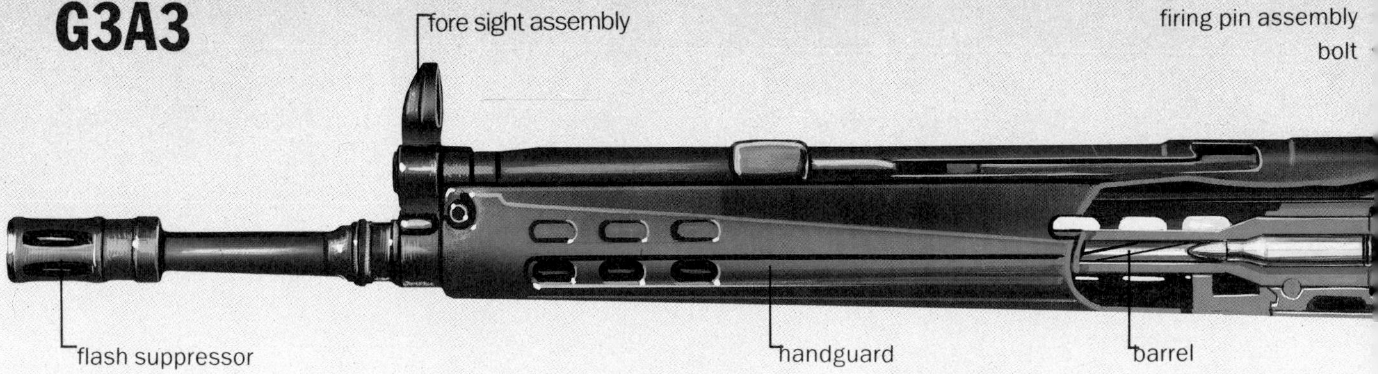

fore sight assembly

firing pin assembly
bolt

flash suppressor

handguard

barrel

patrol would carefully feel the ground for soft area that might indicate recent digging. If one was found the *picadors* would then probe the area for the unmistakeable hollow 'clonk' of a mine. Other members of the patrol would remain vigilant as this was often a moment of ambush. Having located a mine the *picadors* would then ensure that no second mine was placed alongside it to trap the unwary.

The Portuguese improvised the use of special trucks with sandbagged floors and tyres half filled with water to lead convoys and deflect mine blast but in the long term an extensive programme of road-tarring was implemented to make it more difficult for the guerrilla to lay his mines undetected. The road building programme reached 8000km in Angola by 1974 and was being completed at a rate of 1400km a year by 1972 in Mozambique, achievements that far exceed those of either the British over 12 years in Malaya or the USA over six years in Vietnam. Rightly, a Portuguese official once commented that 'revolt starts where the road ends'.

Other simple responses by the Portuguese to the

olt head carrier
recoil spring
selector cam
ejector
rotary rear sight
trigger
sear
magazine
hammer
grip
stock

Calibre 7.62mm
Length 102.5cm
Weight (loaded) 5kg
Magazine 20-round box
Cartridge 7.62 x 51mm NATO round
Rate of fire (practical auto) 100rpm
Muzzle velocity 780-800mps
Maximum effective range 400m

Above: The West German Heckler and Koch G3A3 assault rifle. The G3 is manufactured under licence in Portugal and is part of a large 'family' of weapons which includes a light machine gun version, the HK11, and a belt-fed machine gun variant, the HK21. The G3 is constructed from metal stampings, making it cheap and easy to manufacture, and is fitted with a tough plastic stock and forward handguard. It is easy to strip down and can be fitted with a range of accessories, including rifle grenades, making it ideally suited to the conditions of small-unit actions. Left, top: A column of Portuguese trucks swings off the road to avoid an uncovered pit dug by guerrillas. Booby traps, pits and mines took a heavy toll on the Portuguese forces and convoys had to be constantly on the alert for signs of recent digging in the roads. Left, centre: Portuguese soldiers leap into action against a suspected guerrilla ambush position in the bush by the roadside. Left, below: A Portuguese soldier stands ready to provide supporting fire for his comrades going in to root out a guerrilla detachment hiding in the long bush grass.

threat of guerrilla ambush included ringing their own positions with wires hung with empty beer bottles, an early-warning system just as effective as sensors. A standard anti-ambush technique was to hurl grenades into the bush when dismounting from vehicles under fire, in case guerrillas were lying in ambush close to the road to catch the Portuguese as they took cover. Apart from mines, the ambush was the most deadly weapon of the guerrillas – the frequent long-range bombardments with mortars or 122mm rockets were rarely effective.

The Portuguese discovered that small operations on foot offered far better chances of thoroughly disrupting guerrilla activities than large-scale raids, which tended only to shift the guerrillas to somewhere else. In 1968, for example, one observer in the heavily forested Dembos mountains of Angola found that 30-man patrols of three-to-five-days duration had become the norm: in Guinea in 1971 the same observer found that the *Commandos Africanos*, elite black troops formed in 1968, had organised themselves into similar patrols. To examine them more closely, let us follow two such patrols, the first based at Zemba in Angola, the second at Tite in Guinea and led by Captain Joao Bacar, who held the highest Portuguese military decoration, the gold Order of the Tower and the Sword.

Moving out of Zemba in 1968, each of the 30 men in the patrol had a distinct function, and would also know the duties of the two men directly in front and behind him in the single file. All communication would be in sign language to maintain strict silence. All metal parts of their uniforms and equipment would be bound in cloth, while the canvas boots with rubber soles worn by the Portuguese minimised any sound of movement over the rotting vegetation on the jungle floor. So effective were these precautions that the guerrillas in Angola came to describe the men as 'the death walkers'. A variety of weapons would be carried, often three heavy machine guns and a bazooka or mortar or, alternatively, three mortars and a recoilless rifle. Those who were not responsible for the heavier weapons would carry ammunition, their rifles and, from 1969, two Instalaza rifle grenades.

In eastern Angola a five-day patrol might cover as much as 100km or even more in the open savannah. Tracks would be avoided if possible to minimise the risk of booby traps such as grenades attached to trip wires, or the Chinese anti-personnel mines, known to American veterans of the Vietnam War as 'Bouncing Betties', which would come spinning out of the earth to explode at groin height when men trod on their prongs. Approaching a village where guerrillas might be encountered, scouts would be sent ahead to determine its size and approaches. The patrol, split into three sections, would then go into the assault.

In the case of Bacar's Guinea patrol in 1971, the men followed a predetermined course over the five days in order to avoid both their own minefields and the possibility of attack by Portuguese air sorties that had been planned for the time. Three 'walkie-talkies' were carried and Bacar was able to call up air support if required. Such patrolling became a deadly cat-and-mouse game as Portuguese and guerrillas alike worked to outwit the other in cunning ambushes. Again, a patrol might return without having once made contact with the enemy. As it happened, Bacar himself ran out of luck during a patrol in April 1971. Caught by the detonation of a

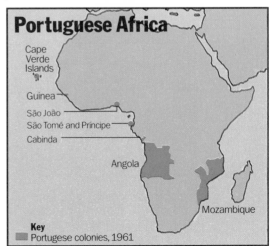

Portuguese Africa

Cape Verde Islands
Guinea
São João
São Tomé and Principe
Cabinda
Angola
Mozambique

Key
Portugese colonies, 1961

Above: The hardship and strain of prolonged anti-guerrilla warfare is clearly visible on the faces of these Portuguese troops as they wait in ambush for a guerrilla column. Long periods of isolation, poor living conditions and basic rations tested their powers of endurance to the full.

Portuguese Paratrooper, Angola 1975

Most Portuguese soldiers wore camouflage uniforms in the African colonies and this soldier wears fatigues cut from a French camouflage pattern. A distinctive feature is the camouflage cap. Black army boots are worn although civilian footwear was popular. This soldier is armed with a West German designed 7.62mm G3A3 rifle, the main smallarm of Portuguese infantry in Africa, and one of the most effective. Ammunition pouches for holding spare G3 magazines are worn on his webbing waist belt. Although Portuguese troops lacked heavy support weapons they were adequately equipped on a personal level.

mine and a subsequent hail of fire his men had dived for cover. In trying to throw grenade, Bacar slipped on wet ground and threw himself on his own grenade to save his men.

The Portuguese wars in their African coloni lasted for over 10 years in Mozambique, 11 years Guinea and 13 years in Angola. The Portuguese d not lose the wars in Guinea and Angola in a milita sense, for the campaigns developed into stalemate the one in Guinea effectively containing the mo successful guerrilla group, PAIGC, by 1974. Only Mozambique were the Portuguese problems stead ly increasing. Then, as it turned out, the outcome w not decided on the battlefield at all, but by unexpected coup d'etat which swept the Caetan regime from power in Portugal in April 1974. The w had undoubtedly caused strain in Portuguese soci ty and had cost an estimated 13,000 dead, the majo ty of whom had been serving in Portugal's eli fighting units. Ironically, the very fact that profe sional soldiers and not conscripts had done most the fighting was a significant factor in the coup origin. Prime Minister Marcello Caetano had i advisedly introduced a new system that, while e couraging conscript officers, caused anger and di content among the professional men who we fighting his war in Africa, eventually leading them participate in the coup against him.

Before political events in Portugal had radical changed the situation in the African colonies, th forces of intervention had been remarkably su cessful in carrying out their brief. Portugal claime that less than two per cent of Angolan territory w controlled by the guerrillas in 1973. In Guinea, whe the PAIGC was steadily accumulating ever mor sophisticated equipment, guerrilla losses still grea ly outnumbered those of the Portuguese. In Mozan bique guerrilla losses were also high, about 125 annually compared to, for example, Portugal's loss 200 men in 1972. In spite of the guerrillas' fierce an resourceful campaigns in the three countries, th Portuguese proved themselves in each case to b the superior fighting force.

THE AUTHOR Ian Beckett, a lecturer in the Departmer of War Studies at The Royal Military Academ Sandhurst, is a leading specialist in guerrilla warfar and counter-insurgency operations. He has writte several books, including *Politicians and Defence*

RANGERS AT WAR

Formed in the early spring of 1943, when 500 men were selected from some 2000 volunteers, the US Army's 2nd Ranger Battalion completed its basic training by the following November and was then despatched to England. During the build-up to D-day, the battalion was stationed in Cornwall, on the Isle of Wight and in Dorset, where the rangers put the finishing touches to their cliff-assault drill.

On D-day, three of the unit's companies, D, E and F, were detailed to capture a large coastal battery at the Pointe du Hoc, a chalk promontory overlooking Omaha beach. Despite heavy losses and fierce German counter-attacks, the rangers, led by Colonel Jim Rudder, held the position for two days until relieved.

After receiving several drafts of replacments in July and August, the battalion was then thrown into the battle for the Brittany port of Brest. On 9 September, Rudder's men took the Lochrist (Graf Spee) battery and captured nearly 2000 enemy troops during the subsequent mopping-up operations. After the fall of the port on the 18th, the battalion participated in the Allied drive to the German frontier, passing through Paris and Luxembourg on the way east.

Fighting inside the Third Reich in December, the rangers were heavily involved in the battle for Bergstein. Taking on a superior enemy force, the battalion was able to capture a vital hill, a position the men held until early March 1945. As the war drew to a close, the rangers advanced through Leipzig and pushed into Czechoslovakia. At Pilsen, the unit was stood down and was finally disbanded in July.

Above: The shoulder flash worn by members of the 2nd Ranger Battalion during World War II.

On D-day the men of the US 2nd Ranger Battalion went in to assault a German gun battery that threatened the main landings on Omaha beach

D-DAY, 6 June 1944. An Allied landing ship, the *Ben My Chree*, rolled in a heavy swell as she swung into the fierce gale blowing towards the Normandy beaches. From her bridge, Colonel Jim Rudder, the commanding officer of the US Army's 2nd Ranger Battalion, could just make out another landing vessel, the *Amsterdam*, as she also came up to drop anchor. Together, the two ships carried the three ranger companies whose job was to scale the massive chalk cliffs of the Pointe du Hoc and take out a large-calibre coastal battery whose guns overlooked Omaha beach and could pour fire down on the fleet lying offshore.

The rangers had breakfasted an hour before – at least those men who could face bacon and eggs – and had packed away most of their kit. The assault teams, facing a tricky climb up a 100ft cliff face, could only carry their carbines and a few Browning automatic rifles. Speed was vital, the rangers had to reach the battery and spike the guns, before the Germans could bring up reinforcements; too much equipment would only delay their ascent. Their preparations completed, Rudder's men began boarding the six assault craft that would take them to their objective. Five of the craft were specially equipped LCAs (Landing Craft, Assault); the sixth carried demolition charges, reserves of ammunition and rations.

Technical Sergeant John I. Cripps clambered aboard *LCA887* as the little craft swayed on the falls of the *Ben My Chree*'s davits. The crew seemed unperturbed by the motion, but Cripps was surprised by the rough water, four-foot waves were sloshing into the LCA, and was worried that the dousing might soak the rocket lines she carried. Six of these three-quarters-of-an-inch-thick ropes were coiled up in open boxes that lay next to the rocket-powered grappling hooks mounted on the stern of the assault craft. With so much equipment onboard, there was little room for the 20 rangers who the LCA was to carry to the shore. The men had all rehearsed their boatwork and, once onboard, settled themselves under the side-decks, crouching on low slats.

Another ranger, Sergeant Bill Petty, supervised the loading of several alloy ladder sections. Each four-foot length of ladder weighed four pounds, but *LCA887* carried 28 and they took up plenty of room. If the rangers' long-practised assault drill paid off, the sections would be slotted together to form a ladder long enough to top the cliff.

The four other grapnel-carrying LCAs and the other stores-carrier, all from the *Amsterdam*, hit the

dark waters of the Channel at 0415 hours. Despite the relative protection offered by the two landing ships, the rangers were relieved to be off; the coxswains moved out to circle off the *Ben My Chree*'s stern. There, the rest of the flotilla joined up with *LCA887*, in readiness for the 10-mile run to Pointe du Hoc. When all was ready, Rudder, in the lead craft, had a message flashed out to a motor launch, the *ML194*, that would guide the assault teams to their target. Astern of the launch was a Landing Craft, Tank, the *LCT415*, with four DUKW amphibians aboard. Two were modified to carry turntable ladders that could be extended up the cliffs and fitted with Lewis guns to provide covering fire during the assault. The other pair carried the assault teams' support weapons that would be used to hold the cliff-top position until infantry units had fought their way off Omaha beach to the east of the battery and relieved the rangers.

The little convoy started out for the enemy-held

Below: In the Allied build-up to D-day, members of the US Army's 2nd Ranger Battalion practise unarmed combat. Their mission on 6 June was to climb the Pointe du Hoc cliffs to take out a coastal battery. Right and below right: Rangers learn rock-climbing techniques. Above right: On their way to France, Rangers smile for the camera.

STORMING THE HEIGHTS

shore at 0430, while it was still dark. Only the first streaks of pre-dawn light betrayed the course of the assault craft. However, the tossing seas began to take their toll: *LCA860*, swamped by heavy waves, foundered. Despite her rangers bailing like fury with their helmets, one of the store-carrying LCAs was also overwhelmed and ten minutes later, the second store-carrier sank. She had fallen behind the flotilla, her cargo-well waterlogged, and was lost.

The sinking of the two store-carriers was a bitter blow: without their explosives to blast the gun emplacements, without any reserves of ammunition and rations, save for the emergency supplies that each man carried in his pockets, Rudder's men faced a much more dangerous challenge. However, Rudder had watched his rangers train for this operation, in America and later in England, where at Bude in Cornwall, they had perfected their cliff-assault techniques, and had no hesitation in signalling his HQ ship that the landing would take place as planned.

The light was getting stronger as the flotilla closed on the coast. From his vantage point, Rudder could make out the deceptively quiet beaches of Omaha and the grim outline of the cliffs of Pointe de la Percée that linked up with the Pointe du Hoc, lying some three miles to the west. During the next hour, as the assault craft made their final approach, Rudder watched in awe as the mighty USS *Texas* lobbed 14in shells onto the battery. Only at 0600 hours did the fury of the pre-landing bombardment abate, allowing 14 USAAF medium bombers to put in a low-level attack against the German guns.

Rudder could see that all this preparatory activity was taking place some distance to the west of the point on the coast where the flotilla was heading, and at 0630, when the rangers should have been hitting the beach below the chalk cliffs, the LCA officers realised that they were off course and heading for the Pointe de la Percée. In a violent manoeuvre, the flotilla turned westwards and for the next 30 minutes headed on

a track that ran a mere 100yds from the coast. Alerted to the threat, the German defenders opened fire on the vulnerable craft.

Bullets rattled against the armoured sides of *LCA887*; Petty in the bows kept his head down, but took a few, quick 'look-sees' to assess his craft's position, noticing mortar shells bursting around the flotilla. His LCA was seventh in a line of nine craft that were stretched out over a distance of 500 yds. By the time they were level with the little shingle beach below the Pointe du Hoc and had turned at full speed to make the final run in, the rangers were nearly 50 minutes behind schedule. The Germans above had recovered from the bombardment and only fire from two destroyers kept the enemy from manning their defences.

As *LCA887's* ramp hit the shingle, Petty leapt ashore, only to disappear up to his neck in a water-filled crater. The unit photographer and other rangers were in a similar plight, and as they struggled to clamber from these pits, grenades burst on the shore, despite the crew of *LCA861* chasing four Germans from their cliff-top post with their Lewis gun.

The craft's rangers fired her rocket lines, but the ropes travelled less than 30ft, being heavy with seawater. A hand-launched line was more successful and one man, Private Harry Roberts, was able to claw his way up the perpendicular face of the cliff and get a footing on the shallower slope above. He was nearly halfway up the rope when it broke free or was cut, and was sent plunging to the foot of the cliff. However, he went up a second line and reached a crater under the lip of the cliff, but the rope broke

Below left: Sheltering from enemy fire and the spray whipped up by a choppy Channel, US troops head for Omaha beach. Pointe du Hoc, a few miles to the west, overlooked the landing site and the battery's guns could have done considerable execution to the assault forces. The neutralisation of the guns was considered a vital prerequisite to the success of Operation Overlord. Below right: Men of Colonel Jim Rudder's 2nd Ranger Battalion prepare to embark on a small landing craft. Many of these vessels were specially converted for the attack on the enemy's cliff-top position.

Pointe du Hoc
US 2nd Rangers, 6 June 1944

On D-day, 6 June 1944, an Allied armada transported a vast army onto the beaches of Normandy. The US 1st Infantry Division was tasked to establish a bridgehead on Omaha beach — but at Pointe du Hoc, to the west, a German cliff-top battery could have wreaked havoc among the American troops. The US 2nd Ranger Battalion was given the task of securing the position and destroying the enemy's artillery and ammunition — a difficult operation involving a perilous assault up a 100ft cliff face. Early in the morning, as the main invasion force made its way towards the beaches, the Rangers embarked on their assault landing craft for the final run-in. They took the battery and held the position for two days against heavy German attacks before a force of the 5th Ranger Battalion was able to make its way along the coast road and link up with the remnants of the embattled 2nd Rangers.

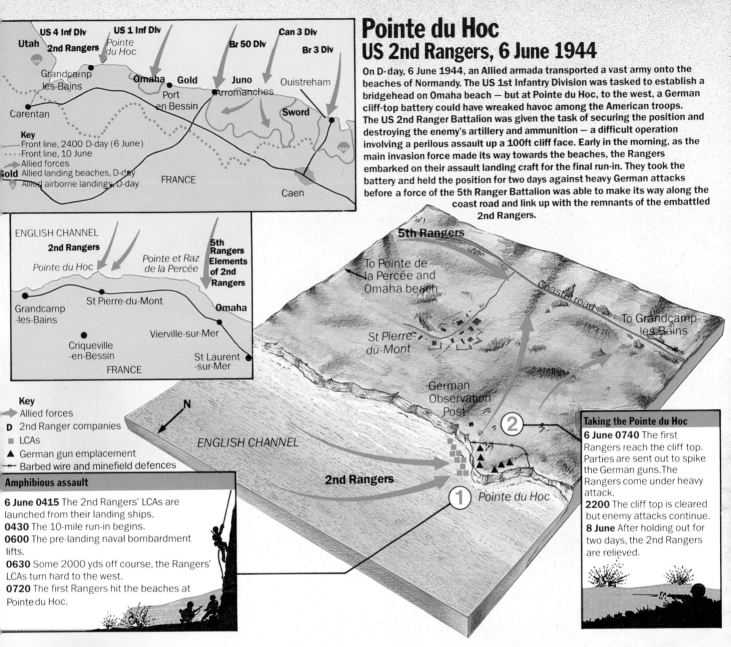

Amphibious assault

6 June 0415 The 2nd Rangers' LCAs are launched from their landing ships.
0430 The 10-mile run-in begins.
0600 The pre-landing naval bombardment lifts.
0630 Some 2000 yds off course, the Rangers' LCAs turn hard to the west.
0720 The first Rangers hit the beaches at Pointe du Hoc.

Taking the Pointe du Hoc
6 June 0740 The first Rangers reach the cliff top. Parties are sent out to spike the German guns. The Rangers come under heavy attack.
2200 The cliff top is cleared but enemy attacks continue.
8 June After holding out for two days, the 2nd Rangers are relieved.

free as another man began the ascent. Only at the third attempt did Roberts' section gain his position, climbing over their comrade as he lay spreadeagled in the crater, holding on to the rope for dear life. Once over the top, he and his men moved eastwards to tackle a German observation post.

Elsewhere, other rangers were also encountering difficulties: Rudder was knocked off the cliff by a great chunk of chalk loosened by the destroyers' fire and other men were caught by a rock-fall produced by the detonation of a 200mm shell that the Germans had slung over the cliff face. Some were more fortunate: Petty, at the second attempt, was able to make some progress, but grenades and fire from machine guns and rifles were taking a grim toll of the men on the beach. The shingle was so badly cratered that the ladder-carrying DUKWs could not reach the foot of the cliff after completing the journey from their LCT, lying some 4000yds offshore.

As there were no ladders available, ropes would have to suffice and Cripps, realising that the closer he could get the rockets to the base of the cliff, the more protected they would be from enemy fire, had them manhandled ashore. There, set up in makeshift mountings, he fired the lines by holding his 'hot box' to the fuzes, knowing that the streak of flames each launch produced would blind him temporarily. However, his sacrifice enabled more men to climb the cliff and, some 30 minutes after the first landings, over 100 rangers were on top of the Pointe du Hoc.

The cliff top resembled a moonscape of destruction, across which the various sections attacked, working their way forward from crater to crater. Petty's Browning, none the worse for its soaking, and other automatic rifles kept the Germans pinned down. As they fired, men advanced by sections: one ranger flinging a grenade in the direction of the enemy as others charged across churned up ground to winkle out the defenders with their bayonets. Sections lost contact with those to their left and right and individual rangers were cut off, but the assault teams pressed the Germans hard until the gun emplacements were cleared. These, however, were empty: the guns had not been mounted.

Left: With their comrades sheltering at the foot of the cliff, the first rangers begin their ascent. Note ranger (below) falling from the cliff in the distance. Below left: US troops begin to move off Omaha beach during the afternoon of D-day. Below, far right: DUKWs fitted with extendable ladders, accompanied the rangers, but could not cross the cratered beach at the foot of the Pointe du Hoc.

After the initial fury of the attack, Rudder established his small HQ on the tip of the Pointe, while his scattered companies organised defensive positions along a line of wire, lying 100yds inland, that the Germans had placed to protect the battery from a landward attack. D Company took up position to the west, with E Company in the centre and F Company to the east. Although all three were short of 50 per cent of their strength, they sent out groups to patrol the road that ran parallel to the coast, a further 800yds inland.

As the rangers moved east and west along the road, two men discovered five guns in an open emplacement, from where they could have shelled the invasion beaches. The guns were spiked – their breeches were destroyed – and later a large stockpile of ammunition was detonated. Another patrol found the guns that were destined to serve as the Pointe du Hoc battery. Still greased, and in their packaging, these 155mm pieces were also spiked.

Despite these successes, the rangers on the cliff top were still in a perilous position: from the west, the 88mm guns of an anti-aircraft battery were pounding the area. Rudder ordered his men to neutralise the threat. First one, and then another sub-section, all the men who could be spared, attacked. Each attack reached the enemy's perimeter wire but was bloodily repulsed. The situation was grim, but not untenable, and Rudder signalled to his superiors that his mission was accomplished. However, he added that to hold the perimeter against counter-attacks he would need ammunition and reinforcements.

After two attacks in which 30 men had been killed or captured, Rudder had about 70 men under orders. Early in the afternoon, enemy patrols had isolated some of the rangers' forward positions and only a well-aimed barrage from the faithful destroyers dealt with the threat. The early evening was relatively quiet and the rangers were able to clear the cliff top of enemy infiltrators by 2200 hours. Although the immediate danger of being overwhelmed had evaporated, Rudder remained concerned about the plight of his wounded, who could not be evacuated, and the acute shortage of smallarms ammunition.

Just after midnight, the contest was resumed with the Germans putting in an attack after an intense, but inaccurate, bombardment. Controlled fire from the rangers contained this threat and a subsequent onslaught. However, an attack at 0130, the third in 90 minutes, overran E Company's positions. F Company, down to a mere handful of men by this time, was equal to the situation, holding its own sector of the perimeter and covering the withdrawal of the hard-pressed rangers. Aware that his command was overstretched, Rudder withdrew his sections into a tighter perimeter around his HQ.

US Ranger, D-day 1944

Armed with a 30-calibre M1903 Springfield rifle, this man wears olive green herringbone twill fatigues, the standard M1 helmet and boots with cleated soles. A compass hangs around his neck.

AMPHIBIOUS WORKHORSE

One of a whole host of supply craft used during waterborne operations during World War II, the DUKW (D indicated that it was a 1942 model; U for an amphibian; K for an all-wheel drive vehicle; and W denoted twin rear axles) was simply a sea-going conversion of the standard GMC 6x6 utility truck. Although the DUKW was primarily designed to transport supplies from ships to the invasion beaches, it proved much more flexible in its applications. Aside from its capacity to carry up to 5175lb of cargo, the DUKW was often used to transport troops or heavy weapons. Some DUKWs were converted to take on specialist tasks: as floating gun platforms and as rocket-equipped fire-suppression vehicles. For the assault on the Pointe du Hoc on D-day, two amphibians were fitted with turntable-mounted extendable ladders that could reach the top of the promontory. To assist in the silencing of enemy opposition, the top of each ladder was fitted with a Lewis machine gun. Based on a tried-and-tested chassis, the DUKW gained a reputation for ruggedness and battlefield reliability. In action, crews found that the amphibian was easy to drive, whether on land or sea, and that minor mechanical failures could be easily rectified. Powered by a GMC Model 270 engine, the DUKW could reach speeds of up to 50mph on land and 6mph at sea. Something like 20,000 DUKWs saw service in World War II, with over 2000 involved in the Normandy landings, and, due to its record, the amphibian has become recognised as one of the unsung war-winners. It did have its faults – a small payload and poor performance in rough conditions – but its ability to carry men and equipment from ships to the front line, whatever the distance, marked the humble DUKW as an outstanding logistical support vehicle.

Bottom: An American soldier, his face blank with shock, sits impassively as a medical officer bandages his injured hand. For many GIs, the carnage of Omaha was a bloody introduction to the grim realities of modern warfare.

Below right: Some of the survivors of the Pointe du Hoc battle, including Colonel Jim Rudder (left), pose for the camera after receiving bravery awards. Only 25 per cent of the 200 rangers who landed survived unscathed.

While the Rangers were battling for the Pointe du Hoc, the main landing on Omaha, a few miles to the east, had met strong resistance and it was not until the late afternoon of D-day that a firm beach-head was established. Although Rudder's men had received a few reinforcements from the 5th Ranger Battalion and a little ammunition during the day, the perilous situation on Omaha meant that they would have to hold out for longer than anticipated. Nothing daunted, Rudder opted to take the fight to the enemy, sending patrols out from the foothold on the cliff top.

At 1700 hours on the 7th, Rudder was ordered to break out and try to link up with men from the 5th Rangers, who were battling their way towards the Pointe from Vierville, a small town on the western flank of Omaha. The Germans, however, were wise to this move and, after heavy fighting, prevented the link-up from taking place; Rudder's men would have

to sit tight for another anxious night. Early in the morning of 8 June, the 5th Rangers, supported by other units from Omaha, recommenced their drive up the coast road, using tank fire to deal with a particularly stubborn enemy strongpoint. Sadly, some shells missed the mark and fell on the Pointe, killing several rangers. Nevertheless the relief force broke through to Rudder's position.

The sight that greeted the relief column was one of massive destruction: enormous craters, blasted and shell-pocked concrete, and a battlefield covered with the obscene litter of war. From their defensive positions, the grim, weary survivors of the 2nd Ranger Battalion rose to greet their brothers-in-arms. Only 50 of the original force of 200 men remained to enjoy the celebrations.

THE AUTHOR James D. Ladd is one of the acknowledged experts on the Special Forces of World War II. His works include *Inside the Commandos*.

INTO THE CAULDRON

In the searing heat of the Western Desert, Rommel's 90th Light Division led the Afrika Korps' offensive against the British Eighth Army during the frontier battles of May 1942

THE 90TH LIGHT DIVISION was born out of the Afrika Korps' need for extra infantry to support its panzer divisions. In July 1941 it was decided that a large number of miscellaneous units based in Libya should be grouped around a nucleus of the 3rd Battalion of the 147th Regiment and six independent companies. One of the three motorised infantry regiments which eventually formed the 90th Light was, perhaps, the most exotic formation in the whole Afrika Korps: the 361st Regiment. Composed of Germans who had served in the ranks of the French Foreign Legion, its men, hardened in battle and wise in the ways of the desert, soon demonstrated their abilities, and gave the whole division a reputation for élan in attack and tenacity in defence.

In November 1941, the new division was thrust into action against the British Eighth Army's Crusade[r] Offensive. The tough ex-Legionnaires of the 361st Regiment courageously attacked British tanks wi[th] close quarter weapons, including Molotov cocktail[s] and then recovered lost ground by launching the[ir] own attack. One group was overrun by Britis[h] armour and taken prisoner, but was soon released [in] a spirited counter-attack. A second drive by th[e] British, however, succeeded in recapturing thes[e] men within the hour, but once again they wer[e] released as another counter-attack went in. Th[e] survivors were grouped with other under-manne[d] units to form Holbeck Battalion, and were deploye[d] to great effect as shock troops, both in assault an[d] defensive operations.

By the end of Field Marshal Erwin Rommel['s] January 1942 offensive, the 90th Division was equip[p]ed largely with British vehicles captured in th[e] advance – its soldiers had taken heed of the

Below: A staff-car ploughing through thick sand at speed. Rommel pushed men and machines to the limits of their endurance in pursuit of victory. Right: German and Italian troops, their faces etched with confidence, co-operate in positioning an artillery piece before the battle of Gazala.

The 90th Light Division was one of the foremost units under Rommel's command during the Desert War. Organised initially from units in Africa in August 1941 as the Special Purposes Division (Afrika), it was rechristened on 28 November of the same year. Its core was three motorised infantry regiments; the 155th, 200th and 361st, and the Panzer Grenadier Regiment 'Afrika'. Other forces, including anti-tank and artillery detachments, were added to the division as needs dictated.

Although the 90th Light did not pack the punch of an armoured division, it was well-equipped and highly mobile and ideally suited to Rommel's war philosophy. The Desert Fox rejected the strategy of fighting along the narrow coastal strip of North Africa in favour of wide, sweeping movements through the 'impassable' desert interior. This vulnerable flank was often weakly defended by the British and susceptible to any sudden thrust carried out with overwhelming strength.

The 90th Light's mobility was utilised to the full by Rommel during the Gazala battles; its motorised regiments were ordered to deliver the knock-out blow around the British left flank.

It was, however, an operation fraught with danger as the British were aware of this favoured manoeuvre, and deep drives behind enemy lines always placed a heavy burden on the Afrika Korps' logistical support.

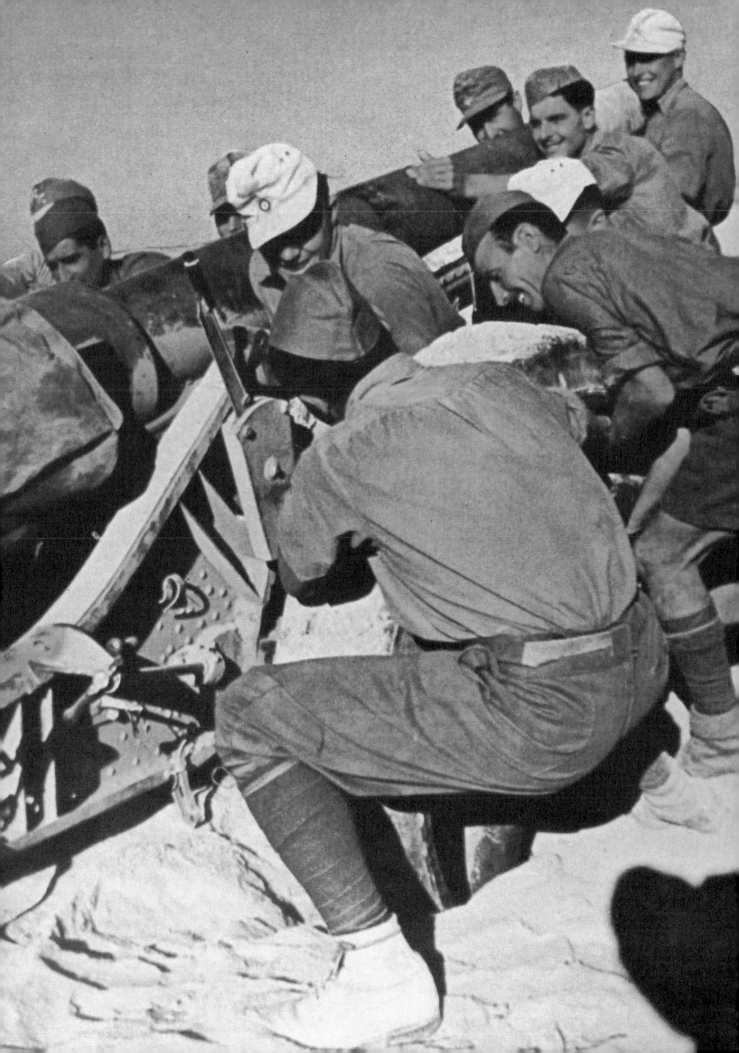

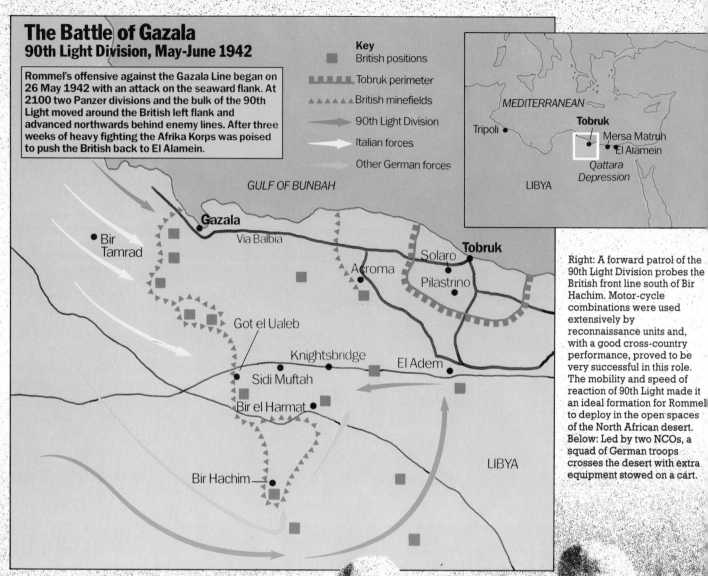

The Battle of Gazala
90th Light Division, May-June 1942

Rommel's offensive against the Gazala Line began on 26 May 1942 with an attack on the seaward flank. At 2100 two Panzer divisions and the bulk of the 90th Light moved around the British left flank and advanced northwards behind enemy lines. After three weeks of heavy fighting the Afrika Korps was poised to push the British back to El Alamein.

Key
- British positions
- Tobruk perimeter
- British minefields
- 90th Light Division
- Italian forces
- Other German forces

MEDITERRANEAN

Tripoli
Tobruk
Mersa Matruh
El Alamein
Qattara Depression
LIBYA

GULF OF BUNBAH

Bir Tamrad
Gazala
Via Balbia
Acroma
Solaro
Pilastrino
Tobruk
Got el Ualeb
Knightsbridge
El Adem
Sidi Muftah
Bir el Harmat
Bir Hachim
LIBYA

Right: A forward patrol of the 90th Light Division probes the British front line south of Bir Hachim. Motor-cycle combinations were used extensively by reconnaissance units and, with a good cross-country performance, proved to be very successful in this role. The mobility and speed of reaction of 90th Light made it an ideal formation for Rommel to deploy in the open spaces of the North African desert. Below: Led by two NCOs, a squad of German troops crosses the desert with extra equipment stowed on a cart.

commander's advice to those who complained that they lacked equipment: 'If you are short of anything go across and take it from the enemy. He has plenty.'

From February until mid-May 1942 there was a lull in the fighting as both sides contented themselves with reinforcing their depleted forces and stockpiling essential supplies. By late May, however, both sides felt strong enough to resume hostilities; Rommel was anxious to press on after his reconquest of Cyrenaica and Churchill, thirsting for a decisive victory that would smash the aura of invincibility that surrounded Rommel, the 'Desert Fox', was pressing the British commanders to resume their offensive operations.

Although less than happy with Prime Minister Winston Churchill's interference in military matters, the British C-in-C, General Auchinleck, was able to draw some comfort from the defensive line that his men had built between Gazala, on the coast, and Bir Hachim, 64km south. An extensive minefield ran along its western edge, and a series of heavily-defended outposts, known as 'boxes', had been built on commanding positions to cover possible German attack routes. Each box was held by a brigade-strength force, lavishly supplied with ammunition, artillery and foodstuffs. A second line, stretching east to west from Sidi Muftah to El Adem, was also in the process of being built, but was far from complete by the time the German offensive was launched. Auchinleck had 100,000 men of the XXX and XIII Corps, 849 tanks, including American-built Grants mounting the powerful 75mm gun, and 200 aircraft to hold the line.

The Desert Fox, with only 560 tanks and 90,000 troops at his command, was considerably weaker than the British, but his armoured formations did contain 109 tanks of the latest design and he fielded a frontline strength of 500 aircraft, likely to guarantee air superiority over the battlefield. Rommel, moreover, was prepared to place his trust in good planning and plain luck to see him through to victory. By late evening of 26 May 1942, the preparations for his offensive, Operation Theseus, were complete and Axis success in North Africa depended upon it.

Armed to the teeth, with bandoliers holding extra rounds or magazines, the men were formidable in attack

The following day, the German offensive against Gazala was opened. The 90th was deployed in the scorching, waterless desert hinterland to protect the open flank of the Axis armoured forces; reconnaissance battalions were taken from the panzer divisions and grouped with the Light Division to locate the British armour and warn the Afrika Korps of its position. The 90th's infantry regiments also had the gruelling task of leading the Afrika Korps' opening attack of Operation Theseus.

The core of the division's assault troops was small, tightly-knit groups of infantry that were taught to advance making the greatest use of the local terrain.

Armed to the teeth, with bandoliers holding extra rounds or sub-machine gun magazines, and carrying the standard issue Mauser 98K 7.92mm rifle or the MP38 sub-machine gun, these men proved to be formidable in attack and indefatigable in defence. The MP38, with a rate of fire of 500rpm, was a superb weapon for close-quarter combat and was much feared by the British. Also, most men carried a bunch of hand grenades. The Steilhandgranate 24 was ideally suited to the needs of assault troops, and it could be used as an anti-tank and anti-emplacement charge by lashing six grenades together. Heavy support in the form of MG34 machine guns and a

RECONNAISSANCE IN THE DESERT

Rommel's ability to meet and defeat a succession of British offensives in North Africa owed much to the quality and volume of the information supplied by the Afrika Korps' reconnaissance units.

Each division had its own force to carry out these operations and, as they were expected to patrol the desert for long periods, they had to be self-contained, all-arms groups. They were not briefed to seek battle actively with the enemy; their role was to discover his dispositions and report on unusual movements.

In the early months of the Desert War, PzKpfw II tanks were pushed up to 13km – the maximum range of their wireless sets – in advance of the main body. Armoured cars, with a faster speed and better cross-country performance, under certain conditions later replaced the ageing tanks and performed the same function more effectively.

Light artillery, anti-tank guns and troops carried in half-tracks or trucks worked in conjunction with their more heavily armoured brethren.

Reporting sightings of the British, however, was only a small part of the unit's effort and special detachments of linguists, well-versed in the call-signs of individual British units, listened to the communications that flowed between senior commanders and their junior officers.

Some of the intelligence gathered by reconnaissance units was likely to be of limited military value, but the energy they expended in deciphering messages was never wasted effort. The discovery of one vital piece of information could make the difference between victory or defeat, and Rommel was undoubtedly aware that he could ill-afford to ignore their findings.

MG34 GPMG

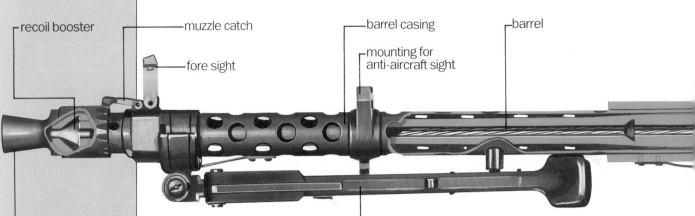

recoil booster — muzzle catch — barrel casing — barrel

fore sight — mounting for anti-aircraft sight

flash hider — bipod (folded position)

THE MG34

After its debut in 1934, the German-built MG34 proved to be one of the finest weapons to see service in World War II and was widely recognised as a revolutionary design. Its most remarkable feature was that the gun worked by an unusual combination of recoil and gas. When a round was fired the barrel recoiled and the bullet was given extra thrust by some of the gases trapped in the muzzle being deflected backwards.

The MG34 had several features that made it an ideal battlefield weapon: a quick way of changing the barrel, easy stripping for cleaning and, like most German machine guns, ease of carrying. The weapon had a two-piece trigger which fired either single rounds or automatic, according to whether the upper or lower portion was pressed.

The most far-reaching aspect of the gun, however, was tactical; fitted with a tripod it functioned as a medium machine gun, while it was deployed also as a light support weapon when mounted on a bipod. The MG34 was also the first belt-fed light machine-gun and its effectiveness did much to prove the concept.

The MG34 did have defects: it was difficult to manufacture in any great quantity and, because its tolerances were very fine, it was liable to malfunction in the dry, dusty conditions of North Africa. Nevertheless, the 90th Light Division used the weapon in large numbers in the Desert War.

variety of mortars was deployed to keep defenders pinned down while the assault groups rushed forward.

Rommel's battle plan was to distract the attention of the Eighth Army by launching infantry attacks against Gazala and, while the town was put under pressure, an armoured group, moving at night, would pass down the front, swing round the British left flank, and then position itself for the kill. In the words of Rommel's operational order, the force was to destroy: 'the British Field Army which is positioned in the Bir Hachim-Acroma-Gazala sectors, after which Panzerarmee Afrika will take the fortress of Tobruk.' Rommel's orders for the 90th Light stressed that it was to 'drive at fastest speed, advancing relentlessly and not allowing (itself) to be diverted by the enemy.' He expected the greatest sacrifices from the troops of his motorised infantry division. Men suffering from heat exhaustion and low on water were expected to defeat a superior, well-rested enemy.

The men, bloody but unbowed, prepared to return to the field of battle

Although the offensive opened with part of the 90th Light supporting the attacks at Gazala, the bulk of the division moved to the south with the armour on 26/27 May. A German with the 90th wrote of the pleasure of a journey, 'lit by a full moon and with firm going, practically free from rocks and stones'. At the correct time the mass of tanks cruised round the British flank in a wide, sweeping movement.

The divisional objective for the 90th was El Adem, a crossing point of two native tracks that was expected to hold a small garrison. El Adem, however, turned out to be a strongly-held brigade box. The division, divided into three battlegroups, roared confidently towards the objective unaware of the danger they faced until an accurate and intensive bombardment crashed down. Behind the barrage came the British armour. The 90th Light dispersed, and contact was lost, not merely between the battle groups but also with the Afrika Korps. The panzer divisions also had struck trouble and were under pressure, but the 90th could offer no help because its own units, advancing across the barren desert wastes towards El Adem were isolated and unsupported. The Headquarters Group moved towards

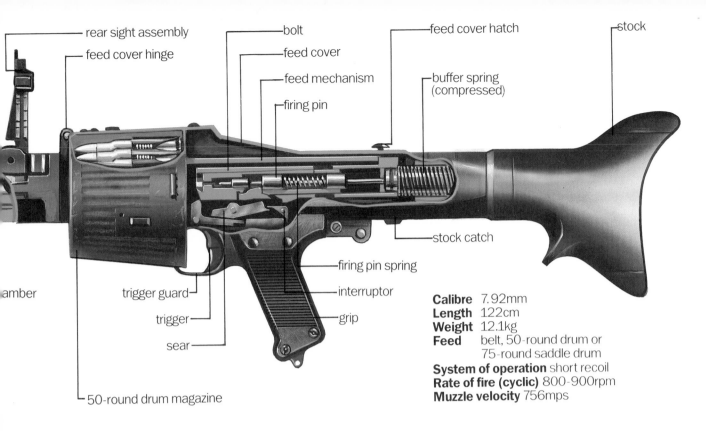

rear sight assembly
feed cover hinge
bolt
feed cover
feed mechanism
firing pin
feed cover hatch
stock
buffer spring (compressed)

amber
trigger guard
trigger
sear
50-round drum magazine
firing pin spring
interruptor
grip
stock catch

Calibre 7.92mm
Length 122cm
Weight 12.1kg
Feed belt, 50-round drum or 75-round saddle drum
System of operation short recoil
Rate of fire (cyclic) 800-900rpm
Muzzle velocity 756mps

eft: With faces masked against the ferocity of a sandstorm, two men of an observation unit wait to continue pin-pointing the position of British gun emplacements. Below: Heavy firepower in the front line. This gunner is sighting a tripod-mounted MG34. Its high rate of fire made it invaluable.

the objective, dispersing enemy supply columns and driving off armoured car patrols. At last light the Headquarters laagered in the middle of a mass of British tanks, still 10km short of the objective. To defend the group against the enemy armour concentrating to the north and east of the laager, Headquarters could call on only a single battery of light artillery. The men were almost defenceless.

Their isolation, however, was not to last. During the morning of 28 May, first one and then the other missing battle group reported in, to be followed during the day by the divisional artillery. The 90th renewed their advance and drove westwards to join the Afrika Korps. The way forward was found to be blocked by a vast minefield. The 90th halted and formed laager. The first attempts by the 900th Engineer Battalion to gap the defences were smashed by destructive and accurate artillery fire. The sappers were switched to a new sector, and managed to clear a corridor within three hours. The mass of the 90th's vehicles were channelled through this narrow funnel. The close-packed columns moved forward slowly. Then there was a halt and a long wait. The men out in the open fretted with impatience at the delay, and were noticeably nervous. The delay was caused by the discovery that beyond the minefield just cleared by the sappers lay another field, which also had to be gapped. Before any order arrived, a lone British bomber, flying across the battlefield, released flares and then dropped a small cluster of bombs. There was a sudden panic among the 90th – the leading group of vehicles drove forward, running over the working sappers and into uncleared ground. Several immediately blew up. The ear-splitting explosions spread the belief that the RAF was bombing the column. It was an ideal bombing target – a mass of immobile trucks unable to escape. Chaos ensued as drivers, completely exhausted from lack of sleep and unable to think clearly, drove their

lorries over the marker tapes into the uncleared areas of the minefield and were blown up. Forty lorries were lost within minutes, but order was soon restored and the troops, bloody but unbowed, prepared to return to the field of battle.

During what remained of the night (28/29 May), the division regained contact with the Afrika Korps and its men were able to snatch a few hours sleep.

Fifty per cent of the division's officers and 25 per cent of its rank and file were casualties

On the following day, however, the battle, which had developed so badly for the Germans, slowly moved in their favour. Instead of the Afrika Korps being trapped between the minefields and British armour, the Germans were actually in a commanding position. The British minefields had been gapped to allow convoys to bring forward fuel, ammunition and supplies to the panzer divisions. Refuelled, rearmed, and firmly under control, the Afrika Korps beat off the unsupported assaults of a succession of British armoured brigades. The box at Got el Ualeb was cut off. The 90th took part in the fighting to crush the defences but, before the operation had been completed, Rommel ordered the division southwards to capture the Bir Hachim box. The eight-day battle that the Italian and German troops fought against the Allied Forces for this stretch of harsh desert was more than a battle of units. It was a fight to the finish, during which the anti-tank and flak battalions of the 90th suffered massive casualties. Driven to desperation, Rommel ordered dive-bombing raids on the garrison, but these failed to break the morale of the defenders. They continued to fight tenaciously and losses to the infantry regiments of the 90th seriously weakened its ability to conduct strong attacks. It was not until 11 June that the box at Bir Hachim fell, but its capture did not signal an end to the fighting. In the short pause before moving back to attack the British 29th Indian Brigade box at El Adem,

WATER SUPPLY IN THE DESERT

The daring, cut and thrust battles of the North African campaign placed an almost insupportable strain on the logistical services of both the German and Allied forces, and nowhere was this pressure felt more than on the supply of water. Throughout the Desert War, the Afrika Korps had to rely on five main sources of water; none was entirely reliable and all were liable to interruption. Although most areas of the desert were served by wells, many produced water spoilt by oil seeping from underground, and water taken from the more fertile coastal areas was too salty. A few towns, notably Benghazi and Tobruk, however, had their own clear springs.

Most of Rommel's offensives, however, were made well inland and so the water supplies nearer the coast were of little use to the advancing forces of the Afrika Korps. Water was brought in by the German Navy, but the Royal Navy and RAF's successes in attacking convoys made it difficult to maintain the flow. To off-set these losses, the Afrika Korps developed its own distillation plants to purify sea water and several units were engaged in water divining, but the demand for water was satisfied rarely. Captured supplies, taken from the British, were always a welcome addition to their often meagre rations, yet successive offensives were forced to the point of collapse on a number of occasions due to shortages.

Above: Purifying water supplies.

the division was regrouped. Checks showed that 50 per cent of the division's officers and 25 per cent of its rank and file were casualties – more than 1300 men had been lost since the offensive had begun.

The resolute defence at El Adem by the 29th Indian Brigade almost crippled the infantry units of the division, and, as even the most determined assaults by the 90th had little effect, a new order from Rommel brought the division hurrying back to join the main elements of the Afrika Korps. The battalions arrived hungry, thirsty and exhausted, but were ordered straight back to El Adem. The terrible losses suffered by the Eighth Army, particularly in armour, had changed the situation. Although the Indians fought on against a superior enemy, Rommel brought forward the 21st Panzer Division. With tank support the infantry of 90th Light went in again. Some gains were made, but it was not a complete and total victory. The attack of the von Loewen battlegroup, on 16 June, showed the fury with which the fighting was conducted by both sides. That group formed an assault detachment to beat down the last resistance in the El Adem box. To bring the battle group up to strength, gun crews were taken from artillery batteries to make good the losses of infantry – but only 70 men could be spared from the artillery. At 0900 von

Loewen's men advanced, moving quickly throug heavy artillery barrages and devastating machine gun fire. Led on by their platoon and compan officers, the assault group pressed forward unde the merciless glare of the sun; men died for ever yard gained. Their charge reached the muzzles o the enemy guns, but the attack faltered and died.

The division's losses had been fearful – one man i two had been killed, wounded or was missing. I Sonderverband 200, a regiment made up of Germar émigres and Arab volunteers, more than 100 mer had been lost in a single day's fighting. By the middl week of June the Sonderverband's strength was tha of a weak battalion. The 155th Infantry Regiment ha also suffered badly; there were only three anti-tanl guns in the 3rd Battalion and the 2nd had lost fiv officers during the fighting for El Adem. The box fe at last on 17 June. Immediately, both the 200th and

361st Regiments were ordered to spearhead the assault on Tobruk. The remnants of the 90th were detailed to carry out a march through the desert to Mersa Matruh and cut off the British who, by this stage of the battle, were retreating towards the Nile. Tobruk fell quickly, and the two detached regiments raced to rejoin their parent formation as it advanced, capturing one objective after another. There were many sleepless nights, and the men lost all sense of time. They were in danger of becoming disorientated with fatigue. Illnesses that would have been shrugged off a month earlier struck hard at the exhausted warriors – stomach disorders were common and dysentry was rife.

As far as the eye could see, there were the bloodiest scenes of death and destruction

On 29 June, with Mersa Matruh in German hands, a beaming Rommel told the exhausted warriors of the 90th: 'Your leave passes are waiting for you in Cairo.' But one last effort was needed. He concentrated the best fighting elements of the 90th under the command of Major Briel, the senior officer of the 606th Flak Battalion and gave him the details of his assignment. He was to lead an advance guard of the battalion and self-propelled guns on a raid through the British lines. The objective was the Nile and Advanced Group Briel was the spearhead of the whole Afrika Korps. Rommel's parting words to Briel were: 'Drive for Alexandria. You and I will drink coffee in Shepherd's Hotel in Cairo'.

Although the men of the division had suffered grievous losses and many of the survivors had crippling illnesses, they responded to Rommel's call for one final effort. It was a great tribute to the stamina and professionalism of the officers that the ordinary soldiers under their command carried out the new orders without a murmur of dissent. Their loyalty grew out of mutual

respect, founded on the knowledge that each man, of whatever rank, knew what was expected of him.

Briel divided his group into three detachments of equal strength and composition – their orders were to by-pass the enemy but if this proved impossible the force was to encircle and destroy any opposition using standard battle tactics. These were a simplification of Rommel's own methods. One group was

Above: For two youthful members of the 90th Light, a moment of relaxation. Below: A German half-track rushing a 5cm PAK 38 anti-tank gun into a forward area. Mobility played a vital part in Rommel's defeat of the British.

to hold the enemy's attention, while a second made a flank attack. A reserve group would then overrun and destroy the shattered enemy. The first hours of the advance were made without encountering serious opposition. Many units of the Eighth Army were pulling back and Briel's group was able to thrust ahead. Post-battle accounts were filled with descriptions of huge, black clouds of greasy smoke from the stores of petrol and supplies that the Eighth Army had brought into the desert, and had been forced to destroy by the German advance. For kilometre after kilometre, as far as the eye could see, there were the bloodiest scenes of death and destruction.

By the early evening of 29 June, Briel Group had

gained their first objectives but, acting on his own initiative, the commander brought his men forward, driving them through the night. Men shivered in inadequate greatcoats and thin trousers, but by midnight the advance guard had crossed the Abd el Rahman track. In less than 12 hours, over 120km had been covered, and Alexandria lay only 100km away. The men were totally exhausted; there had been no proper rest since the offensive opened in the last week of May.

A bewildering order came in to Briel during the night: Rommel directed him to halt his advance and wait until the rest of 90th Light arrived. Briel waited for his support to arrive and watched several large units of the Eighth Army retreat past his positions towards El Alamein. A new order came in. The Briel Advance Group was to be disbanded on 1 July and reorganised into a battlegroup with its own anti-tank guns, artillery, sappers and infantry. At first light on 1 July the Afrika Korps, concentrated along the El Alamein front, was ordered to attack in the hope of achieving a quick break-through. The German assault moved off under cover of a sandstorm. German Intelligence, however, did not know that the Alamein Line, extending across the narrow gap between the sea and the Qattara Depression, had been prepared as a last-ditch position.

'It was as if the jaws of hell had opened when the guns began to fire'

The 90th swung into an assault against an outpost position at Deir el Shein and captured the ground in a day-long fight that cost the division its whole artillery strength. The battle orders for 2 July demanded that the attack be continued, but by now much of the German Army was too exhausted and too weak to carry out Rommel's orders. The weary infantry of the 90th, however, rose out of their slit trenches at dawn on 2 July and made their final effort. One soldier of the division remembered the attack:

'It was as if the jaws of hell had opened when the British guns began to fire. We had all experienced really savage bombardments, but those of 2 July destroyed us completely. Not only in the casualties which we suffered, but in morale as those guns fired and fired with no let up.'

Under cover of another sandstorm the shattered battalions of the 90th Light withdrew from the attack. The division had shot its bolt. Its men, exhausted after weeks of continuous battle, could do no more; the total strength of the 90th had been reduced to just 58 officers, 247 NCOs and 1023 men by the severe fighting of the Gazala offensive and the First Battle of Alamein.

Under Rommel's skilful command, it had all but achieved the vital breakthrough demanded of it, but in the end, had been ground into defeat. The Allied troops had fought with dogged determination, and the RAF had dealt a series of body-blows to German supply columns, making it impossible for the 90th Light to carry out its mission. Without precious water and vital fuel, men and machines, having been stretched to the limit of endurance, were forced to a halt.

THE AUTHOR James Lucas served with the Queen's Own Royal West Kent Regiment during the North African Campaign and is currently Deputy Head of the Department of Photographs at the Imperial War Museum, London.

Captain, 90th Light Division, North Africa 1942

The assignment of Luftwaffe units to ground formations was a standard practice in the German armed forces and this *Hauptmann* would have commanded an anti-aircraft unit within the 90th Light. Jacket and trousers are Luftwaffe tropical pattern and other notable service features include the Luftwaffe version of the national insignia (worn above his right breast pocket) and the ground combat badge attached to the left breast pocket. Rank is denoted by the two pips on the shoulder strap and the red piping around the strap reveals his Flak artillery arm of service. A map case hangs from his leather belt as does the standard issue 9mm P38 pistol. Just above his binoculars is the ribbon of the Iron Cross 2nd Class.

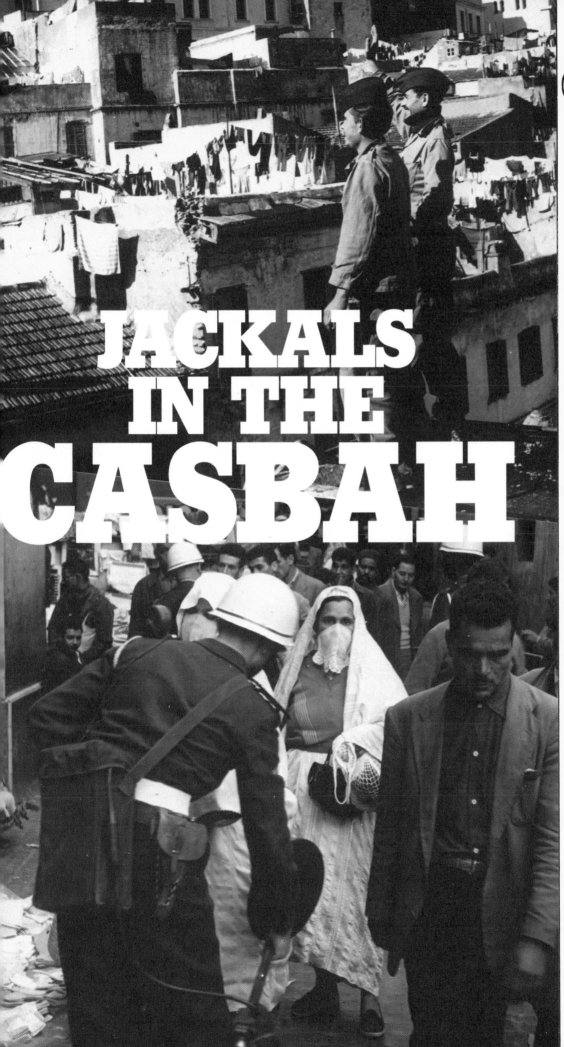

JACKALS IN THE CASBAH

THE ZOUAVES

On 15 August 1845, just a few days after the French captured Algiers, the first 500 Zouaves were paraded in the city. They came from a single Kabyle tribe, the Zwawa. These volunteers were soon formed into a formal battalion and seven years later they were at the head of the attacking force which took the city of Constantine. In following years, Algerian Muslims served in *tirailleur* regiments, while European immigrants joined the Zouave regiments that were raised.

There were three Zouave regiments during the Second Empire and they fought in the Crimean War – suffering 50 per cent casualties during the attack on the Malakof fort at Sebastapol. They went on to fight in Italy, Mexico and, of course, in Algeria where they were engaged in every 19th century campaign. They fought on French soil during the Franco-Prussian War of 1870-71, went to China in 1900, and again played a major part during World War I.

Seventeen Zouave regiments were raised for World War II; the 9th Regiment fought heroically on 8 and 9 June 1940 at La Ferme-Pouy and then continued resistance to the German offensive in the following days.

During the liberation of France in 1944, the 9th Regiment was part of the French First Army and was notable for its contribution to the fighting in the Jura. The motto of the regiment, which originated in World War I, and was very apt for the Zouaves who fought in the Casbah in the 1950s, translates as 'Jackals in Algeria and Tigers at Verdun.'

The French Zouaves who took up positions in Algiers in 1956 were at the heart of a bloody urban war fighting the guerrillas of the FLN

THE CASBAH was the district at the centre of the ancient city of El-Djazair, the place that became known in English as Algiers, and was the heart of the French-ruled province of Algeria. The Casbah remained a unique district during the period of French rule – a labyrinth of narrow alleys, of enclosed passageways, of hidden terraces rising on a hill, where the inhabitants seemed to live a lifestyle that had not changed for centuries. Shopkeepers, artisans, vagabonds, beggars, and their families lived a life that was based on the rules of the Koran, in a teeming world that offered a ready refuge for fugitives from justice – a place where such fugitives could swim like fish in a bustling, overstocked human sea.

In 1956, such a comparison was particularly apt, for the Casbah was providing a refuge for men who did indeed see themselves as fish swimming in a human sea. The guerrillas of the FLN (Front de Libération Nationale, the national liberation front fighting against French rule) used the Casbah as a safe haven. The authorities were hesitant about moving in to try to destroy the FLN structure. They saw the Casbah as both an ant-hill and a powder keg. If it was kicked, then there could easily be an explosion. In effect, the army restricted itself to a few patrols, in

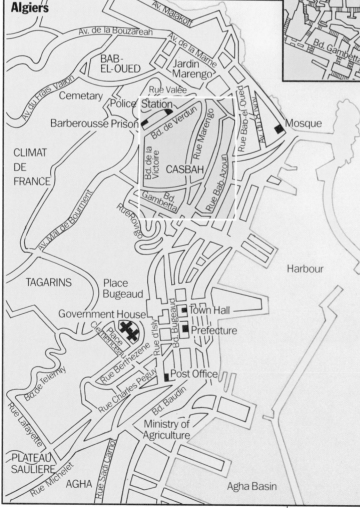

Into the Casbah
4th Company, 9th Regiment of Zouaves
1956–1957

In the summer of 1956 the 9th Zouave Regiment was deployed in the city of Algiers. The regiment's 4th Company was given the task of moving against the FLN rebels in the city's Casbah, which had so far been a safe guerrilla haven. Over the next few months, Captain Sirvent's Zouaves familiarised themselves with the Casbah's inhabitants and its labyrinth of streets. When the time came to go on the offensive, the Zouaves were ready.

ing Algerians of European extraction (known as *colons* or *pieds noirs*), and conscripts from mainland France itself. To this polyglot force was given a major responsibility in a grim guerrilla war and to the 4th Company of the regiment was given the particular task of trying to restore authority in the seemingly impenetrable Casbah, where the FLN had long operated unchallenged.

The arrival of the 4th Company of the 9th Regiment of Zouaves was to change all that. This company, under Captain Sirvent, set up its headquarters in the Rue de l'Intendance, at the very centre of what had been considered almost a forbidden city. Sirvent, whom the inhabitants of the Casbah called 'el Capten' was of European immigrant stock, one of the million or so *pieds noirs* who had been born and bred in Algeria. He was a veteran of the Indochinese war that had ended in 1954; he had been wounded there and had become a specialist in counter-insurgency during his time in the Far East. In addition, he knew the Islamic world perfectly, and spoke Arabic. He didn't look particularly threatening, with his round face and heavy body, and he played up his physical appearance with a jovial, good-hearted manner. But this façade masked a hard, pitiless soldier who knew that he could not afford to give his adversaries an inch if he were to win.

Sirvent's company, of 100 men, soon moulded itself in his image; active and extremely aggressive. To a certain extent this was surprising, because most of his 'jackals' (the nickname came from their motto) had no special military background and initially there was no reason to expect them to excel at carrying on a battle in the enclosed hostile world of the fearsome Casbah of Algiers. Many, indeed, were conscripts from northern France. But they proved a potent fighting force.

Captain Sirvent began by enclosing the zone that he had to organise and pacify. Barbed wire and sandbags were used to facilitate his regulation of the streets, and patrols were sent throughout the Casbah. These first steps were designed to undermine the rebels' feeling of security. The Zouaves and police agents carried out a constant round of searches, day and night.

Both sides realised that their aim must be to control the people of the Casbah

By the end of 1956 Sirvent's men were beginning to sort things out: arrests began to increase, and rebels were often shot on sight. By the end of the year about 80 FLN members had been killed. However, Mohammed Larbi Ben M'hidi, head of the FLN in Algiers, and his assistant, Yacef Saadi, had been busy forming special shock groups. These units were designed to cross Sirvent's blocks and spread terror outside the Casbah by killing both Europeans and Algerian Muslims loyal to France. At the same time, the FLN deployed its own police force to organise, protect and control the inhabitants of the Casbah, for both sides, the French authorities and the FLN rebels, realised that their aim must be to control the people of the Casbah.

The situation in Algeria became even more tense after the assassination, at the end of December 1956, of Amédée Froger, the mayor of the town of Boufarik, and also president of the Federation of Mayors of Algeria. For after this assassination some Europeans decided upon vengeance and they carried out a series of indiscriminate terror attacks on the Mus-

vious page above: On the ch over the rabbit warren treets that composed the bah of Algiers. Previous e below: As the 'Battle of iers' increased in nsity, all those leaving the bah had to be searched. : Searching cars for nbs. Above right: Music in Casbah. The Zouaves e a ceremonial menade through the Arab rt of Algiers.

which soldiers gingerly and rather ineffectually marched through one of the most mysterious and extraordinary urban environments of the Islamic world.

In August 1956, the French authorities decided that they would make a major effort to root out the FLN in Algiers, and as part of this effort, the 9th Zouave Regiment was moved into the city, with its four companies given specific areas to control. The 4th Company was assigned to the Casbah. The Zouaves, with their distinctive red ceremonial headgear, had originally been raised from among Algeria's Islamic population, but by the 1950s consisted of men from a variety of backgrounds: includ-

lims. There was, henceforth, a line of blood that separated the two communities.

Governor-General Robert Lacoste, the head of the French authorities, was a militant socialist and a firm upholder of the French presence in Algeria. From Paris he was ordered to use further military units to re-establish order in Algiers. General Jacques Massu was to be employed in this task; his 10th Colonial Parachute Division, whose men were nicknamed the 'leopards', was moved into the city.

The arrival of the parachutists was just the back-up that Sirvent and his Zouaves needed. They knew the Casbah and its meandering streets very well, and they were now to be in the very front line of the new, more intense phase of the war. Two other companies of Zouaves were called to reinforce them, as well as troops from the French Black African colonies, line infantry, and three squadrons of Gendarmes.

Perhaps the most important single incident of the whole battle of Algiers came early in 1957, when the FLN sent out an order for a general strike in the Casbah for the week beginning 28 January. The parachutists and the Zouaves now had to meet head on the power that the FLN held over the population of the Casbah. Their response to the FLN's call for a strike was swift and effective. During the night of 14/15 January, well before dawn, about 15,000 'suspects' were arrested in their homes in an enormous round-up operation conducted while the Casbah slept. These men, dragged from their beds, were taken to special interrogation centres set up by the counter-insurgency forces. The French operations were under way, and this large-scale pre-emptive action testified to the will of the army to destroy its enemy, the FLN.

The corrugated iron shopfronts were pulled apart; the Casbah was made to come back to life

When the first day of the strike, 28 January, arrived, everyone knew that the moment of truth had come. If the shops and small businesses failed to open, then the French would have lost enormous prestige. But if any tradesmen opened their shops, they risked reprisals from the commandos of the FLN. This was where the Zouaves came in. They knew the Casbah; they knew its inhabitants. Captain Sirvent was able to test the water and see what the shopkeepers and artisans really thought. Certain representative tradesmen told Captain Sirvent (strictly off the record) that they wouldn't mind if they were pushed around a bit by the Zouaves in order to keep their shops open – but they didn't want it to look as if they were opening voluntarily.

The operation mounted by the French forces to break the strike worked extremely well. Men whose place of work was outside the Casbah were forced into military convoys of trucks, and even some of the unemployed were dragged out (they returned to the Casbah later the same morning!) The corrugated iron fronts over shops that stayed closed were pulled apart; the Casbah was made to come back to life. By noon, the Casbah was back to normal – getting ready for the afternoon siesta after an unusual morning. Massu's 'leopards' had provided the military force that had broken the strike; but Sirvent's 'jackals' had been the men on the ground who knew how to direct the military force, and where it would best be employed.

In the wake of its victory over the strike, the French authorities decided upon a demonstration of the new

Above: The result of a car bombing in Algiers. One of the most unpleasant aspects of this urban war was that innocent civilians were frequently the victims. Right: Arrested FLN members are paraded for the cameras of the world press. Above right, Yacef Saadi, director of the FLN terrorist network in Algiers and, bottom right, Ben M'hidi, head of the FLN in Algiers. Far right: The 'jackals' (left foreground) and the 'leopards' (right foreground) acting together in the Casbah as suspects are led out.

order in the Casbah. Men of the 9th Zouaves marched into the Casbah in dress uniform, complete with red head-dress, striding through the narrow alleys. But this time, they weren't heavily armed, nor intent upon raiding houses where rebels were hiding: they were carrying musical instruments, for a different set of operations. They played military marches and popular tunes, and distributed sweets to the children. The people of the Casbah were being shown that the Zouaves were not just a force of repression.

The strike may have been broken, but the problem of terrorism still remained after January 1957. The FLN's commandos could still slip out of the Casbah, plant bombs and then disappear back into its welcoming bustle. Just a few men could still terrorise all of Algiers. Victory would necessitate more action in the Casbah.

Caught between the leopards and the jackals, the prey had little chance of escape

Once again, the fight had to be carried on at various levels. Massu's soldiers (and especially the 3rd Colonial Parachute Regiment led by Colonel Marcel Bigeard) became the most well-known troops there, but they were heavily dependent upon the Zouaves for information and day-to-day policing. Once things began to happen, they happened quickly – caught between the leopards and the jackals, the prey had little chance of escape.

The head of the FLN, Ben M'hidi, was caught on 25 February, and most of the other members of the Algiers leadership found that they had to flee the Casbah, which had now become a trap rather than a refuge. But Yacef Saadi still remained at large. His organisation had suffered severe losses; probably over 100 leaders of 'cells' (the basic FLN unit) and 150 active terrorists had been arrested, and in custody, faced with the brutally effective interrogations of Bigeard's men, they were forced to impart information needed by the authorities to piece together the structure of the nationalists in Algiers. Over 500 ordinary FLN members had also been identified, and 653 smallarms and 87 bombs in the process of preparation had been seized.

Yacef Saadi refused to consider himself beaten. From mid-April 1957, terrorist attacks multiplied. The most serious one was on 9 June, when a bomb was thrown into the Cassino cafe where couples were dancing. Nine people were killed and 85 wounded. The 'Battle of Algiers' was resumed with a vengeance, this time fought as a ferocious underground struggle.

In this new phase of the struggle, the Zouaves played an even more important part than before. They knew, more than other units, the people on whom pressure could be brought to bear. The cadres of the FLN were successfully infiltrated, and Yacef Saadi himself was arrested on 23 September. The battle could finally be said to have been won in October, when the hiding place of the last of Saadi's lieutenants, Ali la Pointe, was discovered. Ali himself refused to give up, and was blown to pieces. But from then on, the Casbah returned to its normal way of life. The jackals had proved that they were real dogs of war.

THE AUTHOR Jean Mabire is one of France's best-known military historians. He served on the Tunisian frontier during the Algerian war.

The tough artillerymen of the Viet Minh 351st Division dug themselves in and smashed the French defences at Dien Bien Phu

ON 7 MAY 1954, in a remote fortress in French Indo-china, small groups of men began scrambling onto the top of a series of bunkers. They were Viet-namese, and they carried the red flag of communist Vietnam. As the flags were waved for the benefit of photographers, the cameras recorded the men's historic victory, ending a siege that has since gone down as one of the most decisive battles in world history. The place was Dien Bien Phu, and the proud flag-wavers were the soldiers of the Viet Minh; the army they had defeated was that of France, and it had included some of the most redoubtable soldiers the world had ever seen – the French Foreign Legion.

Bottom left: Vo Nguyen Giap, commander of the Viet Minh, briefs his planning staff during the battle. Below left: Hardened Viet Minh troops. Below: Shells crash onto the airstrip at Dien Bien Phu, cutting off supplies to the garrison.

GIAP'S GUNNERS

The Viet Minh had, by the early 1950s, become
generally accepted name for the armed forces of
Viet Nam Doc Lap Dong Minh Hoi (League for the
Independence of Vietnam), an organisation set up in
1 by the ardent communist Ho Chi Minh. How-
er, Ho was a politician rather than a military
der, and from 1944 Vo Nguyen Giap became the
ving force behind the organisation that was finally
oust the French from one of their possessions.

The mortars, bazookas, bangalore
orpedoes and machine guns began
o spit flame in a deafening roar...'

der Giap's leadership, the Viet Minh developed
m a small guerrilla band, armed with little more
n shotguns and a few captured rifles, into an army
able of operating against the military might of a
ropean nation. Some Western observers have
ded to belittle the achievements of the Viet Minh:
at was, by any standards, supreme bravery, has
en been described as mere fanaticism.
At first, the French tended to sneer at the Viet
inh as fighters, making jokes concerning the slight
ysical build of their opponents – for example, it
s very difficult for French troops to tell whether a
man passing a checkpoint might not be a com-
nist soldier, and only an intimate examination
could provide the answer. It was not long, however,
before the French learnt to treat their enemies with
the highest regard as soldiers in the field. A reading
of the personal accounts of Viet Minh soldiers makes
it abundantly clear that these were troops who
reached heights of professionalism equal to those of
any army. A radio operator, deployed in the central
mountains to the south of the decisive battle of Dien
Bien Phu, gave the following description of a night
action in which his unit was involved:

'The mortars, bazookas, bangalore torpedoes and
machine guns began to spit flame in a deafening
roar. I woke up completely and with a few twinges
in my stomach began to open my papers, ready to
work.

'The hand generator which fed the radio set
began to crank with the noise of a rattle: as a matter
of principle we were authorised to operate our
radio only after the first shooting had begun. Two
minutes later, the messenger handed me a message from Zone Headquarters... At first I thought I
had made a mistake decoding, and verified the
message immediately. But there was no error; the
text was correct. I leapt up and ran over to the CO.

'I can no longer remember the exact tenor of the
message, but the essential parts read as follows –
"Enemy has brought to Plei-Rinh, GM100 [a
French mobile unit], the 4th Battalion of the 2nd
French Foreign Legion Regiment and one
armoured unit..." This meant that we were attacking a force eight times the size of ours... We had
now to inflict a defeat on the enemy this very night
or he would be able to counter-attack tomorrow
morning. In this flat terrain, favourable to his
artillery and air force, he could make things
enormously difficult for us.

'Volley upon volley, the 81mm and 60mm mortars, the bazookas and the machine guns tore the
atmosphere in response to the given order.
GM100 was an old acquaintance of ours... It was
the third time we had faced this unit, which had
borne the United Nations insignia in Korea. The
first engagement had been on the Kontum-Kon
Brai road, where GM100 had lost a platoon. The
second had been the capture of Dak-Doa where it
had lost a company...'

It was intelligence work of this calibre, relaying to
front-line troops valuable information on the size and
deployment of the enemy, that stood the Viet Minh in
good stead during the difficult battles of the Indochina War.
The decision to fight a large-scale battle at Dien
Bien Phu was taken by the French. Hard-pressed to
defeat the elusive Viet Minh forces, that always
seemed able to fight on terrain of their own choosing,
the French high command planned to set up a large
base upon a route commonly used by the Viet Minh to
infiltrate Laos. The French saw the key to success as
superior firepower. They fully expected that, in any

THE VIET MINH

Since their defeat in the Red
River Delta in 1951, the Viet
Minh were determined not
to give the French another
opportunity to use their
military superiority to such
devastating effect. Between
1951 and 1954, Giap
reconstituted his forces in a
pyramid structure, at the top
of which was an elite
division intended for
beating the French at their
own game. At the bottom of
Giap's pyramid was the
village militia. Essentially,
this consisted of all the able-
bodied men and women in
regions controlled by the
Viet Minh. By 1954 the
militia possessed a strength
of some 350,000
Vietnamese, and, though
often unarmed, they were
invaluable for preparing
defensive positions,
carrying equipment and
gathering intelligence.
Their mobilisation into a
transport system was to play
a crucial role at Dien Bien
Phu.
Above the militia were the
so-called regional troops.
Mostly equipped with
smallarms, they were
controlled by the
commanders of the six
'inter-zones' into which
Vietnam had been divided
by the communist high
command in 1948. These
troops were responsible for
maintaining strict control
over the population in Viet
Minh dominated areas, and
pursued a campaign of
constant harassment against
the enemy – a ploy that
eventually tied down the
vast bulk of French units in
Indochina. By 1954, the
regional troops probably
numbered around 75,000.
The cutting edge of the Viet
Minh, however, was the
regular force, or Chuc Luc.
In the remote mountains of
the Viet Bac in northern
Tonkin, Giap had carefully
prepared the Chuc Luc as
the spearhead of his army.
By 1954, there were six
divisions including the
heavily armed 351st.

war of position, where they could promulgate a battle in a fixed terrain, they would be capable of dealing with any number of enemy troops by virtue of artillery and air superiority. Indeed, in 1951 the French had already achieved such a victory – in the battle for the Red River Delta, the great rice-bowl and population centre surrounding the cities of Hanoi and Haiphong. Fresh from successes the previous year against remote French outposts on the Lang Son ridge, in the mountains of the Viet Bac near the Chinese border, Giap had launched his troops against the heart of French authority in what he hoped would be a decisive offensive. However, under Marshal Jean de Lattre de Tassigny, the forces of the colonial power held fast, deploying the full weight of their armament to shatter three successive waves of attack.

French forces had occupied the valley around Dien Bien Phu late in 1953, and, after pushing patrols into the outlying hills, they fully expected a Vietnamese build up, followed by a full-scale attack. The Viet Minh responded with sporadic shelling of the base and its airstrip, but despite the build up of enemy forces, Colonel Charles Piroth, the officer in charge of the French artillery, was confident that his 105mm and 155mm guns, together with three heavy mortar batteries and suppressive aircraft fire, would be fully capable of locating and destroying the Viet Minh artillery positions.

However, supported by the regional militia, the men of the 351st Division had been making a

monumental effort to transport their heavy weapons to hills surrounding the French base. With only 600 lorries at his disposal, and faced with distances of up to 800km, by the beginning of March 1954, Giap had deployed the ammunition and armament necessary for the siege of Dien Bien Phu. Bicycles had been modified in order to carry up to 200kg of equipment each, and during the first two months of 1954 it supplied the communist forces.

The heavy guns were dismantled and carried by hand to prearranged positions

'Sweat saves blood' was one of the British Army's mottoes – and it could equally have been applied to the 351st. The heavy guns, including 75mm and 105mm weapons, were dismantled and carried by hand to pre-arranged positions, where each was sited in a camouflaged and shell-proof dug-out. These dug-outs were meticulously planned in order not to disturb the foliage cover on the hillside – the French were totally unaware of the steady accretion of enemy forces around their garrison. In addition, the Viet Minh guns were surrounded by anti-aircraft units – by the end of the battle, 80 Soviet-made 37mm AA guns were in position, plus over 100 0.5in heavy machine guns and several 'Katyusha' rocket launchers.

By 11 March, Giap's preparations were complete, and a message from him was read out to the assembled troops:

'Remember this historic battle. Determined to destroy the enemy, keep in mind the motto: "Always attack, always advance." Master fear and pain, overcome obstacles, unite our efforts, fight to the very end, annihilate the enemy at Dien Bien Phu. Win a great victory!'

On 12 March, the French senior officer in Tonkin, General René Cogny, landed at the airstrip on a tour of inspection of the defences. As Cogny's aircraft took off following his brief visit, the airstrip was hit by a salvo of 105mm shells. Cogny made it back to Hanoi, but the Viet Minh gunners had found their range.

A low cloud cover on 13 March made French air operations hazardous, and the Viet Minh artillery knew that their moment had arrived. At precisely 1700 hours, they plastered the whole French position

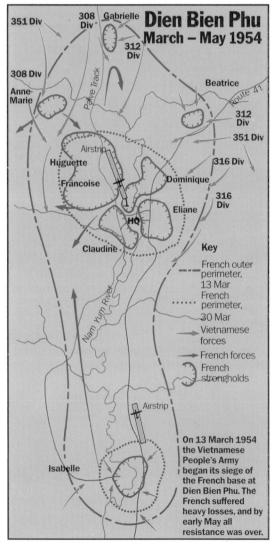

Key
- - - French outer perimeter, 13 Mar
...... French perimeter, 30 Mar
→ Vietnamese forces
→ French forces
⌒ French strongholds

On 13 March 1954 the Vietnamese People's Army began its siege of the French base at Dien Bien Phu. The French suffered heavy losses, and by early May all resistance was over.

Bottom: Specially converted bicycles bring up arms and ammunition together with food and supplies to the Viet Minh forces surrounding the French at Dien Bien Phu. To obtain the number of bicycles needed, Viet Minh agents secretly purchased large quantities of Peugeot bicycles from French dealers in Hanoi. Right: Viet Minh gunners in training, using captured Japanese 75mm field guns. The surrender of the Japanese in 1945 had allowed the communists to take over much of their equipment. Centre right: Streaming across the airstrip at Dien Bien Phu, Viet Minh infantry garner the harvest sown by the devastating bombardment of their artillerymen. Below main picture: Equipped with scaling ladders, the final wave of attackers prepares to take the last French bunkers. Bottom right: Triumph for the Viet Minh as their flag flies over shattered French position.

Viet Minh irregular, Dien Bien Phu, 1954

Wearing the characteristic Vietnamese black pyjamas and a French Army tropical hat, this soldier carries a 9mm MAT 49 sub-machine gun with butt extended.

Below: The French guns that failed to deliver the goods. Colonel Charles Piroth had claimed that his artillery would destroy any Viet Minh gun enplacements, but the shattered 105mm guns shown here proved unable to contain the hail of fire that the 351st Heavy Division unleashed on 13 March. Piroth took personal responsibility for the failure, and committed suicide in his bunker. He had lost his right arm during World War II, and so the method he chose was to pull the pin out of a grenade and hold it against his chest. Bottom: A carefully staged victory photograph on the stricken remains of a transport aircraft.

with a devastating hail of fire that continued almost until dawn the following day. A member of one of the Foreign Legion mortar units described the terrifying scene:

'We thought we'd been at the centre of a catac-lysm, but we quickly found that things were the same all over. Everything was smoke-blackened, broken, demolished. All round, wandering silhouettes bore witness to the disaster.'

In the wake of the bombardment came the infantry assaults. Giap hurled his men into an attack on the northern strongholds of 'Béatrice', which fell on 13 March under the first rain of artillery shells, and 'Gabrielle', which fell on the morning of the 15th.

Concealing their guns from the enemy artillery observers, the 351st kept up the pressure, steadily refining their range and homing in on the airstrip – the garrison's link with the outside world. The last aircraft to fly into Dien Bien Phu was an ambulance plane. It landed on 28 March, but never took off again.

However, the defenders of Dien Bien Phu were tough, and when Giap launched the next wave of infantry attacks in late March, they put up a stout defence and one of the para officers, Marcel Bigeard, achieved a remarkable success on the 28th, when he stormed a Viet Minh anti-aircraft position some 3km to the west of the French defences. Following this and other defensive successes, Giap was forced to abandon the 'human wave' tactics. Giap himself has described the change in tactics as one he readily welcomed: Chinese advisers, he later explained, had wished to bring the battle to a speedy conclusion and preferred massive infantry assaults to Giap's siege and trench warfare – regardless of the cost to the Viet Minh.

Carrying scaling ladders, the Viet Minh overran the bunkers

French attempts to destroy Viet Minh gun posi-tions using low-flying aircraft were foiled by the elaborate cave and tunnel system the Viet Minh had laboriously excavated over the previous two months: as soon as the aircraft were sighted, the artillerymen would move their pieces back into shelter. When napalm was employed in an attempt to prise the enemy gunners from the hillsides, the dense clouds of smoke produced by the napalm falling on damp foliage afforded even more cover for the Viet Minh.

Under the mounting weight of shell-fire (French gunners believed that over 130,000 shells had fallen on their positions during the siege), the beleaguered Foreign Legion was inexorably pounded into defeat. The end came on 7 May. After the final artillery bombardment, shock troops used bangalore torpe-does to break their way through into the last line of French defence. Carrying scaling ladders, the Viet Minh overran the bunkers, and the cream of the French expeditionary force in Indochina – mainly legionnaires and paras – could only surrender.

A guerrilla army the Viet Minh may have been in 1945; by 1954, however, its elite artillery division had demonstrated that, in a classic battle of position, it was more than able to hold its own.

THE AUTHOR Ashley Brown is an historian who has contributed a number of articles to military publica-tions, specialising in the history of the French Army since 1789. He was editor of the military partwork, *War in Peace,* and is author of the book, *Modern Warfare.*

SHOCK ARMY

Soviet tank armies are trained and equipped as the spearhead for a high-speed offensive designed to sweep aside NATO armour

THE TANK is the main battle weapon of the Soviet [Red] Army, with a proven combination of firepow[er], mobility and protection that will make it the linch[pin] of any future high-speed offensive. No other elem[ent] in the Red Army plays such a decisive role in [the] attack. Indeed, the Soviets believe that only arm[our] can assure the rapid destruction of the enemy – [Red] Army tactics are tank tactics. In total contrast to [the] defensive role of NATO armour, Soviet tank for[ces] are primarily attacking formations – designed [to] outflank, envelop and pursue the enemy – and [to] them, defence is only a secondary consideration[.]

The modern Soviet reliance on the concep[t of] offensive armour has its origin in the enormous los[ses] and defeats sustained during the first year of [the] Great Patriotic War. Following the German invas[ion] of the Soviet Union in 1941, the Red Army was forc[ed] to reassess its tactics on the battlefields of [the] Ukraine and Belorussia. As doctrines and meth[ods] were discarded or adopted according to result[s in] the field, gradually the concept of the Tank Ar[my]

evolved. From a disorganised mass of vehicle[s it] developed into an effective force that relied [on] mobility to defeat the enemy.

Today, as NATO and Warsaw Pact forces confr[ont] one another across the North German Plain, [the] Soviet concept of victory in any future offensiv[e is] dominated by an estimation of the number of [Red] Army tanks that can attack per kilometre of fronta[ge] – in an effort to outflank and crush enemy defenc[es.] The main attack is expected to be directed we[st]wards from East Germany – a springboard fr[om] which the Warsaw Pact forces can launch the[m]selves into the initial stages of a campaign that th[ey]

expect will carry them to the Atlantic coastline.

Responsible for maintaining the Warsaw Pa[ct] offensive military posture in East Germany [are] several combat-ready formations, known in [the] West as the Group of Soviet Forces Germ[any] (GSFG). The headquarters of this formidable c[on]centration of firepower is at Zossen-Wunstorf, 30[km] south of Berlin, and it controls no less than five arm[ies.] The first of these is 3 Shock Army, which, as its na[me] suggests, would be in the vanguard during the e[arly] stages of any combined-arms offensive. The ot[her] elements of GSFG are 1 Guards Tank Army, 2 Gua[rds] Tank Army, 8 Guards Tank Army and 20 Gua[rds] Army. The latter is similar to an enlarged motori[sed] infantry formation, but also possesses a powe[rful] tank increment – enabling it to secure objectives [that] can be exploited by the tank armies.

Augmenting the tank armies are a large numbe[r of] support units that include helicopter regime[nts,] enlarged bridging battalions and specialised c[om]bat engineer regiments. Probably the largest s[up]porting arm is the artillery, represented by [34] Guards Artillery Division. Western experts beli[eve]

Left: An experienced tank driver glances at the camera, confident in the knowledge that he is part of the world's largest armoured fleet. Bottom left: On manoeuvres. As their tank column halts, young conscripts, part of the new generation of Red Army 'tankies', enjoy a letter from home. The harsh climatic conditions of the northern European winter demand that tank crews are well-practised in the techniques of winter warfare (main picture), and the flat training areas of East Germany provide ample space for rehearsing the basic element of Soviet battle doctrine – the high-speed shock offensive. Inset below: Eastern bloc tank crews take a brief rest while on exercise. The manoeuvres took place in 1980 and marked the 25th anniversary of the Warsaw Pact treaty.

this to be at least three times the size of a normal artillery division, able to call upon over 600 guns and a number of multiple rocket launchers to lay down direct or indirect fire prior to a tank assault.

The headquarters of 3 Shock Army is located at Magdeburg, in full view of the railway that connects Berlin to West Germany. For the British Army of the Rhine, 3 Shock Army has a special significance – in any future conflict it can be expected to confront the Chieftains and Challengers of the British 1 (BR) Corps.

3 Shock Army Headquarters commands a number of large battle formations up to division level, and its spearhead comprises 10, 12 and 47 Guards Tank Divisions. To these can be added the 207 Motorised Rifle Division and an artillery brigade with a total complement of 162 guns, most of them self-propelled. One SCUD surface-to-surface missile brigade, two brigades of surface-to-air launchers and a regiment of smaller SAM-6 launchers completes the division's air and ground defence capability. Engineer units include an entire engineer brigade, a pontoon bridging regiment and a special assault river crossing brigade. Back-up for 3 Shock Army comprises the usual 'admin' units such as traffic control, logistic support, medical posts, tank trans-

porters and missile support units. In addition, there is a special signals intercept and jamming battalion.

Despite the impressive array of military strength within 3 Shock Army, the tank divisions comprise the army's cutting edge, and their deployment forms a pivot around which all other elements must revolve.

12 Guards Tank Division earned its coveted 'Guards' title during the latter stages of the Great Patriotic War, and is now based at Neuruppin, 60km northwest of Berlin. In the event of a Warsaw Pact offensive, it will be one of two divisions leading the attack on 1 (BR) Corps. Used as an exploitative force, the division will be responsible for creating and maintaining shock action in the enemy rear, thereby reducing the likelihood of counter-attacks by NATO armour. Soviet tank divisions are designed to engage in fast-moving and intense continuous combat – up to six days of sustained operations – and this large logistic requirement is reflected in the division's structure. It has the usual divisional headquarters and its associated company, three tank regiments, a motorised rifle regiment with BMP mechanised infantry fighting vehicles, an artillery regiment and a host of other formations ranging from surface-to-air missile units to a multiple rocket launcher battalion. There is even a helicopter squadron and a mobile

During the 1973 Arab-Israeli war, the T-62 (left main picture) proved inferior to the Israeli-crewed Centurions. However, Soviet defence priorities provide for a new tank to be developed every 10 years and the T-64/72 series was already on hand to replace the ageing T-62. This new generation of battle tanks incorporated the novel feature of an autoloader (bottom left), and the T-72 possesses the most sophisticated fire-control system ever to appear in Soviet armour. The technical differences between the T-64 and T-72 appear to be largely cosmetic. For example, the searchlight on the T-64 (left) has been moved across the turret to improve the gunner's field of vision. Far left: T-72s conduct manoeuvres through broken terrain.

field bakery. The total commitment to combat, inherent in any Red Army tank division, is reflected by the provision of a chemical defence battalion of some 225 men, equipped to carry out all stages of chemical defence from reconnaissance to vehicle decontamination.

The bulk of the regiments and sub-units of 12 Guards Tank Division are clustered around Neuruppin, housed in ageing Wehrmacht barracks and often using the same firing ranges once employed by the pre-1945 German armies. Each regiment comprises three tank battalions, together with about one-third of every unit strength within the division – from engineers and surface-to-air missiles to signals and motor transport. Each tank battalion has an approximate strength of 135 officers and men, and in any attack two battalions will usually comprise the regimental first echelon, with the third battalion (reinforced by motorised rifle support) serving as the advance guard during the march towards contact with the enemy.

The battalion is seen by the Soviets as the 'weapon of decision', and its complement of 31 T-72 tanks is deployed in three companies, each possessing 10 tanks, leaving one tank for the battalion headquar-

ters and service platoon. The latter performs the usual headquarters functions of command and communication, but also arranges re-supply, medical evacuation and catering. The command T-72 acts as a forward command vehicle, with the remaining headquarters personnel operating from two BMP vehicles usually found at the rear of the battalion. There are also several trucks, trailers and fuel tankers – one day's approach march is sufficient to expend the T-72's fuel. Each company is further divided into three tank platoons, each with three T-72s, and a support and stores section comprising a single truck and light vehicle. However, the tank company normally fights as a complete unit, with all the tanks and armoured fighting vehicles operating within sight of the company commander, who travels in the tenth T-72 and directs the battle formation and firing of each platoon.

The T-72 main battle tank is a potent weapon, and its introduction into the Soviet arsenal in 1971 – replacing the T-62 – signalled to NATO that the Red Army had achieved a level of technical sophistication in tank development to complement their existing numerical superiority. Armed with a 2A46 125mm smoothbore main gun, the T-72 possesses a

SOVIET TANK DEVELOPMENT

Soviet tank development since 1941 has been evolutionary, rather than revolutionary, consisting of an updating of the T-34/85 tank – with its 85mm gun and low silhouette – to meet modern conditions.
The T-54 entered service in 1949 (followed by the T-55), and, in addition to a 100mm gun and 105mm armour, its variants incorporated night-fighting equipment in the form of an infra-red searchlight.
The T-62 was a further development of the T-54/55 series, with a longer, wider hull, a new 115mm smoothbore gun, more sophisticated infra-red equipment and an NBC system.
The introduction of the T-64 in 1967 marked a break with the past, and demonstrated a Soviet capacity for innovation in tank development. Like its successor, the T-72, the T-64 has a crew of three and is armed with a 125mm main gun. Both tanks are technically similar and appeared to have been developed in parallel, although the T-72 has been modified in order to eliminate the engine, transmission, suspension and loading difficulties that plagued the early T-64s. The improved T-72 entered production in 1971, and its variants have been identified in service with many countries including Algeria, Bulgaria, Cuba, Czechoslovakia, East Germany, Libya and Iraq. The successor to the T-72, known in the West by the designation T-80, entered service in early 1986. It has improved cross-country capability and armour, along with the main features of the T-64/72 series.

T-72 MAIN BATTLE TANK

Crew: 3
Dimensions: length 9.24m; width 4m; height 2.37m
Weight: Combat loaded 41,000kg
Engine: V-46 water-cooled diesel developing 780bhp

Armament: One 125mm 2A46 smoothbore gun; 7.62mm PKT co-axial machine gun; 12.7mm NSVT anti-aircraft machine gun
Performance: Maximum road speed 70km/h; range 1000km; vertical

obstacle 0.91m; trench 3.07m; gradient 60 per cent; fording 1.4m
Armour: Composite 220-240mm maximum, with a skin layer of lead-based foam as protection from nuclear contamination

secondary armament of a 7.62mm PKT co-axial machine gun, and a 12.7mm NSVT anti-aircraft machine gun over the commander's cupola. The T-72 is unusual in its class by having a crew of only three – commander, gunner and driver. The fourth crew member, the loader, has been replaced on the T-72 by an autoloader that selects, and loads, the projectiles and their separate propellant charges. The size of the ammunition limits the number of rounds carried to 39: 12 armour-piercing fin-stabilised discarding sabot (APFSDS) for engaging enemy armour; 21 high explosive (HE) for general use; and six high-explosive anti-tank (HEAT). These rounds are carried in a carousel system on the floor of the turret. The autoloader is one of the T-72's main features, and theoretically it can improve the fire rate to eight rounds per minute. However, the system's reliability is doubted by Western experts – in the early days at least, the autoloader would sometimes attempt to grab the gunner and load him into the breech! Nevertheless, the latest reports suggest that these difficulties have largely been overcome, seriously undermining NATO's belief in the qualitative superiority of its own armour.

The T-72 armour affords excellent front protection against anti-armour missiles such as the standard TOW

There are several variations on the T-72 theme, and the nature of the tank's sloping armour remains something of a mystery in the West. On some models, there are side-plates designed to detonate hollow charge warheads at a safe distance from the main armour. Extra protection is provided by smoke grenade dischargers on the turret – the smoke contains an infra-red screening component designed to defeat enemy infra-red detectors. Soviet defence spokesmen maintain that the T-72 armour affords excellent front protection against anti-armour missiles such as the standard TOW, one of NATO's most powerful long range anti-tank weapons. Well-armoured, the T-72 is also extremely

mobile. Long-range fuel tanks carried over the hull rear provide a road range of 1000km, and a V-46 diesel engine gives a maximum speed of 70 kilometres per hour. The speed of a Red Army tank advance would be rapid, and the T-72 has been designed with this in mind. Assault bridging for crossing every water obstacle could waste valuable time, and thus the T-72 is able to wade through water up to 5.5m deep with the aid of a snorkel tube.

For the driver, seated centrally well back from the front of the hull, the job of driving the T-72 requires great skill. As with most Soviet tanks, the controls are awkward to operate and gear changing involves a great deal of double de-clutching. Some reports indicate that the later models of the T-72 series have an automatic transmission, but this has yet to be confirmed. The driver is also responsible for the maintenance of the vehicle, assisted by the gunner, commander and personnel from the support section.

The other two crew members are seated in the cast turret, the gunner on the left and the commander on the right under his rotating cupola. Day and night sights are provided for all three crew members, in addition to an infra-red searchlight on the right-hand side of the turret. The gunner's day sight is the TPD-2, equipped with a complex graticule system, and for emergencies the commander also possesses a limited aiming capability through his own gun sight.

Although the T-72 is one of the most technically advanced of Soviet main battle tanks, the crews often experience difficulties in mastering its fire control system. This problem is not helped by the allocation of only two or three full-calibre rounds per year for live gunnery training. For the rest of the year, gunners train using 'dry' shoots or sub-calibre devices mounted over the gun barrel.

Soviet tanks are designed with offensive capabilities first and foremost, and the silhouette of the T-72 – 2.37m high – reduces its vulnerability to NATO defences. While this has resulted in a rather cramped environment for the tank crews, the Red Army 'tankie' is a resilient breed of soldier, the result of a rigorous training programme, and is committed

The success of a Soviet shock offensive would hinge on the co-ordination of heavy armour – used as the spearhead – artillery and infantry to pre-empt NATO deployment. Left: Emphasising the importance that the Red Army attaches to combined-arms tactics, the T-72 main battle tank (foreground) is photographed here with two BMP infantry combat vehicles and an SA-13 surface-to-air missile launcher (background). Main picture: A D-30 howitzer artillery unit runs through its drill. The 122mm D-30 has a maximum range of 15,400m and is capable of a rapid 360-degree traverse. Top left: A SCUD-B surface-to-surface missile on its MAZ-543 launch vehicle. This weapon can be equipped with conventional and nuclear warheads, and would play a crucial role in weakening enemy defences prior to the tank offensive.

to his role within the Red Army.

The most extensive training schedule within the tank divisions is reserved for the tank commanders – a six-month intensive course is followed by additional specialised training for platoon commanders. Theoretically, only the commander is instructed in the use of the radio, emphasising the rigid command structure, though a substantial amount of cross-training is believed to occur in most fields at unit level. The gunner and driver both receive four months' specialist training. Three 7.62mm AKMS assault rifles comprise the crew's personal weapons.

When serving with the Third Shock Army few soldiers are allowed leave, since all units are maintained on a permanent combat footing – ready to move at least 80 per cent of their vehicles and manpower into battle positions within a matter of hours. Training, maintenance duties and general education therefore play a very important role in a formation dedicated to the concept of high-speed offensive operations in the event of a conflict.

Battle tactics, like many other factors in Red Army life, have been moulded into simple formulae that demand immediate response from the tank commanders in the field. Once the attack has been planned, at regimental or divisional level, a massive artillery assault will provide fire support – timed to hit enemy front-line defences from the moment the T-72s enter direct-fire range. This will continue until the tanks and their accompanying all-arms combat support team are 150 to 200m away from the enemy positions. During the advance, the tank battalion moves forward in a column before altering to company column with two companies side-by-side (the other in support) for the attack. For the company attack, the standard formation of two platoons forward with one in support is retained.

Soviet tanks rarely fire on the move, other than in the final stages of the attack, although targets may be acquired during the advance. For the final aiming, the tank will halt and accurately lay its gun before firing. The maximum combat range is expected to be 2000 to 1500m from the enemy positions, depending on the terrain.

The head-on steam roller attack, employed by the Soviets during World War II, has largely been discarded as a viable offensive tactic. Instead, reflecting the complexity of the modern battlefield, the tank army is supported by a formidable array of firepower in the form of artillery and infantry. Similarly, the technical innovation exemplified by the new generation of Red Army tanks has demonstrated Soviet ability to match that of the West. Although variants of the T-72 (known as 'monkey models') have been exported, the Soviets often remove most of the sophisticated weapons systems, leaving Western experts in the dark concerning the tank's true offensive capability. Below: A Soviet 'tankie', part of the Red Army's most important combat echelon.

During the climax of the assault, all available tanks move into a line-abreast formation, with battalions using some sub-units to provide direct fire support from a static position. The role of 12 Guards Tank Division is to surprise and outflank the enemy, and as a general rule any enemy strongpoints will be bypassed and left to the rifle formations and their armour and artillery.

All operations and tactics have been carefully drilled into the tank crews, leaving no room for misunderstanding regarding objectives and methods. The crews, therefore, have the benefit of a 'timetable' that allows them to move forward in a series of rehearsed movements with artillery and combat engineer support. Each battalion and company within the division has a precise knowledge of its duties and is confident of being able to accomplish them along well-practised lines.

One factor that will doubtless remain from the days of the Great Patriotic War is the seemingly heedless acceptance of manpower and equipment casualties inherent in the concept of a massive high-speed offensive against NATO defensive positions. However, the Red Army is estimated to possess a force of over two million trained soldiers and some 50,000 tanks – if the spearhead of the Third Shock Army is blunted within the opening days of hostilities, the loss can easily be absorbed by the enormous reserves at the disposal of the high command.

Such knowledge is no doubt of little comfort to the men of the tank battalions within 12 Guards Tank Division, but they are more than ready to carry out their orders – however draconian these may seem to their counterparts in the West. If departing from their Neuruppin barracks and fighting westwards towards the Atlantic coastline will help the Soviet Union to secure a worldwide communist state, the Red Army tank crews are more than ready to pledge themselves to the cause.

THE AUTHOR Terry Gander is a freelance writer on military affairs and is the author of the *Encyclopedia of the Modern British Army*, now in its third edition.

COMBAT SKILLS OF THE ELITE

CAMOUFLAGE

If an enemy can see you, he can hit you. In the natural world, many creatures have evolved their own particular brand of camouflage to hide them from the prying eyes of marauding predators, but man has no such natural defences. In the hostile environment of the battlefield, the arts of camouflage and concealment are fundamental to your survival, whether you are engaged in clandestine forward reconnaissance, behind-the-lines operations, or fighting from a prepared position.

When applying personal camouflage, that is, making your body, weapon and equipment blend into the environment you are fighting in, there are two main things to consider. First, you should make sure that your colouring is as close as possible to that of your immediate environment, and second, you should try to break up the tell-tale outline of your body and weapon. Most soldiers are issued with uniforms that will provide a good basis for camouflage. Sandy colours, browns and dull greens will help you merge into a northern European countryside, while the white smocks worn by mountain and arctic warfare troops blend into the background of a snowfield. DPM (disruptive pattern material) will also help break up the obvious shape of an arm or a leg. However, your uniform is only the foundation on which to construct a successful camouflage.

One of the most easily recognisable shapes is your helmet, and while an issue helmet-cover will help to conceal it, the addition of a little local mud, plus a few twigs and leaves, will make it all the more difficult for an enemy to spot. Natural camouflage materials should always be gathered from your immediate surroundings and should be held in place by strips of hessian material, string or rubber bands. Be careful not to overdo it – a walking bush will always attract attention – and change it regularly, making sure that it is in keeping with your current surroundings.

Your face is the next area to attend to, especially if

Continued overleaf

Below: When possible, camouflage cream should be applied by a colleague. Bottom: Soviet sub-machine gunners camouflaged to blend in with their surroundings. Below left: Applied camouflage breaks up the outline of a sniper's rifle and helmet.

Continued from back cover

you are operating at night. The natural oil in your skin will reflect light, whether you have dark or light skin, so cover is most important. Camouflage cream should be applied in a combination of two colours, a light colour for the shadow areas – under your nose, chin and eyes – and a dark colour for the shiny areas – your cheek bones, nose, forehead and chin. Your hands, forearms and the back of your neck should also be painted. If you do not have any ready-made camouflage cream to hand, you can make do with burnt cork, charcoal, lamp black or mud. It is very important to make the patterns you apply as irregular as possible. In the field, it is usually best to get someone else to apply it for you, while you do the same for him.

Just as applies to your helmet, it is very important to break up the outline of your weapon, especially if you are a sniper. This can be done by wrapping hessian or netting material around it, but you must take great care not to allow the camouflage materials to get anywhere near the moving parts of the weapon.

Another important factor to consider when making yourself invisible to enemy observation is the reflection of light from polished surfaces. This is especially dangerous in conditions of bright sunlight, or of full moonlight in a night operation. Any metal or glass object can create a light flash that will be visible over long distances, so care must be taken

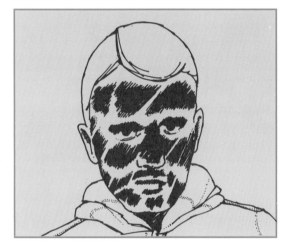

to keep objects like metal watches and straps, compasses, cigarette lighters, dog tags, belts, buckles and the blades of knives or bayonets under wraps, especially when moving. Much modern equipment is manufactured with a 'subdued' finish in dark green or black non-reflective plastic to minimise the risk of flash, but if such gear is not available reflecting surfaces can be dulled with a layer of boot polish, camouflage cream or mud. Take great care when using optical devices such as binoculars or sniper sights, making sure that the lenses are kept in deep shadow as much as possible. When using the sniper's Starlight Scope, for example, it is wise to press the eyepiece as close as possible to your eye. This will prevent light from the scope illuminating your face and revealing your position to the enemy.

While personal camouflage is as important in an offensive action as it is in a defensive operation, if you are digging in or occupying static positions these too must be camouflaged. On the modern battlefield, where the enemy will be using sophisticated surveillance and night-vision equipment to try to detect you, your skill at camouflaging your fighting position or your forward observation post will be crucial to both the success of your mission and your personal

survival.

Before camouflaging a position, make a careful study of the surrounding terrain and then gather your materials from a wide area – a single spot stripped of all vegetation will attract the attention of an experienced observer. Again, be very careful not to overdo the amount of material you use since an over-camouflaged position may actually disclose your whereabouts. If you are fighting from a gun pit or a dug-in fighting position, make sure that the piles of earth removed when building it are well hidden. These are particularly visible from the air. When your camouflage is complete, inspect it carefully from every angle, paying particular attention to what the position will look like from the air.

Visual camouflage, however, is only one aspect of the art of concealment and must go hand in hand with strict discipline. The careless use of a cigarette lighter or torch at night, sudden movement or undue noise will surely ruin all the work you have put in to make yourself as invisible as possible, and may well cost you your life.

Below: Two-colour camouflage breaks up the shadow pattern and shape of a soldier's face. Bottom: US Special Forces on a jungle operation in Vietnam. The colouring of the tiger-stripe camouflage uniform allows them to lose themselves against the foliage, while its design repeats the high-contrast pattern of light and shade created by strong sunlight pouring through the trees.